Elements of Formal Semantics

Edinburgh Advanced Textbooks in Linguistics

Series Editors
Peter Ackema, Reader in Linguistics (University of Edinburgh)
Mitsuhiko Ota, Reader in the Phonetics and Phonology of Language
Acquisition (University of Edinburgh)

Editorial Advisory Board
Ricardo Bermudez-Otero (University of Manchester)
Kersti Börjars (University of Manchester)
Greville Corbett (University of Surrey)
Anastasia Giannakidou (University of Chicago)
Caroline Heycock (University of Edinburgh)
Jack Hoeksema (University of Groningen)
Miriam Meyerhoff (University of Edinburgh)
Geoffrey Pullum (University of Edinburgh)
Andrew Spencer (University of Essex)
Donca Steriade (MIT)
Susi Wurmbrand (University of Connecticut)

TITLES IN THE SERIES INCLUDE
Essential Programming for Linguistics
Martin Weisser

Morphology: From Data to Theories
Antonio Fábregas and Sergio Scalise

*Language and Logics: An Introduction to the Logical Foundations
of Language*
Howard Gregory

*Elements of Formal Semantics: An Introduction to the Mathematical
Theory of Meaning in Natural Language*
Yoad Winter

Visit the Edinburgh Advanced Textbooks in Linguistics website at
www.euppublishing.com/series/EATL

Elements of Formal Semantics

An Introduction to the Mathematical Theory
of Meaning in Natural Language

Yoad Winter

EDINBURGH
University Press

In memory of Paula Frank-Boas
1916 Amsterdam–2015 Haifa

Edinburgh University Press is one of the leading university presses in the UK. We publish academic books and journals in our selected subject areas across the humanities and social sciences, combining cutting-edge scholarship with high editorial and production values to produce academic works of lasting importance. For more information visit our website: www.edinburghuniversitypress.com

Edinburgh University Press Ltd
The Tun - Holyrood Road, 12(2f) Jackson's Entry, Edinburgh EH8 8PJ

Typeset in 12/14 Minion by
by Nova Techset Pvt Ltd, Bangalore, India, and
printed and bound in Great Britain by
CPI Group (UK) Ltd, Croydon CR0 4YY

A CIP record for this book is available from the British Library

ISBN 978 0 7486 4044 7 (hardback)
ISBN 978 0 7486 7777 1 (webready PDF)
ISBN 978 0 7486 4043 0 (paperback)
ISBN 978 0 7486 7779 5 (epub)

CONTENTS

ACKNOWLEDGMENTS

This book has benefited from the generous feedback that I got over the years from many colleagues and students. For their detailed comments and extensive help, I am especially grateful to Philomena Athanasiadou, Gilad Ben-Avi, Chris Blom, Sophie Chesney, Rogier van Dinther, Gianluca Giorgolo, Eyal Hurvits, Theo Janssen, Heidi Klockmann, Larry Moss, Kirsten Oosterom, Ya'acov Peterzil, Eddy Ruys, Remko Scha, Assaf Toledo, Hanna de Vries and Joost Zwarts. I am grateful to many other colleagues and students who have helped my work on this book since its early versions took shape. I would also wish to thank an anonymous Edinburgh University Press reviewer, as well as the rest of the EUP team, for their help and patience during the preparation of the manuscript. The quotation on page 1 appears by kind permission of BD Music Co. Work on this book was partially supported by VICI grant 277-80-002 of the Netherlands Organisation for Scientific Research (NWO), which is gratefully acknowledged.

Most of all, I am grateful to Yael and Dana Seggev and the rest of my family. I wouldn't find any meaning without you.

Utrecht, June 2015

NOTATIONS

For standard set-theoretical notation see pages 9 and 10.

$\star$	ungrammaticality
#	semantic incoherence
$\top$	truth-value for *true*
$\perp$	truth-value for *false*
$S_1 \Rightarrow S_2$	sentence S_1 entails sentence S_2
$S_1 \nRightarrow S_2$	sentence S_1 does not entail sentence S_2
$S_1 \Leftrightarrow S_2$	sentences S_1 and S_2 are equivalent
$S_1 \nLeftrightarrow S_2$	sentences S_1 and S_2 are not equivalent
blik$_\tau$	arbitrary denotation of a word *blik*, of type τ
BLIK$_\tau$	constant denotation of a word *blik*, of type τ
$[[exp]]^M$	denotation of an expression *exp* in model M
$\varphi : \tau$	denotation φ of type τ
$[\upsilon_1 \mapsto r_1\ \upsilon_2 \mapsto r_2 \dots]$	a function that maps υ_1 to r_1, υ_2 to r_2 etc.
χ_Y	the characteristic function of a set Y
$f^\star$	the set characterized by a function f
e	type of semantic entities
t	type of truth-values
f	type of phonetic entities
D_τ	domain of type τ
$\mathcal{F}^E$	frame over an entity domain E
E	domain of semantic entities (D_e)
F	domain of phonetic entities (D_f)

ix

$(\tau\sigma)$	for any type τ and σ, the type of functions from D_τ to D_σ, abbreviated '$\tau\sigma$'
$\lambda x_\tau.\varphi_\sigma$	the function mapping any x in D_τ to the corresponding element of D_σ described by φ
$\sim$	propositional negation
$\wedge$	propositional conjunction
$\vee$	propositional disjunction
$\rightarrow$	implication/functional constructor between abstract types
AND^τ	conjunction for denotations of type τ
OR^τ	inclusive disjunction for denotations of type τ
OR_{in}	inclusive denotation of *or*
OR_{ex}	exclusive denotation of *or*
adj^{mod}	modificational denotation of adjective of type $(et)(et)$
adj^{arb}	arbitrary denotation of adjective of type $(et)(et)$
MON↑/MON↓	upward/downward monotone generalized quantifier, upward/downward right-monotone determiner
MON¬	non-monotone generalized quantifier, non-right-monotone determiner
$\mathbf{D}_f$	determiner relation corresponding to a function f of type $(et)((et)t)$
↑MON/↓MON	upward/downward left-monotone determiner
¬MON	non-left-monotone determiner
$x \cdot y$	concatenation of strings x and y (also multiplication of numbers x and y)
I_x	individual substitute for entity x
$P^w_{e(st)}$	extension in world w of property denotation $P_{e(st)}$
IS^I_{id}	intensional *be* of identity
$[\varphi]^i$	hypothetical assumption φ with index i
ε	empty phonetic entity

ABBREVIATIONS

A	adjective
ACG	Abstract Categorial Grammar
def.	definition/definition of
DRT	Discourse Representation Theory
FA	function application
f-denotation	phonetic denotation
f-type	phonetic type
GQ	generalized quantifier
iff	if and only if
MP	Modus Ponens
N	noun/nominal
NP	noun phrase
NPI	negative polarity item
S	sentence
s-denotation	semantic denotation
s.t.	such that
s-type	semantic type
TCC	Truth-Conditionality Criterion
TCC^E/TCC^I	extensional/intensional Truth-Conditionality Criterion
VP	verb phrase

CHAPTER 1

INTRODUCTION

One of the most striking aspects of human language is the complexity of the meanings that it conveys. No other animal possesses a mode of expression that allows it to articulate intricate emotions, describe distant times and places, study molecules and galaxies, or discuss the production of sophisticated tools, weapons and cures. The complex meanings of natural language make it an efficient, general-purpose instrument of human thought and communication. But what are meanings? And how does language convey them?

To illustrate one aspect of the problem, let us consider a phrase in one of Bob Dylan's famous love songs. The phrase opens the song's refrain by describing a woman, whose identity is not disclosed. It goes like this:

(1.1) sad-eyed lady of the lowlands, where the sad-eyed prophet says that no man comes

If we want to restate the meaning of this phrase in simpler terms, we can do it as follows:

(1.2) There's a lady. That lady has sad eyes. She is from the lowlands. Some prophet also has sad eyes. That prophet says "no man comes to the lowlands".

Without doubt, this way of paraphrasing Dylan's verse robs it of much of its poetic value. But at the same time it also highlights a remarkable property of meaning in natural language. When we hear a long expression like (1.1), we immediately draw from it all sorts of simple conclusions. This happens even in cases where we miss information that is important for understanding the "true meaning" of what is being said. Dylan's song only gives vague clues about the identity of the lady. Yet upon hearing the refrain we unfailingly draw from (1.1) the conclusions in (1.2). The converse is true as well: when Dylan invented his description of the sad-eyed lady, he must have implicitly assumed the statements in (1.2) as part of its meaning. This kind of back-and-forth reasoning occurs whenever we think and converse. When we hear, utter or think of an expression, we instinctively relate it to other phrases that we consider obvious conclusions. Drawing such trivial-looking inferences using our language is one of the abilities that characterize us as linguistic creatures. No other animal has this linguistic ability, and no current technology can accurately mimic it.

Our effortless manipulation of meaning is highly systematic, and relies on an ingrained ability to recognize structure in language. When we hear the phrase in (1.1), we mentally tack its words into short collocations like *sad-eyed* and *the lowlands*. Further, short expressions are tacked together into longer expressions such as *sad-eyed lady from the lowlands*. These syntactic dependencies between words and expressions lead to a complex hierarchical structure. In the case of (1.1), some main elements of this structure are represented below.

(1.3) [[sad-eyed] lady] [of [[the lowlands], [where [[the [[sad-eyed] prophet]] [says [that [[no man] comes]]]]]]]

The bracketed expressions in (1.3) represent *constituents*: sub-parts of the description in (1.1) that act as syntactic units – noun phrases, verb phrases, clauses etc. As the representation in (1.3) illustrates, constituents are often embedded within one another. For instance, the short sentence *no man comes* is embedded in the verb phrase *says that no man comes*, which is itself embedded within the sentence *the sad-eyed prophet says that no man comes*. In total, the expression in (1.1) has no fewer than seven levels of constituents that are embedded within each other. This complexity does not impair our ability to make sense of the description. Furthermore, it is part and parcel of our ability to understand it. In (1.1), the highly organized way in which the constituents are embedded makes it possible for us to immediately grasp Dylan's complex vision as paraphrased in (1.2). In the case of complicated phrases like (1.1), it is clear that we would not be able to extract even the basic paraphrase in (1.2) if language did not support well-organized hierarchical structures. Furthermore, syntactic hierarchies help us to extract meaning from most other linguistic expressions, including ones that are much more ordinary than Dylan's verse.

The subfield of linguistics known as *formal semantics* studies how linguistic structure helps speakers to manipulate meaning. The word 'formal' stresses the centrality of linguistic forms in the enterprise. At the same time, the token 'formal' also expresses a motivation to account systematically for language meanings by using precise mathematical methods. Formal semanticists have benefited from the many breakthroughs in logic and computer science, two disciplines that constantly develop new artificial languages and address challenging questions about their meanings and forms. The dazzling achievements that logicians and computer scientists achieved in the twentieth century were based on a rich tradition of research in philosophy of language and the foundations of mathematics. It is only natural that in the 1960s, when semanticists started to systematically address questions about meaning and form in natural language, they turned to these neighboring disciplines in search of guiding principles. As a result, formal semantics relies on the mathematical foundations that were laid in major works on logic, philosophy of language and theoretical computer science.

The mathematical foundations of formal semantics give us precise tools for studying natural languages. Mathematical semantic models help us see what meanings are, and, more importantly, why they can be shared by different expressions. By examining meanings under the powerful microscope of mathematical theories, formal semantics has obtained effective methods for uncovering systematic regularities in the everyday use of language expressions.

The scientific value of this linguistic endeavor is further enhanced by recent developments in other branches of cognitive science that study natural language. In the emerging field of *cognitive neuroscience*, mathematical principles are becoming increasingly important for harnessing recent advances in brain imaging. As a leading cognitive neuroscientist puts it: "only mathematical theory can explain how the mental reduces to the neural. Neuroscience needs a series of bridging laws [...] that connect one domain to the other" (Dehaene 2014, p. 163). These laws are also needed in order to understand how the brain enables the semantic dexterity of language speakers. Mental semantic faculties are profitably described by mathematical laws. Recent works in natural language semantics have supported many of these laws by statistically analyzing experimental data. As neuroscience brings more experimental data on the workings of the brain, it is becoming increasingly important to connect statistical generalizations about this data with models of our mental semantic abilities.

Similar procedures of mathematical theorizing are equally critical in current work in *artificial intelligence*. Recent advances in statistical machine learning make it possible to exploit formal semantic principles to enhance algorithms and computing technologies. In a recent state-of-the-art review, the authors describe this new direction, stating that "the distinction between logical and statistical approaches is rapidly disappearing with the development of models that can learn the conventional aspects of natural language meaning from corpora and databases" (Liang and Potts 2015, p. 356). In the new domain of computational semantics, mathematical and logical principles of formal semantics are increasingly employed together with statistical algorithms that deal with the parametrization of abstract semantic models by studying distributions of various linguistic phenomena in ordinary language.

Although these recent developments are not the focus of the current book, they do highlight new motivations for using precise principles and techniques in the study of natural language semantics. The achievements of formal semantics have formed a lively area of research, where new ideas, techniques, experimental results and computer systems appear every day. This book introduces you to some of the most important mathematical foundations of this field.

AIMS AND ORGANIZATION OF THIS BOOK

The two senses of the word 'formal' have a key role in this textbook. The book is a systematic introduction to the study of form and meaning in natural language. At the same time, it capitalizes on the precise mathematical principles and techniques that underlie their analysis. The aim is to help the reader acquire the tools that would allow her to do further semantic work, or engage in interdisciplinary research that relies on principles of formal semantics. Because of that, the book does not attempt to single out any of the current versions of formal semantic theory. Rather, it covers five topics that are of utmost importance to all of them.

Chapter 2 is a general overview of the major goals and techniques in formal semantics. It focuses on the principles of natural language semantics that support meaning relations as in (1) and (2). These semantic relations are called *entailments*. They are described by abstract mathematical *models*, and general principles of compositionality that connect forms with model-theoretical meanings.

Chapter 3 introduces *semantic types* as a means of systematizing the use of models. Typed meanings are derived from simpler ones by a uniform semantic operation of function application. A convenient notation of *lambda-terms* is introduced for describing semantic functions. This notation is illustrated for a couple of modification and coordination phenomena.

Chapter 4 uses the principles and tools of the two previous chapters for treating *quantification*. By focusing on the semantics of noun phrases that involve counting and other statements about quantities, Chapter 4 directly introduces one of the best-known parts of formal semantics: the theory of generalized quantifiers.

Chapter 5 extends the framework of the preceding chapters for treating meaning relations between expressions that appear a certain distance from each other. A principle of *hypothetical reasoning* is added to the system of Chapter 3. This principle works in duality with function application, and complements its operation. The two principles apply within a system of linguistic *signs*, which controls the interactions between forms and meanings.

Chapter 6 treats *intensional expressions*: expressions that refer to attitudes, beliefs or possibilities. Such expressions are treated in semantic models containing entities that represent *possible worlds*. Possible world semantics is introduced as a systematic generalization of the system developed in previous chapters.

Part of the material in Chapters 3 and 6 was covered by early textbooks on "Montague Grammar" (see further reading at the end of this chapter). Here, this material is introduced in a more general setting that takes recent findings into account and capitalizes on the mathematical architecture of type-theoretical grammars. Chapter 4 is unique in being a detailed textbook-level introduction to the central problem of quantification in natural language, which is fully based on the type-theoretical framework of Chapter 3. The treatment of long-distance dependencies in Chapter 5 is the first textbook-level introduction of a general theoretical configuration known as *Abstract Categorial Grammar*.

At the end of each chapter there are exercises (see below) and references for suggested further reading. Further materials can be found through the website of Edinburgh University Press, at the following link:

edinburghuniversitypress.com/book/9780748640430

ON THE EXERCISES IN THIS BOOK

At the end of each chapter you will find some exercises, with model solutions to many of them. Acquiring the ability to solve these exercises constitutes an integral part of studying the material in this book. You will be referred to exercises at various points of the text, and further developments in the book often rely on the exercises in previous chapters. There are two kinds of exercise:

- Technical exercises, which should be solvable by using only the methods explained in the body of the textbook.
- More advanced exercises, which are specified at the beginning of each exercise section. Some of these advanced exercises introduce new notions that were not addressed in the text. These more "notional" advanced exercises are listed in **boldface** at the beginning of the exercises, and are especially recommended among the advanced exercises.

Upon finishing a chapter, and before moving on to the next chapter, it is advisable to make sure that you can correctly solve all of the technical exercises.

WHO IS THIS BOOK FOR?

The book is meant for any reader who is interested in human language and its mathematical modeling. For readers whose main interest is linguistic theory, the book serves as an introduction to some of the most useful tools and concepts in formal semantics, with numerous exercises to help grasp them. Readers who are mainly interested in mathematical models of language will find in the book an introduction to natural language semantics that emphasizes its empirical and methodological motivations.

The book is especially suitable for the following audiences:

- general readers with the necessary mathematical background (see below)
- students and teachers of undergraduate linguistics courses on natural language semantics, which put sufficient emphasis on its set-theoretical background (see below)
- students and teachers of relevant undergraduate courses in artificial intelligence, computer science, cognitive science and philosophy
- researchers and advanced students in linguistics

PRESUPPOSED BACKGROUND

To be able to benefit from this book you should have some basic background in naive set theory. At the end of this chapter, you will find some suggestions for further reading, as well as some standard notation, exercises and solutions. By solving the exercises, you will be able to practice some basic set theory at the required level before you start reading. The book does not presuppose any prior knowledge in logic or theoretical linguistics. However, some general familiarity with these disciplines may be useful. Some suggestions for textbooks that introduce this background are given in the suggestions for further reading at the end of this chapter.

FOR THE INSTRUCTOR

The material in this book has been used for teaching undergraduate and graduate courses in linguistics, computer science and artificial intelligence programs. Different kinds of audiences may benefit from different complementary materials. For linguistics students, the most important additions should include more semantic and pragmatic theories of phenomena like anaphora, plurals, events, ellipsis, presupposition or implicature. In most linguistics programs, a short introduction to basic set-theoretical notions would be necessary in order to allow students to grasp the materials in this book (for materials see the further reading section below). For computer science and AI students, additional material on computational semantics may be useful, especially if it is accompanied by programming assignments. The type-theoretical semantics in this book is especially easy to adapt for programming in strongly typed functional languages like Haskell. Some remarks about recommended literature are made at the end of the further reading section below.

FURTHER READING

Background material on linguistics, set theory and logic: For a general introduction to linguistics, see Fromkin et al. (2014). For a classical introduction to naive set theory, see Halmos (1960). Linguistics students may find the introduction in Partee et al. (1990, chs.1–3) more accessible. For a useful open-source introduction and exercises, see ST (2015). Two classical textbooks on logic are Suppes (1957); Barker-Plummer et al. (2011).

On the history of formal semantics: For a book-length overview, see Partee (2015). For article-length overviews, see Abbott (1999); Partee (1996).

Other introductions to formal semantics: Chapters 3 and 6 overlap in some critical aspects with the early textbooks Dowty et al. (1981) and Gamut (1982), which introduced formal semantics as developed in Montague (1973). Zimmermann and Sternefeld (2013) is a friendly introduction to basic topics in formal semantics. For some of the topics covered in the present book, there are also more advanced textbooks that may be consulted. Carpenter (1997) and Jacobson (2014) are detailed introductions to compositional type-theoretical semantics. Jacobson's book also contains an elaborate linguistic discussion. For introductions to formal semantics as it is often used in generative grammar, see Chierchia and McConnel-Ginet (1990); Heim and Kratzer (1997). For an introduction to formal semantics in the framework of Discourse Representation Theory, see Kamp and Reyle (1993). Readers who are interested in general perspectives on meaning besides formal semantics may consult Elbourne (2011); Saeed (1997).

For the instructor: On further important topics in formal semantics that are not covered in this textbook, see Chapter 7. For a textbook that uses the Haskell programming language to illustrate some of the core problems in formal semantics, see Van Eijck and Unger (2010).

Concepts and notation from set theory

$x \in A$ x is an *element of* the set $A = x$ is a *member of* A

$x \notin A$ x is not an element of A

$\emptyset$ the *empty set* = the set that has no members

$A \subseteq B$ the set A is a *subset* of the set $B = B$ is a *superset* of A = every element of A is an element of B

$A \nsubseteq B$ A is not a subset of B

$\wp(A)$ the *powerset* of A = the set of all subsets of A. Example: $\wp(\{a, b\}) = \{\emptyset, \{a\}, \{b\}, \{a, b\}\}$

$A \cap B$ the *intersection* of A and B = the set of elements that are in both A and B

$A \cup B$ the *union* of A and B = the set of elements that are in A or B (or both)

$A - B$ the *difference* between A and B = the set of elements in A that are not in B

$\overline{A}$ the *complement* of A (in E) = $E - A$, where E is a given superset of A

$|A|$ the *cardinality* of A = for finite sets: the number of elements in A

$\{x \in A : S\}$ the set of elements in A s.t. the statement S holds
Example: $\{x \in \{a, b\} : x \in \{b, c\}\} = \{a, b\} \cap \{b, c\} = \{b\}$

$\{A \subseteq B : S\}$ the set of subsets of B s.t. the statement S holds. Example: $\{A \subseteq \{a, b\} : |A| = 1\} = \{\{a\}, \{b\}\}$

$\langle x, y \rangle$ an ordered pair of items x and y

$A \times B$ the *cartesian product* of A and B = the set of ordered pairs $\langle x, y \rangle$ s.t. $x \in A$ and $y \in B$
Example: $\{a, b\} \times \{1, 2\} = \{\langle a, 1 \rangle, \langle a, 2 \rangle, \langle b, 1 \rangle, \langle b, 2 \rangle\}$

A *binary relation between A and B* is a subset of the cartesian product $A \times B$.

A *function f from A to B* is a binary relation between A and B that satisfies: for every $x \in A$, there is a unique $y \in B$ s.t. $\langle x, y \rangle \in f$. If f is a function where $\langle x, y \rangle \in f$, we say that f *maps x to y*, and write $f : x \mapsto y$ or $f(x) = y$.

Example: the binary relation $f = \{\langle a, 1 \rangle, \langle b, 2 \rangle\}$ is a function from $\{a, b\}$ to $\{1, 2\}$, which is equivalently specified $[a \mapsto 1, b \mapsto 2]$ or by indicating that $f(a) = 1$ and $f(b) = 2$.

B^A is the set of functions from A to B.

Example: $\{1, 2\}^{\{a,b\}}$ = the functions from $\{a, b\}$ to $\{1, 2\}$
$= \{[a \mapsto 1, b \mapsto 1], [a \mapsto 1, b \mapsto 2], [a \mapsto 2, b \mapsto 1], [a \mapsto 2, b \mapsto 2]\}$

EXERCISES

1. Which of the following statements are true?
   (i) $a \in \{a, b\}$ (ii) $\{a\} \in \{a, b\}$ (iii) $\{a\} \subseteq \{a, b\}$
   (iv) $a \subseteq \{a, b\}$ (v) $\{a\} \in \{a, \{a\}\}$ (vi) $\{a\} \subseteq \{a, \{a\}\}$
   (vii) $\{\{a, b, c\}\} \subseteq \wp(\{a, b, c\})$ (viii) $\{\{a, b, c\}\} \in \wp(\{a, b, c\})$
   (ix) $\emptyset \in \{\{a\}, \{b\}, \{c\}\}$ (x) $\emptyset \subseteq \{\{a\}, \{b\}, \{c\}\}$

2. Write down explicitly the following sets by enumerating their members, e.g. $\wp(\{a\}) = \{\emptyset, \{a\}\}$.
   (i) $\wp(\{a, b, c\})$ (ii) $\{a\} \cap \wp(\{a\})$ (iii) $\{\{a\}\} \cap \wp(\{a, b\})$
   (iv) $\wp(\{a, b\}) \cap \wp(\{b, c\})$ (v) $(\wp(\{a\}) \cup \wp(\{b\})) \cap \wp(\{a, b\})$
   (vi) $\wp(\wp(\emptyset))$

3. Write down explicitly the following sets by enumerating their members.
   (i) $(\{a, b\} \times \{c\}) \cap (\{a\} \times \{b, c\})$ (ii) $\wp(\{\emptyset\}) \times \wp(\{a, b\})$
   (iii) $\wp(\{a, b\} \times \{c\}) - \wp(\{a\} \times \{b, c\})$

4. Which of the following binary relations are functions from $\{a, b\}$ to $\{1, 2\}$?
   (i) $\{\langle a, 1 \rangle\}$ (ii) $\{\langle a, 1 \rangle, \langle b, 2 \rangle\}$ (iii) $\{\langle a, 1 \rangle, \langle a, 2 \rangle\}$
   (iv) $\{\langle a, 1 \rangle, \langle b, 1 \rangle\}$ (v) $\{\langle a, 1 \rangle, \langle a, 2 \rangle, \langle b, 1 \rangle\}$

5. How many binary relations are there between $\{a, b\}$ and $\{1, 2\}$? How many of them are functions?

6. Write down the functions in $\{no, yes\}^{\{a,b,c\}}$. For each such function show a member of the powerset $\wp(\{a, b, c\})$ that intuitively corresponds to it.

7. Write down the functions in $\{a, b, c\}^{\{left, right\}}$. For each such function show a member of the cartesian product $\{a, b, c\} \times \{a, b, c\}$ that intuitively corresponds to it.

8. Write down explicitly the following sets of functions:
   (i) $\wp(\{a\})^{\wp(\{b\})}$ (ii) $\{1, 2\}^{\{a,b\} \times \{c\}}$ (iii) $(\{1, 2\}^{\{c\}})^{\{a,b\}}$

9. Consider the following function f in $\{1, 2\}^{\{a,b\} \times \{c,d\}}$:
   $[\langle a, c \rangle \mapsto 1, \langle a, d \rangle \mapsto 1, \langle b, c \rangle \mapsto 2, \langle b, d \rangle \mapsto 1]$.
   Write down the function g in $(\{1, 2\}^{\{c,d\}})^{\{a,b\}}$ that satisfies for every x in $\{a, b\}$, for every y in $\{c, d\}$: $(g(x))(y) = f(\langle x, y \rangle)$.

10. Write down explicitly the members of the following sets:
    (i) $\{f \in \{a, b\}^{\{b,c\}} : f(b)=b\}$ (ii) $\{A \subseteq \{a, b, c, d\} : |A| \geq 3\}$
    (iii) $\{\langle x, y \rangle \in \{a, b, c\} \times \{b, c, d\} : x \neq y\}$

SOLUTIONS TO EXERCISES

1. i, iii, v, vi, vii, x

2. (i) $\{\emptyset, \{a\}, \{b\}, \{c\}, \{a, b\}, \{a, c\}, \{b, c\}, \{a, b, c\}\}$ (ii) $\emptyset$
   (iii) $\{\{a\}\}$ (iv) $\{\emptyset, \{b\}\}$ (v) $\{\emptyset, \{a\}, \{b\}\}$ (vi) $\{\emptyset, \{\emptyset\}\}$

3. (i) $\{\langle a, c \rangle\}$ (ii) $\{\langle \emptyset, \emptyset \rangle, \langle \emptyset, \{a\} \rangle, \langle \emptyset, \{b\} \rangle, \langle \emptyset, \{a, b\} \rangle, \langle \{\emptyset\}, \emptyset \rangle,$
   $\langle \{\emptyset\}, \{a\} \rangle, \langle \{\emptyset\}, \{b\} \rangle, \langle \{\emptyset\}, \{a, b\} \rangle\}$ (iii) $\{\{\langle b, c \rangle\}, \{\langle a, c \rangle, \langle b, c \rangle\}\}$

4. ii, iv

5. 16; 4

6. $[a \mapsto no, \ b \mapsto no, \ c \mapsto no] : \emptyset$
   $[a \mapsto yes, \ b \mapsto no, \ c \mapsto no] : \{a\}$
   $[a \mapsto no, \ b \mapsto yes, \ c \mapsto no] : \{b\}$
   $[a \mapsto no, \ b \mapsto no, \ c \mapsto yes] : \{c\}$
   $[a \mapsto yes, \ b \mapsto yes, \ c \mapsto no] : \{a, b\}$
   $[a \mapsto yes, \ b \mapsto no, \ c \mapsto yes] : \{a, c\}$
   $[a \mapsto no, \ b \mapsto yes, \ c \mapsto yes] : \{b, c\}$
   $[a \mapsto yes, \ b \mapsto yes, \ c \mapsto yes] : \{a, b, c\}$

7. $[left \mapsto a, \ right \mapsto a] : \langle a, a \rangle$ $[left \mapsto a, \ right \mapsto b] : \langle a, b \rangle$
   $[left \mapsto a, \ right \mapsto c] : \langle a, c \rangle$
   $[left \mapsto b, \ right \mapsto a] : \langle b, a \rangle$ $[left \mapsto b, \ right \mapsto b] : \langle b, b \rangle$
   $[left \mapsto b, \ right \mapsto c] : \langle b, c \rangle$
   $[left \mapsto c, \ right \mapsto a] : \langle c, a \rangle$ $[left \mapsto c, \ right \mapsto b] : \langle c, b \rangle$
   $[left \mapsto c, \ right \mapsto c] : \langle c, c \rangle$

8. (i) $\{[\emptyset \mapsto \emptyset, \{b\} \mapsto \emptyset], [\emptyset \mapsto \emptyset, \{b\} \mapsto \{a\}], [\emptyset \mapsto \{a\}, \{b\} \mapsto \emptyset],$
   $[\emptyset \mapsto \{a\}, \{b\} \mapsto \{a\}]\}$
   (ii) $\{[\langle a, c \rangle \mapsto 1, \langle b, c \rangle \mapsto 1], [\langle a, c \rangle \mapsto 1, \langle b, c \rangle \mapsto 2],$
   $[\langle a, c \rangle \mapsto 2, \langle b, c \rangle \mapsto 1], [\langle a, c \rangle \mapsto 2, \langle b, c \rangle \mapsto 2]\}$
   (iii) $\{[a \mapsto [c \mapsto 1], b \mapsto [c \mapsto 1]], [a \mapsto [c \mapsto 1], b \mapsto [c \mapsto 2]],$
   $[a \mapsto [c \mapsto 2], b \mapsto [c \mapsto 1]], [a \mapsto [c \mapsto 2], b \mapsto [c \mapsto 2]]\}$

9. $[a \mapsto [c \mapsto 1, d \mapsto 1], b \mapsto [c \mapsto 2, d \mapsto 1]]$

10. (i) $[b \mapsto b, c \mapsto a], [b \mapsto b, c \mapsto b]$
    (ii) $\{b, c, d\}, \{a, c, d\}, \{a, b, d\}, \{a, b, c\}, \{a, b, c, d\}$
    (iii) $\langle a, b \rangle, \langle a, c \rangle, \langle a, d \rangle, \langle b, c \rangle, \langle b, d \rangle, \langle c, b \rangle, \langle c, d \rangle$

CHAPTER 2

MEANING AND FORM

This chapter introduces some of the key notions about the analysis of meaning in formal semantics. We focus on entailments: *relations between premises and valid conclusions expressed as natural language sentences. Robust intuitions about entailment are distinguished from weaker types of reasoning with language. Speaker judgments on entailments are described using* models: *abstract mathematical structures, which emanate from semantic analyses of artificial logical languages. Model-theoretical objects are directly connected to syntactic structures by applying a general principle of* compositionality. *We see how this principle helps to analyze cases of structural ambiguity and to distinguish them from other cases of under-specification.*

What do dictionaries mean when they tell us that semantics is "the study of meaning"? The concept that people intuitively refer to as "meaning" is an abstraction inspired by observing how we use language in everyday situations. However, we use language for many different purposes, and those various usages may inspire conceptions of meaning that are radically different from one another. We cannot reasonably expect a theory of meaning to cover everything that people do with their languages. A more tractable way of studying meaning is by discerning specific properties of language use that are amenable to scientific investigation. These aspects of language use, if stable across speakers and situations, will ultimately guide us toward a theory of language "meaning".

ENTAILMENT

One of the most important usages of natural language is for everyday reasoning. For example, let us consider sentence (2.1):

(2.1) Tina is tall and thin.

From this sentence, any English speaker is able to draw the conclusion in (2.2) below:

(2.2) Tina is thin.

Thus, any speaker who considers sentence (2.1) to be true, will consider sentence (2.2) to be true as well. We say that sentence (2.1) *entails* (2.2), and denote it (2.1)⇒(2.2). Sentence (2.1) is called the *premise*, or *antecedent*, of the entailment. Sentence (2.2) is called the *conclusion*, or *consequent*.

The entailment from (2.1) to (2.2) exemplifies a relation that all English speakers will agree on. This consistency is remarkable, and all the more so since words like *Tina*, *tall* and *thin* are notoriously flexible in the way that they are used. For instance, you and I may have different criteria for characterizing people as being *thin*, and therefore disagree on whether Tina is thin or not. We may also disagree on the identity of Tina. You may think that Tina in sentences (2.1) and (2.2) is Tina Turner, while I may think that these sentences describe Tina Charles. However, we are unlikely to disagree on whether sentence (2.2) is a sound conclusion from (2.1).

We noted that when sentence (2.1) is judged to be true, so is sentence (2.2). However, the converse does not hold: (2.2) may be true while (2.1) is not – this is the case if Tina happens to be thin but not tall. Because of such situations, we conclude that sentence (2.2) does *not* entail (2.1). This is denoted (2.2)⇏(2.1). Just as with positive judgments on entailment, rejections of entailment are also often uniform across speakers and circumstances of use. Therefore, we consider both positive and negative judgments on entailment as important empirical evidence for semantic theory.

When studying simple entailments, we often pretend that our language vocabulary is very small. Still, as soon as our vocabulary has some simple adjectives and proper names, we can easily find entailments and non-entailments by looking at their different combinations with words like *and, or, is* and *not*. For instance:

(2.3) a. Tina is tall, and Ms. Turner is not tall ⇒ Tina is not Ms. Turner.

     b. Tina is tall, and Tina is not Ms. Turner ⇏ Ms. Turner is not tall.

(2.4) a. Ms. Turner is tall, and Tina is Ms. Turner or Ms. Charles
       $\Rightarrow$ Tina is tall or Tina is Ms. Charles.

       b. Ms. Turner is tall, and Tina is Ms. Turner or Ms. Charles
       $\not\Rightarrow$ Tina is tall.

The examples above may look unsurprising for anyone who is familiar with philosophical or mathematical logic. Indeed, similar entailments in natural language have inspired well-known logical formalisms like Propositional Logic and Predicate Logic. Readers may therefore wonder: don't the entailments above demonstrate puzzles that were solved long ago by logicians? The answer is "yes and no". Sure enough, these entailments can be translated to well-understood logical questions. However, logic does not traditionally focus on the details of the translation procedure from ordinary language to logical languages. This translation step is not "pure logic": it also involves intricate questions about the sounds and the forms of human languages, and about the nature of semantic concepts in the human mind. Consequently, in modern cognitive science, the study of entailment in natural language is not the sanctuary of professional logicians. Entailment judgments bring to the forefront a variety of questions about language that are also of primary concern for linguists, computer scientists, psychologists and philosophers. For instance, let us consider the following entailments:

(2.5) a. Sue only drank half a glass of wine $\Rightarrow$ Sue drank less than
       one glass of wine.

       b. A dog entered the room $\Rightarrow$ An animal entered the room.

       c. John picked a blue card from the pack $\Rightarrow$ John picked a
       card from the pack.

The entailments in (2.5) illustrate different aspects of language: measures and quantity in (2.5a); word meaning relations in (2.5b); adjective modification in (2.5c). These kinds of entailment are very common in natural language, but they were not systematically treated in classical logic. By studying the whole spectrum of entailments in ordinary language, formal semantics addresses various aspects of linguistic phenomena and their connections with human reasoning. Ideas from logic are borrowed insofar as they are useful for analyzing natural language semantics. More specifically, later in this book we adopt concepts from type theory and higher-order logics that have proved especially well suited for studying entailment in natural language. As we shall see, incorporating these concepts allows formal semantics to develop important connections with theories about sentence structure and word meaning.

Among the phenomena of reasoning in language, entailment is especially central because of its remarkable stability. In other instances of reasoning with natural language, conclusions are not fully stable, since they may rely on implicit assumptions that emanate from context, world knowledge or probabilistic principles. These lead to meaning relations between sentences that are often fuzzier and less regular than entailments. Consider for instance the following two sentences:

(2.6) Tina is a bird.

(2.7) Tina can fly.

Sentence (2.7) is a likely conclusion from (2.6), and most speakers will not hesitate too much before drawing it. However, upon some reflection we can come up with many situations in which sentence (2.6) truthfully holds without supporting the conclusion in (2.7). Think of young birds, penguins, ostriches, or birds whose wings are broken. Thus, in many natural discourses speakers may accept (2.6) while explicitly denying (2.7):

(2.8) Tina is a bird, but she cannot fly, because ... (she is too young to fly, a penguin, an ostrich, etc.).

We classify the inferential relation between sentences like (2.6) and (2.7) as *defeasible*, or cancelable, reasoning. By contrast, entailments are classified as *indefeasible reasoning*: all of the assumptions that are needed in order to reach the conclusion of an entailment are explicitly stated in the premise. For instance, the entailment (2.1)$\Rightarrow$(2.2) cannot be easily canceled by adding further information to the premise.

A discourse like (2.9) below that tries to contradict sentence (2.2) after asserting (2.1) will normally be rejected as *incoherent*.

(2.9) #Tina is tall and thin, but she is not thin.

A speaker who wishes to support this incoherent line of reasoning would need to resort to self-contradictory or otherwise counter-communicative arguments like "because I am lying when saying that Tina is tall and thin", or "because I am not using English in the ordinary way". The incoherence of (2.9) is marked by '#'. Sentence (2.9) is intelligible but nonsensical: its communicative value is dubious. This sort of incoherent, contradictory sentence should be distinguished from *ungrammaticality*. The latter notion is reserved for strings of words that clearly do not belong to natural language, e.g. *is and tall Tina thin*. Such ungrammatical strings are standardly marked by '*'.

Taking stock, we adopt the following notion of entailment:

---

*Given an indefeasible relation between two natural language sentences S_1 and S_2, where speakers intuitively judge S_2 to be true whenever S_1 is true, we say that S_1 **entails** S_2, and denote it $S_1 \Rightarrow S_2$.*

Just as intuitive judgments about sentence grammaticality have become a cornerstone in syntactic theory, intuitions about entailments between sentences are central for natural language semantics. As in other linguistic domains, we aim to build our semantic theory on judgments that do not rely on training in linguistics, logic or other scholarly disciplines. Entailments that robustly appear in ordinary reasoning give us a handle on common semantic judgments about language.

Entailments between sentences allow us to define the related notion of *equivalence*. For instance, the sentence (2.1)=*Tina is tall and thin* and the sentence S=*Tina is tall and Tina is thin* are classified as equivalent, because they entail each other. We denote this equivalence (2.1)$\Leftrightarrow$S. For more examples of equivalent sentences see Exercise 4. Another classical semantic notion is *contradiction*, which was lightly touched upon in our discussion of sentence (2.9) above. See Exercise 7 for some elaboration on contradictions and their relations to entailment.

MODELS AND THE TRUTH-CONDITIONALITY CRITERION

With this background on entailments in natural language, let us now see how formal semantics accounts for them. As mentioned above, formal semantics relies on some central principles from traditional philosophical and mathematical logic. Most versions of formal semantics account for entailments using theoretical structures that are called *models*. Models are mathematical abstractions that we construct and use as descriptions of hypothetical situations. We call these situations "hypothetical" because they do not necessarily correspond to actual situations in the world. Some of our models may agree with how we look at the world, but some of them will also describe situations that are purely imaginary. For instance, the models that we use for analyzing the sentence *Tina is thin* will describe situations in which Tina is thin, as well as situations where she is not thin. If you know a woman called Tina and you think that she is thin, you will consider the first models as closer to reality than the others. However, this is irrelevant for our purposes. For the sake of our semantic analysis we consider all the models that we construct as hypothetical. As such, they are all equal.

In order to encode hypothetical situations in models, we let models link words to abstract mathematical objects. For instance, since we want our models to describe situations in relation to the word *Tina*, we let each model contain some or other abstract entity that is associated with this word. Similarly, when we analyze the words *tall* and *thin*, we also let our models associate these adjectives with abstract objects. In this chapter we let models link adjectives to *sets* of entities. Thus, in each model we include a set of entities that is associated with the word *tall*. These are the abstract entities in that model that are considered tall in the hypothetical situation that the model describes. Similarly, each model associates the adjective *thin* with the set of entities that are considered thin in the situation.

In addition to dealing with words, models also treat *complex expressions*: phrases and sentences that are made up of multiple words. For example, let us consider the complex phrase *tall and thin*. Just like we did in the case of simple adjective words, we let each model associate this phrase with a set of entities. These are the entities that are considered to be tall and thin in the hypothetical situation that the model describes. Other words, phrases and sentences are associated with all sorts of abstract mathematical objects. The words, phrases and sentences that we treat are collectively referred to as *expressions*. In each of our models, we associate abstract objects with all the expressions that we treat.

Summarizing, we state our general conception of models as follows:

> A **model** *is an abstract mathematical structure that we construct for describing hypothetical situations. Models are used for analyzing natural language expressions (words, phrases and sentences) by associating them with abstract objects.*

Associating language expressions with abstract objects is part and parcel of a model definition. For instance, one of the models that we use, call it M, may associate the word *Tina* with some abstract entity a. In technical terms, we say that in the model M, the word *Tina* denotes the entity a. In all the models that we study in this chapter, the name *Tina* denotes some or other entity, and the adjective *tall* denotes some or other set of entities. Given a particular model M, we refer to those denotations as $[[Tina]]^M$ and $[[tall]]^M$, respectively. Similarly, $[[tall\ and\ thin]]^M$ is the denotation of the phrase *tall and thin* in the model M. In general, we adopt the following notational convention:

> Let exp *be a language expression, and let M be a model. We write* $[[exp]]^M$ *when referring to the* **denotation** *of* exp *in the model M.*

To have a more concrete view on models and denotations, let us consider Figure 2.1. This figure describes two models, each of them containing three entities: a, b and c. In model M_1, the name *Tina* denotes the entity a, and the adjective *thin* denotes the set $\{a, b\}$. In model M_2, the denotation of *Tina* is again the entity a, but this time, the set denotation of *thin* is the set $\{b, c\}$. We formally write it as follows:

$$[[Tina]]^{M_1} = a \quad [[thin]]^{M_1} = \{a, b\}$$
$$[[Tina]]^{M_2} = a \quad [[thin]]^{M_2} = \{b, c\}$$

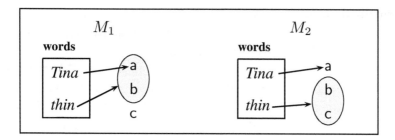

Figure 2.1   *Models map words and other expressions to abstract mathematical objects. M_1 and M_2 are models with an entity denotation of* Tina *and a set denotation of* thin. *The arrows designate the mappings from the words to their denotations, which are part of the model definition.*

Figure 2.1 only illustrates the assignment of denotations to simple words. However, as mentioned above, models are used in order to assign denotations to all expressions that we analyze, including complex expressions that are made of multiple words. In particular, models specify denotations for *sentences*. There are various ideas about what kinds of abstract objects sentences should denote. In most of this book, we follow the traditional assumption that sentences denote the two abstract objects known as *truth-values*, which are referred to as 'true' and 'false'. In more technical notation, we sometimes write '$\top$' for 'true' and '$\bot$' for 'false'. Yet another convention, which is most convenient for our purposes, is to use the number 1 for 'true' and the number 0 for 'false'.

Models assign truth-value denotations to sentences on the basis of the denotations they assign to words. For instance, the way we use models such as M_1 and M_2 in Figure 2.1 respects the intuition that the sentence *Tina is thin* is true in M_1 but false in M_2. Thus, we will make sure that M_1 and M_2 satisfy:

$$[\![\textit{Tina is thin}]\!]^{M_1} = 1 \qquad\qquad [\![\textit{Tina is thin}]\!]^{M_2} = 0$$

As we move on further in this chapter, we see how this analysis is formally obtained.

The truth-value denotations that models assign to sentences are the basis for our account of entailment relations. Let us return to the entailment between the sentence *Tina is tall and thin* (=(2.1)) and the sentence *Tina is thin* (=(2.2)). When discussing this entailment, we informally described our semantic judgment by saying that whenever sentence (2.1) is true, sentence (2.2) must be true as well. By contrast, we observed that the intuition does not hold in the other direction: when (2.2) is true, sentence (2.1) may be false. For this reason we intuitively concluded that sentence (2.2) does *not* entail (2.1). When analyzing (non-)entailment relations, we take into account these pre-theoretical intuitions about 'truth' and 'falsity'. We analyze an entailment $S_1 \Rightarrow S_2$ by introducing the following requirement: if a model lets S_1 denote *true*, it also lets S_2 denote *true*. When truth-values are represented numerically, this requirement means that if a model lets S_1 denote the number 1, it also lets S_2 denote 1.

Specifically, in relation to the entailment $(2.1) \Rightarrow (2.2)$, we require that for every model where sentence (2.1) denotes the value 1, sentence (2.2) denotes 1 as well. Another way to state this requirement is to say that in every model, the truth-value denotation of (2.1) is *less than or equal to* the denotation of (2.2). Let us see why this is indeed an equivalent requirement. First, consider models where the denotation of (2.1) is 1. In such models, we also want the denotation of (2.2) to be 1. Indeed, requiring $[[(2.1)]] \leq [[(2.2)]]$ boils down to requiring that $[[(2.2)]]$ is 1: this is the only truth-value for (2.2) that satisfies $1 \leq [[(2.2)]]$. Further, when we consider models where the denotation of (2.1) is 0, we see that such models trivially satisfy the requirement $0 \leq [[(2.2)]]$, independently of the denotation of (2.2).

To conclude: saying that $[[(2.2)]]$ is 1 in every model where $[[(2.1)]]$ is 1 amounts to saying that $[[(2.1)]] \leq [[(2.2)]]$ holds in every model. Accordingly, we translate our intuitive analysis of the entailment $(2.1) \Rightarrow (2.2)$ to the formal requirement that $[[(2.1)]] \leq [[(2.2)]]$ holds in every model. More generally, our aim is to account for entailments using the $\leq$ relation between truth-values in models. This leads to a central requirement from formal semantic theory, which we call the *truth-conditionality criterion* (TCC):

A semantic theory T satisfies the **truth-conditionality criterion** (TCC) *for sentences S_1 and S_2 if the following two conditions are equivalent:*

   (I)   *Sentence S_1 intuitively entails sentence S_2.*

   (II) *For all models M in T: $[[S_1]]^M \leq [[S_2]]^M$.*

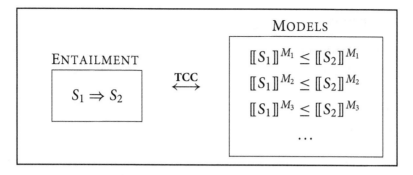

Figure 2.2 *The TCC matches judgments on entailment with the $\leq$ relation. When the entailment $S_1 \Rightarrow S_2$ holds, the $\leq$ relation is required to hold between the truth-value denotations of S_1 and S_2 in all the models of the theory.*

Table 2.1:   Does $x \leq y$ hold?

	$y=0$	$y=1$
$x=0$	**yes**	**yes**
$x=1$	**no**	**yes**

Clause (I) of the TCC postulates an entailment between sentences S_1 and S_2. This is an *empirical* statement about the semantic intuitions of native speakers. By contrast, clause (II) is a statement about our *theory*'s treatment of sentences S_1 and S_2: the formal models we use indeed rely on intuitive notions of 'truth' and 'falsity', but they are purely theoretical. By imposing a connection between the empirical clause (I) and the theoretical clause (II), the TCC constitutes an *adequacy criterion* for semantic theory.

By way of recapitulation, Figure 2.2 illustrates how the TCC emulates the intuitive relation of entailment ('$\Rightarrow$') between sentences, by imposing the $\leq$ relation on sentence denotations in the models that our theory postulates. Table 2.1 summarizes how the requirement $x \leq y$ boils down to requiring that if x is 1, then y is 1 as well. Readers who are familiar with classical logic may observe the similarity between Table 2.1 and the truth table for *implication*. We will get back to this point in Chapter 5.

ARBITRARY AND CONSTANT DENOTATIONS

We have introduced the TCC as a general criterion for the empirical
adequacy of formal semantics. Obviously, we want our theory to
respect the TCC for as many intuitive (non-)entailments as possible.
This will be our main goal throughout this book. Let us start our
investigations by using the TCC to explain our favorite simple entailment: $(2.1) \Rightarrow (2.2)$. We want to make sure that the models that
we construct respect the TCC for this entailment. Thus, we need to
define which models we have in our theory, and then check what truth-
values each model derives for sentences (2.1) and (2.2). The models
that we define fix the denotations of words like *Tina*, *tall* and *thin*. In
technical jargon, words are also called *lexical items*. Accordingly, we
will refer to the denotations of words as *lexical denotations*. Based on
the lexical denotations that models assign to words, we will define the
truth-values assigned to sentences containing them. To do that, let us
explicitly state the assumptions that we have so far made about our
models:

1. In every model M, in addition to the two truth-values 0 and 1, we
   have an arbitrary non-empty set E^M of the entities in M. We refer
   to this set as the *domain* of entities in M. For instance, in models
   M_1 and M_2 of Figure 2.1, the entity domains E^{M_1} and E^{M_2} are the
   same: in both cases they are the set {a, b, c}.
2. In any model M, the proper name *Tina* denotes an arbitrary entity
   in the domain E^M (cf. Figure 2.1).
3. In any model M, the adjectives *tall* and *thin* denote arbitrary <u>sets</u> of
   entities in E^M (cf. Figure 2.1).

When the model is understood from the context, we often write
E for the domain of entities, suppressing the subscript M. We say
that the domains of entities in the models we define are 'arbitrary'
because we do not make any special assumptions about them: *any* non-
empty set may qualify as a possible domain of entities in some model.
Accordingly, we also treat the entity denotation of *Tina* as an arbitrary
element of E. Whether this entity corresponds to a real-life entity like
Tina Turner or Tina Charles is not our business here. We are not even
insisting that the entity for *Tina* has 'feminine' properties, as might be
suitable for a feminine English name. All we require is that in every
model, the name *Tina* denotes *some* entity. In a similar fashion, we let

the adjectives *tall* and *thin* denote arbitrary sets in our models. This arbitrariness is of course an over-simplification, but it will do for our purposes in this book. Here we study the meanings of words only to the extent that they are relevant for the study of entailment. Of course, much more should be said on word meanings. This is the focus of research in lexical semantics, which deals with many other important aspects of word meaning besides their contribution to entailments. For some readings on this rich domain, see some recommendations at the end of this chapter.

From now on we will often use words in **boldface** when referring to arbitrary denotations. For instance, by '**tina**' we refer to the element $[\![Tina]\!]$ of E that is denoted by the word *Tina* in a given model. Similarly, '**tall**' and '**thin**' are shorthand for $[\![tall]\!]$ and $[\![thin]\!]$: the *sets* of entities in E denoted by the words *tall* and *thin*. Putting words in boldface in this way is a convenience that spares us the use of the double brackets $[\![\,]\!]$. When we want to be more specific about the model M, we write $\textbf{tina}^M$ or $[\![Tina]\!]^M$.

In our discussion of Figure 2.1, we noted that the sentence *Tina is thin* is intuitively true in M_1 but false in M_2. We can now see how this intuition is respected by our precise definition of models. To achieve that, we make sure that the sentences *Tina is thin* reflects a *membership assertion*. We only allow the sentence to be true in models where the entity denoted by *Tina* is a member of the set denoted by the adjective. Therefore, we analyze the word *is* as denoting a *membership function*. This is the function sending every entity x and set of entities A to the truth-value 1 if x is an element of A. If x is not an element of A, the membership function sends x and A to the truth-value 0. When referring to the membership function that the word *is* denotes, we use the notation 'IS'. Formally, we define IS as the function that satisfies the following, for every entity x in E and every subset A of E:

$$\text{IS}(x, A) = \begin{cases} 1 \text{ if } x \in A \\ 0 \text{ if } x \notin A \end{cases}$$

For example, let us reconsider the models M_1 and M_2 that we saw in Figure 2.1. With our new assumption on the denotation of the word *is*, we now get:

In M_1: $[\![Tina\ is\ thin]\!] = \text{IS}(\textbf{tina}, \textbf{thin}) = \text{IS}(a, \{a, b\}) = 1$ *since* a ∈ {a, b}

In M_2: $[\![Tina\ is\ thin]\!] = \text{IS}(\textbf{tina}, \textbf{thin}) = \text{IS}(a, \{b, c\}) = 0$ *since* a ∉ {b, c}

Thus, in M_1 the sentence *Tina is thin* denotes 1, and in M_2 it denotes 0, as intuitively required. More generally, in (2.10) below we summarize the denotation that the sentence *Tina is thin* is assigned in every model:

$$(2.10) \quad [\![\textit{Tina is thin}]\!]^M \;=\; \textsc{is}(\textbf{tina}, \textbf{thin}) \;=\; \begin{cases} 1 \text{ if } \textbf{tina} \in \textbf{thin} \\ 0 \text{ if } \textbf{tina} \notin \textbf{thin} \end{cases}$$

When referring to denotations, we have made a difference between the font for the denotations **tina, tall** and **thin**, and the font for the denotation IS. There is a reason for this notational difference. As mentioned, the denotations of the words *Tina, tall* and *thin* are arbitrarily chosen by our models. We have presented no semantic 'definition' for the meaning of these words. Models are free to let the name *Tina* denote any of their entities. Similarly, the adjectives *tall* and *thin* may denote any of set of entities. By contrast, the denotation of the word *is* has a constant definition across models: in all models we define this denotation as the membership function. We will have more to say about this distinction between denotations in Chapter 3. In the meantime, let us summarize our notational conventions:

Let blik *be a word in a language. When the denotation* $[\![\text{blik}]\!]^M$ *of* blik *is arbitrary, we mark it* **blik**. *When it has a constant definition across models we mark it* BLIK.

ANALYZING AN ENTAILMENT

In order to analyze the entailment (2.1)$\Rightarrow$(2.2), let us now also look at the denotation of the sentence *Tina is tall and thin*. Since we let the sentence *Tina is thin* denote the truth-value of a membership assertion, it is only natural to analyze the sentence *Tina is tall and thin* in a similar way. Thus, we want this sentence to be true if the entity **tina** is a member of a set denoted by the conjunction *tall and thin*. But what should this set be? The same semantic intuitions that supported the entailment (2.1)$\Rightarrow$(2.2) can guide us to the answer. Obviously, for Tina to be tall and thin, she has to be tall, and she also has to be thin. And vice versa: if Tina is tall, and if in addition she is also thin, there is no way to avoid the conclusion that she is tall and thin. Elementary as they are, these considerations suggest that if we are going to let the conjunction *tall and thin* denote a set, it had better be the *intersection* of the two sets for the adjectives *tall* and *thin*. Formally, we write:

$$[\![tall\ and\ thin]\!]^M = [\![tall]\!]^M \cap [\![thin]\!]^M = \textbf{tall} \cap \textbf{thin}.$$

Thus, we define the denotation of the word *and* to be the *intersection function* over E. This is the function AND that satisfies the following, for all subsets A and B of E:

$$\text{AND}(A,\ B) = A \cap B$$

$$= \text{the set of all members of } E \text{ that are both in } A \text{ and in } B$$

Now there is also no doubt about the denotation of the sentence *Tina is tall and thin*. Using the same kind of membership assertion that we used for the sentence *Tina is thin*, we reach the following denotation for this sentence:

(2.11) $[\![Tina\ is\ tall\ and\ thin]\!]^M = \text{IS}(\ \textbf{tina},\ \text{AND}(\textbf{tall},\textbf{thin})\ )$

$$= \begin{cases} 1 \text{ if } \textbf{tina} \in \textbf{tall} \cap \textbf{thin} \\ 0 \text{ if } \textbf{tina} \notin \textbf{tall} \cap \textbf{thin} \end{cases}$$

In words: in every given model M, the sentence *Tina is tall and thin* denotes the truth-value 1 if the entity **tina** is in the intersection of the sets **tall** and **thin**; otherwise the sentence denotes 0.

We have now defined the truth-value denotations that the sentences *Tina is tall and thin* and *Tina is thin* have in every model. These are the truth-values specified in (2.11) and (2.10), respectively. Therefore, we can use the TCC in order to verify that our theory adequately describes the entailment between the two sentences. As a matter of set theory, the truth-value (2.10) must be 1 if the truth-value in (2.11) is 1: if the entity **tina** is in the intersection **tall** ∩ **thin**, then, by definition of intersection and set membership, it is also in the set **thin**. This set-theoretical consideration holds for all possible denotations **tina**, **tall** and **thin**. Thus, it holds for all models. This means that our assignment of denotations to sentences (2.1) and (2.2) has been successful in meeting the TCC when accounting for the entailment between them.

At this point you may feel that the games we have been playing with entities, sets, functions and truth-values are just restating obvious intuitions. This is perfectly true. Indeed, there is reason to feel satisfied

about it. Semantic models provide us with a general and mathemati-
cally rigorous way of capturing common intuitions about entailment.
A model is a small but precise description of a particular situation
in which different sentences may be true or false. By specifying the
denotations of the words *Tina, tall* and *thin*, a model describes, in an
abstract way, who Tina is, and what the tall entities and thin entities
are. As we have seen, and as we shall see in more detail throughout
this book, models also take care of more "logical" denotations for
words like *and* and *is*. This assignment of denotations to lexical items
enables us to systematically assign denotations to complex expressions,
including conjunctive phrases like *tall and thin* and sentences like
Tina is tall and thin. If we are successful in assigning denotations to
such complex expressions, we may be reasonably hopeful that our
strategies will also be useful for much higher levels of hierarchical
embedding (e.g. Dylan's description of the sad-eyed lady on page
1). In fact, by defining truth and falsity in models for two simple
sentences, we have been forced to dive rather deep into the meanings
of conjunction, predication, adjectives and proper names, and the ways
in which they combine with each other. As we shall see in the following chapters, much of our elementary set-theoretical maneuvering
so far is valuable when tackling more advanced questions in formal
semantics.

When looking at a class of models that is heterogenous enough, we
can "see", so to speak, whether one sentence must denote 1 when
another sentence does. Let us get a feel of what is going on in the
simple example we have been treating, by playing a little with some
concrete models. Let us consider Table 2.2, which summarizes our
assumptions so far and illustrates them concretely in the three models
described in the rightmost columns. Each of these models has the set
$E = \{a, b, c, d\}$ as its domain of entities. In model M_1, the word *Tina*
denotes the entity a, and the word *thin* denotes the set of three entities
$\{a, b, c\}$. Model M_2 assigns different denotations to these words: *Tina*
denotes the entity b, and *thin* denotes the set $\{b, c\}$. In model M_3, the
denotation of *Tina* remains the entity b, as in model M_2, while the
adjective *thin* denotes a set of three entities: $\{a, c, d\}$. Accordingly, the
truth-values in the three models for the sentence *Tina is thin* are 1, 1
and 0, respectively. Similarly, using the assumed denotations for *tall*,
we can also verify that the truth-values in these three models for the
sentence *Tina is tall and thin* are 0, 1 and 0, respectively. Satisfying

Table 2.2: Denotations for expressions in the entailment (2.1)$\Rightarrow$(2.2).

Expression	Cat.	Type	Abstract denotation	Denotations in example models with $E = \{a, b, c, d\}$		
				M_1	M_2	M_3
Tina	PN	entity	**tina**	a	b	b
tall	A	set of entities	**tall**	{b, c}	{b, d}	{a, b, d}
thin	A	set of entities	**thin**	{a, b, c}	{b, c}	{a, c, d}
tall and thin	AP	set of entities	AND(**tall, thin**)	{b, c}	{b}	{a, d}
Tina is thin	S	truth-value	IS(**tina, thin**)	1	1	0
Tina is tall and thin	S	truth-value	IS(**tina**, AND(**tall, thin**))	0	1	0

Categories: PN = proper name; A = adjective; AP = adjective phrase; S = sentence.

the TCC means that the latter value must be less than or equal to the former value, which is indeed the case.

Model M_1 in Table 2.2 shows that the TCC is also met for the non-entailment (2.2)$\nRightarrow$(2.1). This model makes sentence (2.2) true while making (2.1) false. This means that our theory respects the requirement in the TCC that, if an entailment is missing, then at least one model does not satisfy the $\leq$ relation between the truth-values of the two sentences in question. In formula, model M_1 satisfies $[\![(2.2)]\!]^{M_1} \nleq [\![(2.1)]\!]^{M_1}$. Furthermore, model M_1 also respects our intuition of *why* an entailment is absent in this case. As pointed out above, if somebody tried to convince you that Tina must be tall and thin just because she happens to be thin, you might reasonably object by pointing out the possibility that Tina may *not* be tall. Model M_1 highlights this possibility.

DIRECT COMPOSITIONALITY

So far we have been paying little attention to sentence structure. However, as mentioned in the introduction, one of our main interests is how meanings of natural language expressions are related to the syntactic forms of these expressions. For instance, let us consider the following two sentences:

(2.12)   a. All pianists are composers, and Tina is a pianist.
     b. All composers are pianists, and Tina is a pianist.

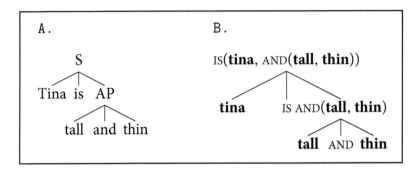

Figure 2.3   Syntactic structure and compositional derivation of denotations for Tina is tall and thin.

Sentences (2.12a) and (2.12b) contain the same words but in a different order. Consequently, the meanings of these two sentences are rather different. In particular, while (2.12a) entails the sentence *Tina is a composer*, sentence (2.12b) does not. The meaning of an expression is not a soup made by simply putting together the meanings of words. Rather, the order of the words in a complex expression and the hierarchical structures that they form affect its meaning in systematic ways. Since entailment relations between sentences reflect an aspect of their meanings, entailments are also sensitive to sentence structure. In the framework that we assume here, entailments are explained by appealing to model-theoretic denotations. Therefore, the question we are facing is: how are syntactic structures used when defining denotations of complex expressions? The general principle known as compositionality provides an answer to this question. According to this principle, the denotation of a complex expression is determined by the denotations of its immediate parts and the ways they combine with each other. For instance, in our analysis of the entailment (2.1)⇒(2.2), we treated the denotation of sentence (2.1) (*Tina is tall and thin*) as derived step by step from the denotations of its parts: the name *Tina*, the verb *is*, and the adjective phrase *tall and thin*. Figure 2.3 summarizes our compositional analysis.

Figure 2.3A shows the syntactic part-whole relations that we assume for the sentence. In this structure we group together the string of words *tall and thin* into one adjectival phrase, which we denote *AP*. More generally, tree diagrams as in Figure 2.3A represent the sentence's constituents: the parts of the sentence that function as grammatical units. In this case, besides the sentence itself and the words it contains, the only syntactic constituent assumed is the adjectival phrase *tall and thin*. Figure 2.3B describes how denotations of constituents are derived from the denotations of their immediate parts. The denotation of the adjectival phrase *tall and thin* is determined by combining the denotations of its immediate parts: **tall**, AND and **thin**. The denotation of the whole sentence is determined by the denotations of its parts: **tina**, IS, and AND(**tall**, **thin**). What we get as a result is the truth-value denotation in (2.11). The way in which this truth-value is derived is sanctioned by the compositionality principle on the basis of the structure in Figure 2.3A. Note that compositionality would not allow us to derive the truth-value in any other order. For instance, on the basis of the structure in Figure 2.3A, we would not be able to compositionally define the denotation of the whole sentence directly on the basis of the denotations of the adjectives *tall* and *thin*. These words are not among the sentence's immediate parts. Therefore, according to the compositionality principle, they can only indirectly affect its denotation.

Summarizing, we have adopted the following general principle, and seen how we follow it in our analysis of the entailment (2.1)$\Rightarrow$(2.2).

Compositionality: *The denotation of a complex expression is determined by the denotations of its immediate parts and the ways they combine with each other.*

A word of clarification should be added here about the role of semantic formulas in our analysis. Consider for instance the formula IS(**tina**, AND(**tall**,**thin**)) that we derive in Figure 2.3B. This formula is not a representation of some abstract meaning, independent of the sentence structure. To the contrary, this formula is almost completely identical to the structure in Figure 2.3A, while adding only the necessary semantic details for describing how the denotation is derived for sentence (2.1). Most importantly, the formula specifies the function-argument relations between the denotations of the sentence constituents. Thus, the formula IS(**tina**, AND(**tall**, **thin**)) is simply the syntactic bracketing [*Tina is* [*tall and thin*]] imposed by the tree in Figure 2.3A, with two modifications: (i) symbols for words are replaced by symbols of their denotations; and (ii) symbols for denotations may be shuffled around in order to follow the convention of putting function symbols to the left of their arguments. This respects the highly restrictive nature of compositional analysis: the process only requires a syntactic structure, denotations of lexical items, and a way to glue the denotations together semantically. The real "semantic action" is within these three components of the theory, not within the semantic formulas we use. This version of compositionality is sometimes referred to as *direct compositionality*. In this paradigm, denotations in the model are directly derived from syntactic structures, with no intermediate level of semantic or logical representation.

STRUCTURAL AMBIGUITY

Direct compositionality helps to clarify an important issue in linguistic theory: the phenomenon of *structural ambiguity*. Consider the following sentence:

(2.13) Tina is not tall and thin.

Let us consult our intuitions with respect to the following question: does (2.13) entail sentence (2.2) (=*Tina is thin*) or not? This is much harder to judge than in the case of the entailment (2.1)$\Rightarrow$(2.2). However, there is a common intuition that (2.13) entails (2.2), but only *under particular usages*. A speaker who wishes to convey the entailment (2.13)$\Rightarrow$(2.2) can do so by stressing the prosodic boundary after the word *tall*:

(2.14) Tina is not tall, and thin.

Without such an intonational pattern, a speaker can also use (2.13) felicitously for describing a situation where Tina is not thin. For instance, if we tell Sue that Tina is tall and thin, she may use (2.13) for denying the assertion, by saying something like:

(2.15) Come on, that isn't true! *Tina is not tall and thin*: although she is indeed very tall, you couldn't possibly think of her as thin!

In this reaction, the way in which Sue uses sentence (2.13) clearly indicates that she does not consider it to entail sentence (2.2).

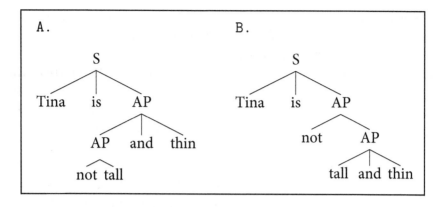

Figure 2.4   Structural ambiguity.

Because the two usages of sentence (2.13) show differences between its "entailment potential", we say that it is *ambiguous*. The "comma intonation" in (2.14) *disambiguates* the sentence. Another way of disambiguating sentence (2.13) is illustrated in (2.15), using the context of our conversation with Sue. In the former disambiguation, sentence (2.13) is used for entailing (2.2); in the latter disambiguation, the entailment from (2.13) to (2.2) is blocked. We refer to the two possible usages of sentence (2.13) as *readings* of the sentence. One reading entails (2.2), the other does not. Another way to describe the "two readings" intuition is to note that sentence (2.13) may be intuitively classified as both true and false in the same situation. Consider a situation where Tina is absolutely not thin. Context (2.15) highlights that sentence (2.13) may be used as true in this situation. By contrast, (2.14) highlights that the sentence also has the potential of being false in the same situation.

The striking thing about the ambiguity of sentence (2.13) is the ease with which it can be described when we assume the compositionality principle. Virtually all syntactic theories analyze sentence (2.13) as having two different syntactic structures, as illustrated in Figure 2.4. A simple phrase structure grammar that generates the structural ambiguity in Figure 2.4 is given in (2.16) below:

(2.16) AP ⟶ *tall, thin, ...*

      AP ⟶ AP *and* AP

      AP ⟶ *not* AP

In words: an adjective phrase (AP) can be a simple adjective, or a conjunction of two other APs, or a negation of another AP. These rules derive both structures in Figure 2.4. When a grammar generates more than one structure for an expression in this way, we say that it treats the expression as *structurally ambiguous*. You may think that the syntactic ambiguity in Figure 2.4 is by itself already an elegant account of the semantic ambiguity in (2.13). However, there is a gap in this account: why does it follow that the structural ambiguity of sentence (2.13) also makes it *semantically* ambiguous? Compositionality provides the missing link. When the two structures in Figure 2.4 are compositionally analyzed, we immediately see that the same model may assign them two different truth-values. Concretely, let us assume that the denotation of the negation word *not* in (2.13) is the *complement function*, i.e. the function NOT that maps any subset A of E to its complement set:

$$\text{NOT}(A) = \overline{A} = E - A = \text{the set of all the members of } E \text{ that are not in } A$$

Figure 2.5 uses the denotation NOT for illustrating the compositional analysis of the two structures in Figure 2.4. As Figure 2.5 shows, the compositional process works differently for each of the two structural analyses of sentence (2.13). For each of the denotations in Figures 2.5A and 2.5B to be 1, different requirements have to be satisfied. This is specified in (2.17a) and (2.17b) below:

(2.17) a. IS(**tina**, AND(NOT(**tall**), **thin**)) = 1
          This holds if and only if (iff) **tina** $\in$ $\overline{\textbf{tall}} \cap \textbf{thin}$.

       b. IS(**tina**, NOT(AND(**tall**, **thin**))) = 1
          This holds if and only if **tina** $\in$ $\overline{\textbf{tall} \cap \textbf{thin}}$.

For the denotation in Figure 2.5A to be 1, the requirement in (2.17a) must hold. When this is the case, the entity **tina** is in the set **thin**, hence the truth-value assigned to the sentence *Tina is thin* (=(2.2)) is also 1. Thus, our compositional analysis of the structure in Figure 2.4A captures the reading of sentence (2.13) that entails sentence (2.2). By contrast, the denotation (2.17b) that is derived in Figure 2.5B does not guarantee that the entity **tina** is in the set **thin**. This is because the entity **tina** may be in the complement set $\overline{\textbf{tall} \cap \textbf{thin}}$ while being in the set **thin**, as long as it is not in the set **tall**. Specifically, consider a model

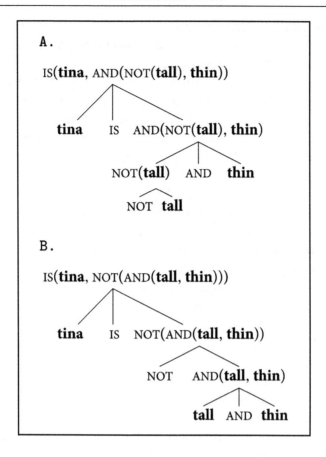

Figure 2.5   Compositionality and ambiguity.

M where the entities **tina, mary** and **john** are t, m and j, respectively. Suppose further that the model *M* assigns the following denotations to the adjectives *thin* and *tall*:

thin = {t, j}   **tall** = {m, j}

The model *M* represents a situation where Tina is thin but not tall, Mary is tall but not thin, and John is both thin and tall. In this model, the denotation in Figure 2.5B is the truth-value 1, but sentence (2.2) denotes the truth-value 0. This means that our compositional analysis of the structure in Figure 2.4B captures the reading of sentence (2.13) that does not entail sentence (2.2).

In compositional systems, the structure that we assume for a sentence strongly affects the entailment relations that our theory expects for it. When a sentence is assumed to be structurally ambiguous, a compositional theory may assign different truth-values to its different structures. As a result, the theory may expect different entailment relations to hold for the different structures. Accordingly, when speakers are confronted with such a sentence, they are expected to experience what we informally call "semantic ambiguity", i.e. some systematic hesitations regarding some of the sentence's entailments. Structural ambiguity is used as the basis of our account of semantic ambiguity. Once we have acknowledged the possibility of ambiguity, we prefer to talk about the entailments that sentence *structures* show, and of the truth-values that are assigned to these structures. However, for the sake of convenience, we often say that sentences themselves have entailments and truth-values. This convention is harmless when the sentences in question are unambiguous, or when it is clear that we are talking about a particular reading.

Semanticists often distinguish the syntactic-semantic ambiguity of sentences like (2.13) from another type of under-specification, which is called *vagueness*. For instance, as we noted above, the sentence *Tina is tall* says little about Tina and her exact height. In some contexts, e.g. if Tina is known to be a Western female fashion model, the sentence may be used for indicating that Tina is above 1.70 meters. In other contexts, e.g. if Tina is known to be member of some community of relatively short people, the sentence may indicate that Tina is above 1.50 meters. However, we do not consider these two usages as evidence that the sentence must be assigned different structures with potentially different denotations. Rather, we say that the sentence *Tina is tall* is vague with respect to Tina's height. Further specification of relevant heights is dealt with by augmenting our semantic treatment with a *pragmatic theory*. Pragmatic theories also consider the way in which sentences are used, and the effects of context on their use. Pragmatic theories aim as well to account for the way speakers resolve (or partly resolve) vagueness in their actual use of language. Classical versions of formal semantics did not aim to resolve vagueness, but current semantic theories often interact with pragmatics and describe the way context helps in resolving vagueness in actual language use.

Vagueness is very prominent in the way natural languages are used, and most sentences may be vague in one way or another. For instance, the sentence *Sue is talking* tells us nothing about Sue's voice (loud or quiet, high or low, etc.), what Sue is talking about, who the addressee is, etc. However, upon hearing the sentence, we may often use the context to infer such information. For instance, suppose that we are at a conference and know that Sue is one of the speakers. In such a context, we may draw some additional conclusions about the subject of Sue's talk and the addressees. Hearers often use context in this way to extract more information from linguistic expressions, and speakers often rely on their hearers to do that. In distinction from entailment, such inferential processes which are based on contextual knowledge are defeasible. For instance, even when the context specifies a particular conference where Sue is a speaker, we may use the sentence *Sue is talking* to indicate that Sue is talking to a friend over the phone. What we saw in sentence (2.13) is quite different from the defeasible reasoning that helps speakers and hearers in their attempts to resolve vagueness of language utterances. The comma intonation in (2.14) illustrated that one phonological expression of sentence (2.13) *indefeasibly* entails sentence (2.2). This convinced us that both structures that we assigned to sentence (2.13) are semantically useful. The theoretical consideration was the key for our treatment of the sentence as semantically ambiguous, more than any "pure" linguistic intuition. Most decisions between ambiguity and vagueness involve similar theoretical considerations, rather than the direct judgments of a speaker's linguistic intuitions.

FURTHER READING

Introductory: For methodological aspects of logical semantics, including truth-values, entailment and compositionality, see Gamut (1982, vol. 1). For more examples and discussion of structural ambiguity, see Zimmermann and Sternefeld (2013, ch. 3), and, in relation to vagueness, Kennedy (2011). For further discussion of compositionality, see Partee (1984). On defeasible reasoning, see Koons (2014). Levinson (1983) is an introductory textbook on pragmatics. On lexical semantics, see Cruse (1986); Murphy (2010). Meaning relations between words and concepts they refer to are extensively studied in the literature on categorization. See Laurence and Margolis (1999); Smith (1988); Taylor (1989) for introductions of these topics.

Advanced: The idea that sentences denote truth-values, and more generally, *propositions* (cf. Chapter 6), was proposed as central for communication (Austin 1962; Searle 1969). The centrality of entailment and the model-theoretic TCC was also highlighted in semantic theories of non-indicative sentences, especially *interrogatives* (Groenendijk and Stokhof 1984, 2011). An alternative to the model-theoretic approach to entailment is *proof-theoretic semantics* (Schroeder-Heister, 2014). In its application to natural language, proof-theoretic approaches are sometimes referred to as *natural logic*. Some examples of work in this area are McAllester and Givan (1992); Sánchez (1991); Moss (2010). Defeasible reasoning in language is related to *common sense reasoning* in work in artificial intelligence (Brewka et al. 1997) and cognitive psychology (Stenning and van Lambalgen 2007; Adler and Rips 2008). For more on pragmatic theories, and specifically the notion of *implicature*, see Grice (1975); Geurts (2010); Chierchia et al. (2012). Much of this work pays close attention to the meaning and use of the word *or* (cf. the choice between 'inclusive' and 'exclusive' denotations in Exercise 6). Direct compositionality in contemporary semantics of natural language was first illustrated in Montague (1970*a*). For further work on compositionality, see Montague (1970*b*); Janssen (1983); Janssen with Partee (2011); Barker and Jacobson (2007); Pagin and Westerståhl (2010); Werning et al. (2012).

EXERCISES (ADVANCED: **4**, 5, **6**, 7, **8**, 9, 10)

1. In the following pairs of sentences, make a judgment on whether there is an entailment between them, and if so, in which of the two possible directions. For directions in which there is no entailment, describe informally a situation that makes one sentence true and the other sentence false. For example, in the pair of sentences (2.1) and (2.2), we gave the judgment (2.1)$\Rightarrow$(2.2), and supported the non-entailment (2.2)$\not\Rightarrow$(2.1) by describing a situation in which Tina is thin but not tall.

   (i) *a.* Tina got a B or a C. *b.* Tina got a B.
   (ii) *a.* Tina is neither tall nor thin. *b.* Tina is not thin.
   (iii) *a.* Mary arrived. *b.* Someone arrived.
   (iv) *a.* John saw fewer than four students. *b.* John saw no students.
   (v) *a.* The ball is in the room. *b.* The box is in the room and the ball is in the box.
   (vi) *a.* Hillary is not a blond girl. *b.* Hillary is not a girl.

(vii) *a*. Hillary is a blond girl. *b*. Hillary is a girl.

(viii) *a*. Tina is a Danish flutist and a physicist. *b*. Tina is a Danish physicist and a flutist.

(ix) *a*. Tina is not tall but taller than Mary. *b*. Mary is not tall.

(x) *a*. Mary ran. *b*. Mary ran quickly.

(xi) *a*. I saw fewer than five horses that ran. *b*. I saw fewer than five black horses that ran.

(xii) *a*. I saw fewer than five horses that ran. *b*. I saw fewer than five animals that ran.

(xiii) *a*. Exactly five pianists in this room are French composers. *b*. Exactly five composers in this room are French pianists.

(xiv) *a*. No tall politician is multilingual. *b*. Every politician is monolingual.

(xv) *a*. No politician is absent. *b*. Every politician is present.

(xvi) *a*. At most three pacifists are vegetarians. *b*. At most three vegetarians are pacifists.

(xvii) *a*. All but at most three pacifists are vegetarians. *b*. At most three non-vegetarians are pacifists.

2. Each of the following sentences is standardly considered to be structurally ambiguous. For each sentence suggest two structures, and show an entailment that one structure intuitively supports and the other structure does not:

(i) I read that Dan published an article in the newspaper.

(ii) Sue is blond or tall and thin.

(iii) The policeman saw the man with the telescope.

(iv) Rich Americans and Russians like to spend money.

(v) Sue told some man that Dan liked the story.

(vi) Dan ate the lettuce wet.

(vii) Sue didn't see a spot on the floor.

3. Table 2.2 shows different denotations for the expressions in sentences (2.1) and (2.2) in different models. We used these models and the truth-values they assign to the sentences to support our claim that the TCC explains the entailment $(2.1) \Rightarrow (2.2)$, and the non-entailment $(2.2) \not\Rightarrow (2.1)$.

The table on the right gives the expressions for the two analyses in Figure 2.5 of the sentence *Tina is not tall and thin*.

   a. Add to this table the missing denotations of these expressions within the three models M_1, M_2 and M_3.

b. Verify that the truth-values that you assigned to the two analy-
ses in Figure 2.5 support the intuition that the analysis in
Figure 2.4A entails sentence (2.2), whereas the analysis in
Figure 2.4B does not entail (2.2).

Expression	Denotations in example models with $E = \{a, b, c, d\}$		
	M_1	M_2	M_3
Tina	a	b	b
tall	{b, c}	{b, d}	{a, b, d}
thin	{a, b, c}	{b, c}	{a, c, d}
not tall			
[not tall] and thin			
Tina is [[not tall] and thin]			
tall and thin			
not [tall and thin]			
Tina is [not [tall and thin]]			
Tina is thin			

4.a. Mark the pairs of sentences in Exercise 1 that you considered
equivalent.
 b. Give three more examples for pairs of sentences that you consider intuitively equivalent.
 c. State the formal condition that a semantic theory that satisfies
the TCC has to satisfy with respect to equivalent sentences.
5. Consider the ungrammaticality of the following strings of words.
  (i) *Tina is both tall   *Tina is both not tall   *Tina is both tall or
thin
  To account for this ungrammaticality, let us assume that the word
both only appears in adjective phrases of the structure both AP_1
and AP_2. Thus, a constituent both X is only grammatical when X
is an and-conjunction of two adjectives or adjective phrases; hence
the grammaticality of the string both tall and thin as opposed to the
ungrammaticality of the strings in (i), where X is tall, not tall and
tall or thin, respectively. We assume further that the denotation
of a constituent both AP_1 and AP_2 is the same as the denotation of the parallel constituent AP_1 and AP_2 as analyzed in this
chapter.

a. With these syntactic and semantic assumptions, write down the denotations assigned to the following sentences in terms of the denotations **tina**, **tall**, **thin**, IS and AND.
(ii) Tina is both not tall and thin.   (iii) Tina is not both tall and thin.

b. Explain why the denotations you suggested for (ii) and (iii) account for the (non-)entailments (ii)$\Rightarrow$(2.2) and (iii)$\not\Rightarrow$(2.2).

c. Consider the equivalence between the following sentences:
(iv) Tina is both not tall and not thin.   (v) Tina is neither tall nor thin.

Suggest a proper denotation for the constituent *neither tall nor thin* in (v) in terms of the denotations **tall** and **thin** (standing for sets of entities). Explain how the denotation you suggest, together with our assumptions in items 5a and 5b above, explain the equivalence (iv)$\Leftrightarrow$(v).

6. Consider the following sentence:
(i) Tina is [tall or thin].
The *inclusive* or *exclusive* analyses for the coordinator *or* involve denotations that employ the *union* and *symmetric difference* functions, respectively – the functions defined as follows for all $A, B \subseteq E$:

$\text{OR}_{in}(A, B) = A \cup B$
$\qquad\qquad$ = the set of members of E that are in A, in B or in both A and B

$\text{OR}_{ex}(A, B) = (A - B) \cup (B - A) = (A \cup B) - (A \cap B)$
$\qquad\qquad$ = the set of members of E that are in A or B, but not both A and B

Consider the following sentential structures:
(ii) Tina is not [tall and thin].
(iii) Tina is not [tall or thin].
(iv) Tina is [not tall] and [not thin].
(v) Tina is [not tall] or [not thin].

a. Assuming that the word *or* denotes the function OR_{in}, write down all the entailments that the TCC expects in (ii)–(v). Answer the same question, but now assuming that *or* denotes OR_{ex}.

   b. Which of the two entailment patterns in 6a better captures your linguistic intuitions about (ii)–(v)?

   c. Under one of the two analyses of *or*, one of the structures (ii)–(v) is expected to be equivalent to (i). Which structure is it, and under which analysis? Support your answer by a set-theoretical equation.

7. A pair of sentences (or readings/structures) is said to be treated as *contradictory* if, whenever one of the sentences is taken to denote 1, the other denotes 0. For instance, under the analysis in this chapter, the sentences *Mary is tall* and *Mary is not tall* are contradictory.

   a. Give more examples for contradictory pairs of sentences/structures under the assumptions of this chapter.

   b. Consider the sentences *The bottle is empty* and *The bottle is full*. Suggest a theoretical assumption that would render these sentences contradictory.

   c. Give an entailment that is accounted for by the same assumption.

   d. Show that according to our account, the denotation of the sentence *Tina is tall and not tall* is 0 in any model. Such a sentence is classified as a *contradiction*. Show more examples for sentences that our account treats as contradictions.

   e. Show that according to both our treatments of *or* in Exercise 6, the denotation of the sentence *Tina is tall or not tall* is 1 in any model. Such sentences are classified as *tautological*. Show more examples for sentences that our account treats as tautological.

   f. Show that the TCC expects that any contradictory sentence entails any sentence in natural language, and that any tautology is entailed by any sentence in natural language. Does this expectation agree with your linguistic intuitions? If it does not, do you have ideas about how the problem can be solved?

8. We assume that entailments between sentences (or structures) have the following properties.

   Reflexivity: Every sentence S entails itself.

   Transitivity: For all sentences S_1, S_2, S_3: if S_1 entails S_2 and S_2 entails S_3, then S_1 entails S_3.

Reflexivity and transitivity characterize entailments as a *preorder* relation on sentences/structures.

Consider the following entailments:

(i) Tina is tall, and Ms. Turner is neither tall nor thin $\Rightarrow$ Tina is tall, and Ms. Turner is not tall.

(ii) Tina is tall, and Ms. Turner is neither tall nor thin $\Rightarrow$ Tina is not Ms. Turner.

Show an entailment that illustrates transitivity together with entailments (i) and (ii).

9. Consider the following structurally ambiguous sentence (=(ii) from Exercise 2).

   (i) *Tina is blond or tall and thin.*

   a. For sentence (i), write down the denotations derived for the two structures using the inclusive denotation of *or* from Exercise 6, and the denotations **tina**, **blond**, **tall** and **thin**.

   b. Give specific set denotations for the words *blond, tall* and *thin* that make one of these denotations *true (1)*, while making the other denotation *false (0)*.

   c. Using the *both… and* construction from Exercise 4, find two unambiguous sentences, each of which is equivalent to one of the structural analyses you have given for sentence (i).

   d. Under an inclusive interpretation of *or*, which of the two sentences you found in 9c is expected to be equivalent to the following sentence?

   (ii) *Tina is both blond and thin or both tall and thin.*

   e. Write down the set-theoretical equation that supports this equivalence.

   f. Using our assumptions in this chapter, find a structurally ambiguous sentence whose two readings are analyzed as equivalent.

10. Consider the following entailment:

    (i) Tina has much money in her bank account, and Bill has one cent less than Tina in his bank account $\Rightarrow$ Bill has much money in his bank account.

    a. We adopt the following assumption: *Tina has m cents in her bank account*, where *m* is some positive natural number. Further, we assume that entailment is transitive. Show that with these assumptions, you can use the entailment pattern in (i) to support an entailment with the following contradictory conclusion: *Ms. X has much money in her bank account, and Ms. X has no money in her bank account.*

b. The ability to rely on transitivity of entailments to support such absurd conclusions is known as the *Sorites Paradox*. Suggest a possible resolution of this paradox by modifying our assumptions in 10a and/or our assumption that entailment relations are transitive.

SOLUTIONS TO SELECTED EXERCISES

3.

Expression	Denotations in example models with $E = \{a, b, c, d\}$		
	M_1	M_2	M_3
Tina	a	b	b
tall	{b, c}	{b, d}	{a, b, d}
thin	{a, b, c}	{b, c}	{a, c, d}
not tall	{a, d}	{a, c}	{c}
[not tall] and thin	{a}	{c}	{c}
Tina is [[not tall] and thin]	1	0	0
tall and thin	{b, c}	{b}	{a, d}
not [tall and thin]	{a, d}	{a, c, d}	{b, c}
Tina is [not [tall and thin]]	1	0	1
Tina is thin	1	1	0

4.c. In any theory T that satisfies the TCC, sentences S_1 and S_2 are equivalent if and only if for all models M in T, $[\![S_1]\!]^M = [\![S_2]\!]^M$.

5.a–b. The truth-values and the accounts of the (non-)entailments are identical to the truth-values for the ambiguous sentence (2.13) and the corresponding (non-)entailment from (2.13) to (2.2).

  c. $[\![$*neither tall nor thin*$]\!] = \overline{\textbf{tall}} \cap \overline{\textbf{thin}} =$
AND(NOT(**tall**), NOT(**thin**)) $= [\![$*both not tall and not thin*$]\!]$

6.a. OR_{in}: (iii)$\Rightarrow$(ii); (iv)$\Rightarrow$(ii); (ii)$\Leftrightarrow$(v); (iii)$\Leftrightarrow$(iv); (iii)$\Rightarrow$(v); (iv)$\Rightarrow$(v).

    OR_{ex}: (iv)$\Rightarrow$(ii); (v)$\Rightarrow$(ii); (iv)$\Rightarrow$(iii).

  c. (v); the OR_{ex} analysis; $(\overline{A} - \overline{B}) \cup (\overline{B} - \overline{A}) = (B - A) \cup (A - B) = (A - B) \cup (B - A)$.

7.a. Mary is neither tall nor thin, Mary is tall or thin; Mary is tall and not thin, Mary is thin; Mary is [not tall] or [not thin], Mary is tall and thin.

b. The adjectives *empty* and *full* denote *disjoint sets*: **empty** ∩ **full** = ∅.

c. The bottle is empty ⇒ The bottle is not full; The bottle is full ⇒ The bottle is not empty.

8. Tina is tall, and Ms. Turner is not tall ⇒ Tina is not Ms. Turner (=(2.3a)).

9.a. IS(**tina**,AND(OR$_{in}$(**blond**,**tall**),**thin**))
IS(**tina**,OR$_{in}$(**blond**,AND(**tall**,**thin**)))

b. **blond** = {**tina**}; **tall** = **thin** = ∅

c. Tina is both blond or tall and thin.
Tina is blond or both tall and thin.

d. Tina is both blond or tall and thin.

e. $(A \cup B) \cap C = (A \cap C) \cup (B \cap C)$

f. Tina is blond and tall and thin

10.a. Consider the following general entailment scheme, based on (i):
(i′) *Ms. n* has much money in *Ms. n*'s bank account and *Ms. n* + 1 has one cent less than *Ms. n* in *Ms. n* + 1's bank account ⇒ *Ms. n* + 1 has much money in *Ms. n* + 1's bank account.

We can deduce from (i′), by induction on the transitivity of entailment, that the following (unacceptable) entailment is intuitively valid:

Ms. 1 has much money in her bank account, and *Ms.* 1 has *m* cents in her bank account ⇒ *Ms. m* + 1 has much money in her bank account, and *Ms. m* + 1 has no cents in her bank account.

TYPES AND MEANING COMPOSITION

This chapter introduces some of the elementary mathematical techniques in formal semantics. We systematize models by organizing denotations in domains *of different* types. *This general type system allows models to describe sets, as well as relations and other operators with multiple arguments. Denotations of complex expressions are compositionally derived by a uniform semantic operation of* function application. *The resulting semantic framework is demonstrated by treating modified noun phrases (a tall man), reflexive pronouns (herself) and coordinations between different phrases. We avoid excess notation by defining denotations set-theoretically and introducing* lambda-*style shorthand when convenient.*

This chapter systematically explains the way in which models allow linguistic expressions to denote abstract objects. This will give us a better insight into our theory of meaning and its relations with syntactic forms. The first step is to describe how denotations are organized in a model. Throughout Chapter 2, we used models freely to describe different mathematical objects. For sentences we used truth-values, for names like *Tina* we used entities, and for adjectives like *tall* we used sets of entities. In addition we used the membership operator for *is*, the intersection function for *and*, and the complement function for *not*. Using various mathematical objects in this manner was useful for expository purposes. However, in general it makes our compositionality principle hard to obtain. With each new mathematical notion we introduce, we need to see how it composes with other denotations. Too much mathematical freedom in the design of the denotations makes it hard to describe how they operate in different natural language expressions. The model structure that we introduce in this chapter helps us to make semantic distinctions between language expressions within well-defined boundaries. In this way we gain a better understanding of denotations in general, and see more clearly how they interact with syntactic forms and with each other.

Some of the foundational themes in this chapter may seem intimidating at first glance. However, none of them is especially hard. To help you follow this chapter with ease, it is divided into four parts. Each of these parts covers a general topic that leads naturally to the topic of the next one. If you are a novice to the field, it is a good idea to solve the exercises referred to at the end of each part before reading on.

- Part 1 ('Types and domains') classifies denotations in models into different domains with different types. An important tool will be functions that characterize sets.
- Part 2 ('Denotations at work') elaborates on the composition of denotations and on how typed denotations in a compositional setting are translated to other set-theoretical concepts. An important tool here is functions that operate on other functions.
- Part 3 ('Using lambda notation') introduces a short notation for functions by using so-called 'lambda-terms'. This helps us to define and use denotations in our analyses.
- Part 4 ('Restricting denotations') is about denotations that are systematically restricted by our models.

The formal system that is developed throughout this chapter is foundational to many works in formal semantics. For this reason, a technical summary of this chapter is included as an appendix to this book (page 239). This appendix gives readers a global overview of some of the most basic technical assumptions in formal semantics.

PART 1: TYPES AND DOMAINS

One of the main goals of this book is to systematically describe semantic distinctions between expressions as they are manifested in entailments. In Chapter 2, the basic difference was between entity denotations of names and truth-value denotations of sentences. Further, we used different functions as the denotations of the words *is, and* and *not*. Now we would like to analyze denotations of many more expressions. Therefore, it is high time to introduce some discipline into our semantic framework. In order to deal with denotations in a more systematic way, we will formally specify the kind of mathematical objects that our models contain. In technical terms, such a specification is referred to as a *type system*.

CHARACTERISTIC FUNCTIONS

Many of the denotations in formal semantics are functions of different types. To illustrate a simple type of function in formal semantics, we start with a maximally simple sentence:

(3.1) Tina smiled.

Intuitively, the intransitive verb *smile* should denote a set of entities, just like the adjectives *tall* and *thin* in Chapter 2. We conceive of the denotation of the word *smiled* in (3.1) as the set of entities that smiled at a given moment in the past. For convenience, we often ignore the tense in our discussion, and refer to the verb *smiled* in (3.1) as being associated with "the set of smilers". But now, how can sentence (3.1) denote a truth-value? Unlike the sentence *Tina is tall*, sentence (3.1) contains no word like *is* that may express the membership function. Thus, the set for *smiled* and the entity for *Tina* do not immediately give a truth-value in (3.1). To allow for their easy composition, we should change perspectives slightly. We still use sets of entities for describing denotations of intransitive verbs, but we do that indirectly using functions. For example, suppose that we want to describe a model with three entities: a, b and c. Suppose further that in the situation that the model describes, entities a and c smiled and entity b did not. In this case the set of smilers in the model, S, is the set $\{a, c\}$. Instead of defining the denotation of the verb *smile* to be the set S itself, we let it be a function that indirectly describes S. This function, which we denote χ_S, is a *function from entities to truth-values*. For each of the two elements in S, entities a and c, the function χ_S returns the truth-value 1. For entity b, which is not in S, we let χ_S return 0. Thus, χ_S is the following function:

(3.2) $\chi_S : a \mapsto 1 \quad b \mapsto 0 \quad c \mapsto 1$

The function χ_S is called the *characteristic function* of the set $\{a, c\}$ over the set of entities $\{a, b, c\}$. In general, we define characteristic functions as follows:

> *Let A be a subset of E. A function X_A from E to the set $\{0, 1\}$ is called the* **characteristic function of** *A* **in** *E if it satisfies for every $x \in E$:*
>
> $$X_A(x) = \begin{cases} 1 & \text{if } x \in A \\ 0 & \text{if } x \notin A \end{cases}$$

For every element x of E, the truth-value $X_A(x)$ indicates whether x is in A or not. Thus, X_A uniquely describes a subset of E. The converse is also true: for every subset of E there is a unique characteristic function. This means that sets of entities and their characteristic functions encode precisely the same information. For this reason we often interchangeably talk about subsets of E or the functions that characterize them. Specifically, in Chapter 4, we will refer by 'f^*' to the set characterized by a function f. Further, we will see that functions can also be used for characterizing subsets of other domains besides E.

For the time being, for the sake of brevity, we use the general term 'characteristic functions' when referring exclusively to functions that characterize sets of entities in E. With this notion of characteristic functions, we can easily describe how the composition process in sentence (3.1) works. We assume that the denotation of the verb *smile* is an arbitrary characteristic function. This corresponds to our assumption that the verb *smile* can be associated with *any* set of entities. Suppose that the denotation of *smile* is the function **smile**. In our analysis of sentence (3.1), this function applies to the entity denotation **tina**. In a formula, sentence (3.1) is analyzed as follows:

(3.3) **smile(tina)**

The expression in (3.3) describes the truth-value that the function **smile** assigns to the entity **tina**. For example, in the model we described above, the denotation **smile** is the function X_S in (3.2). Suppose that in the same model, the denotation **tina** is the entity a. As a result, the denotation (3.3) of sentence (3.1) is $X_S(a)$, which equals 1. If **tina** is the entity b, the denotation (3.3) equals 0. This way, by letting the denotation of the verb *smile* characterize a set, we directly obtain a truth-value denotation for the sentence *Tina smiled.*

In our analysis of sentence (3.1), we have been using three denotations: an entity, a characteristic function and a truth-value. Each of these denotations has a different 'nature', which we distinguish by letting each of them come from a different *domain*. In Chapter 2, we already let every model M contain a domain of entities E^M and a domain of truth-values $\{0, 1\}$. Now it is time to also introduce domains for characteristic functions and other denotations. Each domain we introduce comes with a label that we call a *type*. We use the letter e as the type for the domain E^M in a given model M. Since we want to make an explicit connection between types and their respective domains, we also use the notation 'D_e^M' (the e Domain in M) as an alternative name for E^M. As usual, when the model M is clear from the context, we write 'D_e' rather than 'D_e^M'. The letter t is used as the type for the domain of truth-values. Accordingly, this domain is denoted 'D_t'. Since we fix D_t as the set $\{0, 1\}$ in all models, we do not mention the model when referring to this domain. In our example above, the name *Tina* takes its denotation from D_e, and the sentence *Tina smiled* takes its denotation from D_t. In short, we say that proper names are of type e and sentences are of type t. We refer to the types e and t as the *basic types* of our type system. The domains for these types, D_e and D_t, have been specified with no relation to other domains. For this reason, we refer to them as the *basic domains* in every model.

Now, we also want to define a type and a domain for characteristic functions like the denotation of *smile*. These are defined on the basis of the types e and t, and the domains D_e and D_t. Specifically, a characteristic function in a model M is a function from the entities in M to truth-values. Accordingly, we define the domain of characteristic functions as follows:

(3.4)   The domain of characteristic functions in a model M is the set of all the functions from D_e^M to D_t.

This domain is assigned the type '(et)'. We often omit outermost parentheses, and refer to the same type as 'et'. The corresponding domain is accordingly referred to as 'D_{et}^M', or simply 'D_{et}'.

In set theory, there is a common way to refer to the set of all functions from a set A to a set B. Formally, we use 'B^A' when referring to this set of functions. Thus, the definition of the domain D_{et} in (3.4)

Table 3.1: Subsets of D_e and their characteristic functions in D_{et}.

Subset of D_e	Characteristic function in D_{et}		
$\emptyset$	$f_1:$ $a \mapsto 0$	$b \mapsto 0$	$c \mapsto 0$
$\{a\}$	$f_2:$ $a \mapsto 1$	$b \mapsto 0$	$c \mapsto 0$
$\{b\}$	$f_3:$ $a \mapsto 0$	$b \mapsto 1$	$c \mapsto 0$
$\{c\}$	$f_4:$ $a \mapsto 0$	$b \mapsto 0$	$c \mapsto 1$
$\{a, b\}$	$f_5:$ $a \mapsto 1$	$b \mapsto 1$	$c \mapsto 0$
$\{a, c\}$	$f_6:$ $a \mapsto 1$	$b \mapsto 0$	$c \mapsto 1$
$\{b, c\}$	$f_7:$ $a \mapsto 0$	$b \mapsto 1$	$c \mapsto 1$
$\{a, b, c\}$	$f_8:$ $a \mapsto 1$	$b \mapsto 1$	$c \mapsto 1$

can be formally written as follows:

$$D_{et} = D_t^{D_e}$$

Functions in the D_{et} domain, as well as expressions of type et, are often referred to as one-place predicates over entities. Common alternative notations for the type of one-place predicates are $\langle e, t \rangle$ and $e \rightarrow t$. In this book we will stick to the shorter notation et.

All intransitive verbs like *smile, dance, run* etc. are assigned the type et. In a given model, each of these verbs may have a different denotation. For example, in the model we described above, the verb *smile* denotes the function χ_S, which characterizes the set $S = \{a, c\}$. Other verbs like *dance* and *run* may be associated with different sets in the same model, and hence denote different characteristic functions. For this reason, the domain D_{et}^M in a given model M includes *all* the functions from D_e^M to D_t. To see which functions these are in our example model, we first note that the domain D_e has eight subsets in that model. These are: the empty set $\emptyset$; the singleton sets $\{a\}$, $\{b\}$ and $\{c\}$; the doubletons $\{a, b\}$, $\{a, c\}$ and $\{b, c\}$; and the whole set D_e, i.e. $\{a, b, c\}$. The domain D_{et} includes the eight functions that characterize these sets, as shown in Table 3.1. In such models, where the entities are a, b and c, intransitive verbs like *smile* and *run* must denote one of the eight functions in D_{et}. Specifically, the function f_6 in Table 3.1 is the same function χ_S that we assumed as the denotation of the verb *smile* in our example.

MANY TYPES, MANY DOMAINS

We have seen how to define the domain D_{et} on the basis of D_e and D_t. As we consider more expressions besides intransitive verbs, we will need more types and domains. The methods for defining them are similar to the definition of D_{et}. The construction of the type et and the domain D_{et} illustrates the general principle that we use for defining new types and domains. We have defined the type (et) as the parenthesized concatenation of the basic types e and t. The corresponding domain D_{et} was defined as the set of functions from the domain D_e to the domain D_t. We employ the same method for defining more new types and domains. Once two types τ and σ and domains D_τ and D_σ are defined, they are used for defining another type $(\tau\sigma)$ and a domain $D_{\tau\sigma}$, which consists of all the functions from D_τ to D_σ. More types and domains are defined in a similar way, with no upper limit on their complexity. Since the same method works for defining all types and domains from the basic ones, we refer to it as an *inductive* procedure. Specifically, types e, t and et, and their respective domains, are used inductively for defining new types and domains. For instance, when using type e twice, we get the type ee. The respective domain, D_{ee}, contains all the functions from D_e to D_e. Further, combining the types e and et, we get the type $e(et)$. The corresponding domain $D_{e(et)}$ is the set of functions from D_e to D_{et}. As we will see below, this $e(et)$ domain is useful for denotations of transitive verbs, i.e. verbs that have both a subject and a direct object.

Definition 1 below formally summarizes our inductive method for specifying types:

Definition 1. *The set of* **types** *over the basic types e and t is the smallest set $\mathcal{T}$ that satisfies:*

   (i) $\{e, t\} \subseteq \mathcal{T}$
   (ii) If τ and σ are types in $\mathcal{T}$ then $(\tau\sigma)$ is also a type in $\mathcal{T}$.

This inductive definition specifies the set of types as an infinite set $\mathcal{T}$, including, among others, the types given in Figure 3.1.

For every model M, we specify a domain for each of the types in the set $\mathcal{T}$. Let us summarize how this is done. The domain D_e^M is directly specified by the model. The domain D_t is fixed as $\{0, 1\}$ for

$$e, t,$$
$$ee, tt, et, te,$$
$$e(ee), e(tt), e(et), e(te), t(ee), t(tt), t(et), t(te),$$
$$(ee)e, (tt)e, (et)e, (te)e, (ee)t, (tt)t, (et)t, (te)t,$$
$$(ee)(ee), (ee)(tt), (ee)(et), (ee)(te), (tt)(ee), (tt)(tt), (tt)(et), (tt)(te)$$

Figure 3.1   Examples for types.

all models. Domains for other types are inductively defined, as formally summarized in Definition 2 below:

Definition 2. *For all types τ and σ in $\mathcal{T}$, the **domain** $D_{\tau\sigma}$ of the type $(\tau\sigma)$ is the set $D_\sigma^{D_\tau}$ – the set of functions from D_τ to D_σ.*

The induction in Definition 2, together with our stipulated basic domains D_e and D_t, specify the domains for all the types derived from Definition 1. We have already discussed the domain D_{et} of characteristic functions. Let us now consider in more detail the definition of the domain $D_{e(et)}$. When unfolding Definition 2, we see that it derives the following definition:

(3.5) $D_{e(et)}$ is the set of functions from D_e to D_{et}
         = the functions from entities to D_{et}
         = the functions from entities to the functions from D_e to D_t
         = the functions from entities to the functions from entities
           to truth-values.

Thus, functions of type $e(et)$ return functions (of type et) as their result. This is a result of our inductive definitions. Our definitions above also make another situation possible: functions that take functions as their *arguments*. For instance, the type $(et)e$ describes functions that map et functions to entities. Further, Definitions 1 and 2 also allow functions that take function arguments and map them to function results. Consider for instance the type $(et)(et)$. The corresponding domain, $D_{(et)(et)}$, contains the functions that map characteristic functions to characteristic functions. For instance, suppose that F is a function in $D_{(et)(et)}$. This means that F can receive any characteristic function g in D_{et} and return a characteristic function h in D_{et}, possibly different from g. We describe this situation by writing $F(g) = h$. The functions g and h characterize sets of entities. Thus, we can view functions like F, of type $(et)(et)$, as mapping sets of entities to sets of entities. We already used one such function in Chapter 2, when we let the denotation of the word *not* map sets of entities to their complement. Functions from sets of entities to sets of entities, in their new guise as $(et)(et)$ functions, will often reappear in the rest of this book.

You are now advised to solve Exercises 1, 2 and 3 at the end of this chapter.

PART 2: DENOTATIONS AT WORK

Semantic types and their corresponding domains give us a powerful tool for analyzing natural language meanings: one that is empirically rich, and yet systematically constrained. Equipped with our expressive tool for describing denotations, it is high time to start using it for analyzing linguistic examples. In order to do that, we have to explain what principles allow denotations to combine with each other compositionally. One elementary principle lets functions apply to their arguments. As we will see, functions, and the rule of *function application*, allow us to encode many useful intuitions about meanings, using the technique known as *currying*. After introducing this technique of using functions, we will see how to develop systematic analyses by solving *type equations*. This will allow us to look back at what we did in Chapter 2, and systematically treat the copula *be* and predicate negation as part of our uniform type system.

FUNCTION APPLICATION

Types provide us with a record of the way denotations combine with each other. In our analysis of the simple example *Tina smiled* we saw how an *et* function combines with an entity (type *e*) to derive a truth-value (type *t*). We write it as follows:

$$(et) + e = t.$$

The rule we used for combining denotations in the sentence *Tina smiled* is *function application*: we applied a function **smile** from entities to truth-values to an entity **tina**, and got a truth-value

smile(tina). In terms of denotations, we write it as follows:

$$\textbf{smile}_{et} + \textbf{tina}_e \ = \ \textbf{smile(tina)} : t$$

By the notation '**smile**$_{et}$' we refer to the denotation of the verb *smile*, and state that it is of type *et*. Similarly for '**tina**$_t$'. An alternative notation is '**smile** : *et*' and '**tina** : *e*'. This colon becomes more convenient when we wish to state the type *t* of the result **smile(tina)**, and write '**smile(tina)** : *t*'. Following standard mathematical practice, we let the function **smile** appear to the left of its argument **tina**. However, English verbs like *smile* normally follow the subject, as is the case in the sentence *Tina smiled*. The workings of function application are not affected by this. So we also assume:

$$e + (et) = t.$$

Thus, when wishing to highlight the syntactic ordering, we also describe the composition of denotations in the sentence *Tina smiled* as follows:

$$\textbf{tina}_e + \textbf{smile}_{et} \ = \ \textbf{smile(tina)} : t.$$

In more general terms, our type-based rule of function application is given below:

Function application with typed denotations: *Applying a function f of type τσ to an object x of type τ gives an object f(x) of type σ. In short:*

Types: $\qquad (\tau\sigma) + \tau \ = \tau \ + (\tau\sigma) = \sigma$

Denotations: $f_{\tau\sigma} \ + x_\tau = x_\tau + f_{\tau\sigma} \ = f(x) : \sigma$

The equations that we gave above describe how types are combined with each other. For each type combination, there is a corresponding operation between denotations in the corresponding domains: function application. Such a system, which combines types and denotations, is called a *type calculus*. The type calculus above, which deals with function application, is known as the *Ajdukiewicz Calculus* (after K. Ajdukiewicz). In Chapter 5 we will return to type calculi, and extend their usages for other operations besides function application.

For now, let us see some more examples of the way we use Ajdukiewicz's calculus:

$e + ee = e$ applying a function g_{ee} to an entity x_e gives an entity $g(x)$

$e(et) + e = et$ applying a function $h_{e(et)}$ to an entity x_e gives an et function $h(x)$

$et + (et)(et) = et$ applying a function $F_{(et)(et)}$ to a function k_{et} gives an et function $F(k)$

These equations each contain two types and their combination using function application. However, for many pairs of types, function application cannot work. For instance, function application cannot combine a function f of type $t(et)$ with a function g of type et. The reason is twofold. First, the function f cannot apply to g, since f takes truth-values as its argument, and g is not a truth-value. Second, the function g cannot apply to f, since g takes entities as its argument, and f is not an entity. Such situations, where the type calculus does not produce any result, are referred to as a *type mismatch.*

TRANSITIVE VERBS

Now that we have seen how typed denotations are systematically combined with each other, let us consider the following sentence:

(3.6) Tina [praised Mary]

Sentences like (3.6), which contain both a subject and a direct object, are referred to as *transitive sentences*. In (3.6) we standardly assume that a transitive verb (*praise*) forms a constituent with the object noun phrase (*Mary*). This means that, in order to compositionally derive a truth-value for sentence (3.6), we first need to derive a denotation for the verb phrase *praised Mary*. To do that, we follow our treatment of intransitive verbs. In the same way that the denotation of the verb *smiled* characterizes the set of entities that smiled, we now want the denotation of the verb phrase *praised Mary* to characterize the set of entities that praised Mary. This is the function that sends every entity that praised Mary to 1, and any other entity to 0. How do we derive such an et function from the denotations of the words *praised*

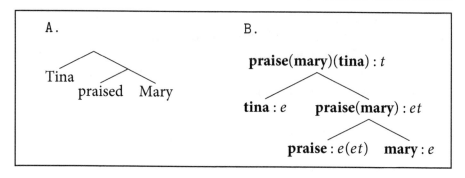

Figure 3.2   Syntactic structure and semantic interpretation for Tina praised Mary.

and *Mary*? The key to doing so is to assume that the verb *praise* denotes a function of type $e(et)$. As we have seen in (3.5) above, functions of type $e(et)$ map entities to et functions. Thus, we let the verb *praise* denote an $e(et)$ function **praise**. Applying this function to the entity **mary**, we get a denotation of type et for the verb phrase *praised Mary*. This is formally written as follows:

(3.7) $\textbf{praise}_{e(et)} + \textbf{mary}_e \;\; = \;\; \textbf{praise}(\textbf{mary}) : et$

Further, in the compositional analysis of the whole sentence (3.6), the et function in (3.7) applies to the entity **tina**. What we get is the following truth-value:

(3.8) $\textbf{praise}(\textbf{mary}) + \textbf{tina}_e \;\; = \;\; (\textbf{praise}(\textbf{mary}))(\textbf{tina}) : t$

In words: when the et function **praise**(**mary**) applies to the entity **tina**, the result is a truth-value. This truth-value is the denotation that our model assigns to the sentence (3.6). To increase readability, we often omit obvious types and parentheses, and write this truth-value as:

(3.9) $\textbf{praise}(\textbf{mary})(\textbf{tina})$

To summarize the compositional process in our analysis of sentence (3.6), we repeat it in Figure 3.2 using tree notation.

Figure 3.2A is the tree notation of the structure we assumed in (3.6). Figure 3.2B is the same tree, but the nodes are now decorated with their types and their denotations. We refer to tree diagrams like Figure 3.2B as *semantically interpreted structures*. In this interpreted structure, the nodes for the words *Tina, praised* and *Mary* are decorated by their lexical types and denotations. In addition, we have two nodes for the constituents assumed in the binary structure: the verb phrase *praised Mary* and the whole sentence. These nodes are decorated by their types and denotations, which are compositionally derived by function application.

Any $e(et)$ function can combine with two entities, one entity at a time, returning a truth-value. Having seen how $e(et)$ functions allow us to derive truth-values for transitive sentences like (3.6), we may still feel that functions that return functions as their result are excessively intricate when analyzing such simple sentences. Fortunately, there is an equivalent way of looking at $e(et)$ denotations of transitive verbs, which better reflects their intuitive simplicity. Intuitively, denotations of verbs like *praised* can be viewed as *two-place relations* between entities, aka *binary* relations. Such relations are sets of *pairs* of entities. In our example, we may view the denotation of the verb *praised* as the set of pairs of entities $\langle x, y \rangle$ that satisfy the condition *x praised y*. For instance, suppose that in our model, the entities t, j and m are the denotations of the respective names *Tina, John* and *Mary*. When the domain D_e is {t, j, m}, we may describe who praised who by the following binary relation U:

(3.10) $U = \{\langle t, m \rangle, \langle m, t \rangle, \langle m, j \rangle, \langle m, m \rangle\}$

The relation U is useful for describing a situation with three people, where Tina only praised Mary, John praised no one, and Mary praised everybody, including herself. In this way, the relation U provides full answers to the following questions:

(3.11) a. Who praised Tina?   Answer: only Mary.
         b. Who praised John?   Answer: only Mary.
         c. Who praised Mary?   Answer: only Tina and Mary herself.

Conversely: anybody who gives the same answers as in (3.11) will have implicitly described the binary relation U.

Now we can get back to $e(et)$ functions, and observe that they give us the same information as binary relations like U. In particular, the

$e(et)$ denotation of *praise* also tells us, for each entity, which entities praised that entity. Thus, when our domain of entities D_e is the set $\{t, j, m\}$, any $e(et)$ function over this domain answers precisely the same questions as in (3.11). In particular, the same situation that the binary relation U encodes is also described by the following $e(et)$ function in our model, which we call X_U:

$$(3.12) \quad X_U : t \quad \mapsto \quad [t \mapsto 0 \quad j \mapsto 0 \quad m \mapsto 1]$$
$$j \quad \mapsto \quad [t \mapsto 0 \quad j \mapsto 0 \quad m \mapsto 1]$$
$$m \quad \mapsto \quad [t \mapsto 1 \quad j \mapsto 0 \quad m \mapsto 1]$$

The function X_U maps each of the three entities in D_e to an et function. More specifically:

- X_U maps the entity t to the function characterizing the set $\{m\}$.
- X_U maps the entity j to the function characterizing the same set, $\{m\}$.
- X_U maps the entity m to the function characterizing the set $\{t, m\}$.

Note the parallelism between this specification of X_U and the question–answer pairs in (3.11). When the denotation **praise** is X_U, our model describes the same situation that (3.11) describes in words, which is the same information described by the binary relation U. More generally, we conclude that $e(et)$ functions encode the same information as binary relations over entities. This is similar to how characteristic functions of type et encode the same information as sets of entities. In mathematical terms, we say that the domain of $e(et)$ functions is *isomorphic* to the set of binary relations over D_e. Because $e(et)$ functions take two entities before returning a truth-value, we sometimes also refer to them as *two-place predicates*.

CURRYING

There is a general lesson to be learned from our treatment of transitive sentences and $e(et)$ predicates. We have seen how a situation that is naturally described by a binary relation can equally be described by a function that returns functions. The general idea is useful in many other circumstances in formal semantics (as well as in computer science). A binary relation between entities is a set containing pairs of entities. We can characterize such a set by a function that takes pairs of entities and returns "true" or "false". Such *two-place functions* occur very often in mathematics. As another example, let us consider one of the most familiar two-place functions: number addition. This function takes two numbers, x and y, and returns their sum, which we normally denote '$x + y$'. To highlight the fact that number addition is a two-place function, let us denote it using the function symbol *sum*. Thus, we use the following notation:

$$sum(x, y) = x + y$$

Now, let us use the letter 'n' as the type for natural numbers. Using this type, we will now see how we can also encode addition as a function of type $n(nn)$: a function from numbers to functions from numbers to numbers. Let us refer to this function as ADD. To define ADD, we need to define the result that it assigns to any given number. This result is an nn function: a function from numbers to numbers. Therefore, to define ADD we will now specify the nn function that ADD assigns to any number. For every number y, we define:

(3.13) The nn function ADD(y) sends every number x to the number $sum(x, y)$.

As we expect from number addition, the function ADD takes two numbers and returns their sum. But it does it step by step: it first takes one number, y, it returns a function ADD(y), and this function applies to another number x and returns the sum $sum(x, y)$, or more simply: $x + y$. As a result, for every two numbers x and y, we get:

$$\text{ADD}(y)(x) = sum(x, y) = x + y$$

For example, let us consider how we calculate the sum of 1 and 5 using the function ADD. We first give ADD the number 1 as an argument, and get the function ADD(1) as the result. This resulting function can take any number and return its sum with 1. Now, we choose to give the function ADD(1) the argument 5. Unsurprisingly, the result of calculating (ADD(1))(5) is $5 + 1$, or 6. Have we gained anything from reaching this obvious result in such a roundabout way? As strange as it may sound, we have! While calculating the sum of 5 and 1, we generated the function ADD(1). This is the *successor* function: the function that sends every natural number to the number that follows it. This function is of course useful for other purposes besides applying it to the number 5.

These different ways of looking at number addition are quite similar to what we saw in our syntactic-semantic analysis of sentence (3.6). In that analysis, we equivalently encoded situations either using binary relations like U or using $e(et)$ functions. Because we adopt the latter method, we got an intermediate result by applying the $e(et)$ denotation of the verb *praise* to the entity denotation of the object *Mary*. This is the et denotation of the verb phrase *praised Mary*. Having such a denotation for the verb phrase is compositionally useful. As we will see later in this chapter, it gives us a natural treatment of conjunctive sentences like *Tina smiled and praised Mary*, where the verb phrase *praised Mary* does not combine directly with the subject *Tina*.

The kind of maneuver we saw above will also be useful for treating many other phenomena besides transitive sentences. In its full generality, the idea is known as *Currying* (after H. Curry) or, less commonly, as *Schönfinkelization* (after M. Schönfinkel). In technical slang we often say that a one-place function like ADD is a *Curried* version of the two-place addition operator *sum*. Conversely, we say that the addition function *sum* is an *unCurried* (or 'deCurried') version of ADD. For more on Currying, see the suggested further reading at the end of this chapter.

SOLVING TYPE EQUATIONS

Using Currying, we now present a revised treatment of the copular sentences with adjectives from Chapter 2. Reconsider the following sentence:

(3.14) Tina [is tall]

In Chapter 2 we analyzed the verb *is* in (3.14) as the membership function. This two-place function sends pairs, of entities and sets of entities, to truth-values. However, now we no longer have two-place functions and sets of entities in our models: we have replaced them by Curried functions and characteristic functions, respectively. Therefore, we need to revise our analysis of (3.14) along these lines. First, as for intransitive verbs, we let adjectives characterize sets of entities. Thus, in our analysis of sentence (3.14) we assume that the adjective *tall* denotes an et function. In many other languages besides English, this allows us to treat sentences of the form *Tina tall*. However, English requires the copula *be* to appear in such sentences. How should we now analyze the semantic role of the English copula? Let us first consider its type. Compositional interpretation of the structure in (3.14) means that the denotation of the constituent *is tall* has to be determined before we determine the denotation of the sentence. To be able to combine with the denotation of the subject *Tina*, the constituent *is tall* has to denote a function that applies to the entity **tina** and derives a truth-value. Therefore, the expression *is tall* should have the same type *et* as the adjective *tall*. We conclude that the denotation of *is* has to be a function of type $(et)(et)$: a function from *et* functions to *et* functions. When such an $(et)(et)$ denotation for the word *is* applies to an *et* function like **tall**, it gives a function of the same type, *et*, which we will use as the denotation for the constituent *is tall*.

What we have done above is a kind of puzzle solving. We assumed solutions to some parts of the puzzle: the types of the words *Tina* and *tall*, and the type *t* of the whole sentence. Using the sentence's structure, we found a suitable type for the word *is* that allows function application to compositionally derive for the sentence a *t*-type denotation. The puzzle can be summarized as follows, with X and Y as the unknown types:

(3.15) [Tina$_e$ [is$_Y$ tall$_{et}$]$_X$]$_t$

In our solution, we found that $X = et$ and $Y = (et)(et)$. The solution process itself is described in Figure 3.3. This figure contains two type equations. One equation is:

Eq. 1: $e + X = t$

　　　　In words: which type(s) X combines with type e and derives type t?

By solving this equation, we see that the type for the constituent *is tall* must be *et*. This leads us to another equation in the compositional analysis of the sentence, which helps us to see how we can derive the type *et* for this constituent:

Eq. 2: $Y + et = et$

　　　　In words: which type(s) Y combines with type *et* and derives type *et*?

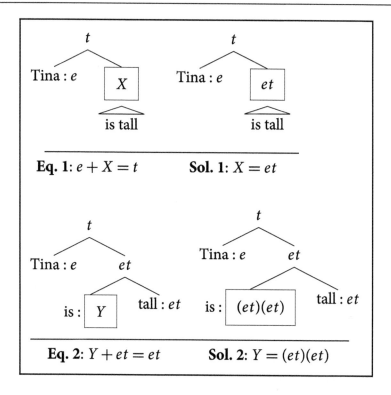

Figure 3.3   Solving type equations for the sentence Tina *is tall.*

Solving this equation as well, we see that the type for the copula *is* must be $(et)(et)$.

BACK TO COPULAS AND PREDICATE NEGATION

Now, after determining the type of the copula *is*, we want its denotation to preserve the welcome results of our analysis in Chapter 2. To do that, we let the constituent *is tall* denote the <u>same</u> *et* function as the adjective *tall*. This is because, intuitively, we still want the sentence *Tina is tall* to be interpreted as a membership assertion, claiming that the entity **tina** is in the set that the function **tall**$_{et}$ characterizes. Thus, we assume that the word *is* denotes the *identity function* for *et* functions: the function of type $(et)(et)$ that maps any *et* function to itself. Formally, we define the denotation IS for the word *is* as the following $(et)(et)$ function:

(3.16) IS is the function sending every function *g* of type *et* to *g* itself.

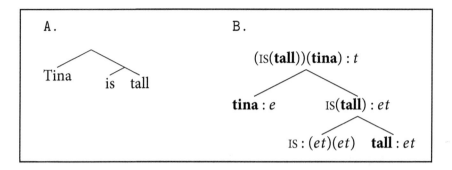

Figure 3.4   Syntactic structure and semantic interpretation for Tina is tall.

Our compositional, type-theoretical analysis is summarized in Figure 3.4.

Because the denotation of the copula *is* is now defined as the identity function, the truth-value that we get for sentence (3.14) can now be analyzed as follows in (3.17):

(3.17) a. IS(**tall**) = **tall**   (by definition of IS in (3.16))

   b. (IS(**tall**))(**tina**) = **tall**(**tina**) (due to the equality in (3.17*a*))

Due to this simple derivation, the truth-value that we derive in (3.17b) for sentence (3.14) is 1 if and only if the entity **tina** is in the set characterized by the function **tall**.

Functions of type $(et)(et)$ are also useful for adjusting our account of predicate negation from Chapter 2. Let us reconsider, for example, the following negative sentence:

(3.18) Tina [is [not tall]]

In Chapter 2 we let the negation word *not* denote the complement function, which sends every set of entities to its complement set. With our characteristic functions substituting sets, we now treat the word *not* as an $(et)(et)$ function, of the same type as the copula *is*. Our definition of the denotation NOT in (3.19) below respects the status of the word *not* in (3.18) as a predicate negator:

(3.19) NOT is the $(et)(et)$ function sending every et function g to the et function NOT(g) that satisfies the following, for every entity x (see next page):

$$(\text{NOT}(g))(x) = \begin{cases} 1 & \text{if } g(x) = 0 \\ 0 & \text{if } g(x) = 1 \end{cases}$$

In words: we define the function NOT, which takes a function g of type et and returns a function $\text{NOT}(g)$ of the same type, separating into the following two cases:

- for any entity x such that $g(x)$ is 0, we define $(\text{NOT}(g))(x)$ to be 1;
- for any entity x such that $g(x)$ is 1, we define $(\text{NOT}(g))(x)$ to be 0.

In this way, the function $\text{NOT}(g)$ reverses the value that g assigns to any entity. Because of that, $\text{NOT}(g)$ is the et function characterizing the *complement set* of the set characterized by g. Thus, by applying the function NOT to an et denotation **tall**, we achieve the same analysis that we got in Chapter 2 by complementing the set characterized by **tall**. More formally, we analyze the structure (3.18) as denoting the following truth-value:

(3.20) $(\text{IS}_{(et)(et)}(\text{NOT}_{(et)(et)}(\textbf{tall}_{et})))(\textbf{tina}_e)$

Because the function IS is the identity function, the truth-value in (3.20) is the same as:

$(\text{NOT}_{(et)(et)}(\textbf{tall}_{et}))(\textbf{tina}_e)$

By definition of the function NOT, this truth-value is 1 if and only if the entity **tina** is in the complement of the set characterized by the et function **tall**. Thus, the structure (3.18) is analyzed on a par with our analysis of the sentence in Chapter 2.

Let us now take stock of what we have done in Part 2. In this part we have aimed to maintain the informal analyses of Chapter 2 within a more structured type system. This system was fully defined by the two simple Definitions 1 and 2 in Part 1. As we have seen, these two definitions are highly expressive: they allowed models to mimic sets by using characteristic functions, and mimic two-place functions by using one-place Curried functions. Despite this expressiveness, so far we have done little to extend the empirical coverage of Chapter 2 besides adding a treatment of transitive verbs. However, by employing types as part of our theory we now have a rather powerful system that elucidates our notions of denotations and compositionality. This unified framework will be employed throughout this book for dealing with new phenomena while relying on the same foundational principles.

You are now advised to solve Exercises 4, 5, 6 and 7 at the end of this chapter.

PART 3: USING LAMBDA NOTATION

Having functions of different types in our semantic framework gives us an extremely powerful tool. In order to use this tool efficiently, it is convenient to have a standard notation for the functions we use, and the way they apply to their arguments. In this part we study the common notation of *lambda terms*, and see how it is used within our semantic system.

DEFINING FUNCTIONS USING LAMBDA TERMS

Below we restate definition (3.16) of the denotation for the copula *is*:

(3.21) the function sending every function g of type et to g itself.

We may feel that (3.21) is an unnecessarily long and cumbersome way of defining the identity function. Indeed, in formal semantics we often use a more convenient notation, by employing *lambda terms*, or 'λ-terms'. Let us illustrate it by rewriting definition (3.21) in our new notation:

- Instead of writing "the function sending every function g of type et," we write "λg_{et}".
- Instead of "to g itself", we write ".g".

After rewriting (3.21) in this way, we get the following formula:

(3.22) $\lambda g_{et}.g$

Since (3.22) is nothing but an alternative way of defining the function in (3.21), it gives us exactly the same information about it:

(i) The letter 'λ' tells us that it is a function.
(ii) The dot separates the specification of the function's argument and the definition of the function's result. Before the dot, writing 'g_{et}'

introduces 'g' as an *ad hoc* name for the argument of the function. The type et in the subscript of g tells us that this argument can be any object in the domain D_{et}.

(iii) The re-occurrence of 'g' after the dot tells us that the function we define in (3.22) simply returns the value of its argument.

From (ii) and (iii) we immediately conclude that the function $\lambda g_{et}.g$ in (3.22) returns an object in the domain D_{et}. Hence this function is of type $(et)(et)$, as we wanted. Now, with our λ-term conventions, we are fully justified in saving space and writing our definition of the denotation for the copula *is* concisely, as in (3.23) below:

(3.23) IS $= \lambda g_{et}.g$

It is important to note that the letter 'g' has no special significance in definition (3.23). If we prefer, we may define the function IS equivalently, as $\lambda h_{et}.h$: "the function sending every function h of type et to h itself". This would not change anything about our definition of the identity function, since it would still do the same thing: return the et function that it got as argument. When defining a function, it hardly matters if we decide to call the argument 'g', 'h', 'x', 'y' or any other name. Any name will do, as long as we use it consistently within the function definition.

With our new lambda notation, we adopt the following convention for writing function definitions:

Lambda notation: *When writing "$\lambda x_\tau.\varphi$", where τ is a type, we mean:*
"the function sending every element x of the domain D_τ to φ".

The expression φ within the lambda term $\lambda x_\tau.\varphi$ specifies the object that we want the function to return. In our definition of the identity function in (3.23), the expression φ was simply the argument g itself. However, in general, any mathematical expression φ that describes an object in one of our domains would be appropriate in such a λ-term. The type of the object that φ describes is the type of the value returned by the function. In (3.23), the type of the value g returned by the function is et, and hence the function is of type $(et)(et)$. Similarly, we have:

$\lambda x_e.x$	the *ee* function sending every entity x to x itself
$\lambda f_{et}.\textbf{tina}_e$	the *(et)e* function sending every *et* function f to the entity **tina**
$\lambda h_{et}.h(\textbf{tina}_e)$	the *(et)t* function sending every *et* function h to the truth-value $h(\textbf{tina})$ that h assigns to the entity **tina**

More generally, when φ describes an object of type σ, the whole λ-term $\lambda x_\tau.\varphi$ describes a function of type $\tau\sigma$: from objects in D_τ to objects in D_σ.

FUNCTION APPLICATION WITH LAMBDA TERMS

Now we can see how λ-terms are used in the semantic analysis. Based on definition (3.23), we can rewrite the equation $\text{IS}(\textbf{tall}_{et}) = \textbf{tall}$ in (3.17a) as follows:

(3.24) a. $\text{IS}(\textbf{tall}_{et})$

        b. $= (\lambda g_{et}.g)(\textbf{tall})$

        c. $= \textbf{tall}$

The move from (3.24a) to (3.24b) is according to the definition of the function IS. The move from (3.24b) to (3.24c) involves applying a function to its argument. As a result, we replace the abstract description in (3.24b) "what the identity function returns when it gets the argument **tall**" by writing more simply and concretely "**tall**". Function application with λ-terms always involves this sort of concretization. Suppose that we have a function f described by the instruction:

> "for every x of type τ do such and such to x and return the result".

Suppose further that we apply f to an argument a of the right type. What we get as the value $f(a)$ is whatever "doing such and such" does to a.

In our lambda notation, the expression φ in a λ-term $\lambda x.\varphi$ describes what the function does with its argument. Within the identity function $\lambda g_{et}.g$ in (3.24), the expression φ is the argument g itself. However, φ may encode a more complex operation on the function argument. For instance, let us again consider operations on numbers. Consider a function DOUBLER that maps any number to its multiplication by 2:

> DOUBLER is the function from numbers to numbers sending every number x to $2 \cdot x$.

In lambda format, this definition is written as follows, where n is again the type of numbers:

(3.25) $\text{DOUBLER}_{nn} = \lambda x_n.2 \cdot x$

Having a name like DOUBLER for this function is convenient when we commonly want to double numbers. However, when using λ-terms we can also avoid giving this function a name, and apply the term that corresponds to the function definition directly to the function's argument, as we did in (3.24b) above. Suppose that we apply the function DOUBLER to the number 17. We get the following term:

(3.26) $(\lambda x_n.2 \cdot x)(17)$

This corresponds to the following verbal description:

"the result of applying the function sending every number x to $2 \cdot x$, to the number 17".

Of course, the result is the value of the arithmetic expression $2 \cdot 17$. We get this expression by substituting '17' for 'x' in the result definition $2 \cdot x$, as it is defined in the λ-term $\lambda x_n.2 \cdot x$. In sum, we get:

(3.27) $(\lambda x_n.2 \cdot x)(17) = 2 \cdot 17$

In general, we describe this kind of simplification as follows:

Function application with lambda terms: *The result $(\lambda x_\tau.\varphi)(a_\tau)$ of applying a function described by a lambda term $\lambda x_\tau.\varphi$ to an argument a_τ is equal to the value of the expression φ, with all occurrences of x replaced by a.*

Consider how this convention works in (3.27). The expression 'φ' within the lambda term $\lambda x_n.2 \cdot x$ is the expression $2 \cdot x$. The argument 'a' is the number 17. Substituting 17 for x in $2 \cdot x$, we get the result $2 \cdot 17$. Something similar happens when we use a λ-term for defining the function ADD that we introduced in (3.13):

$$\text{ADD} = \lambda y_n.\lambda x_n.y + x$$

As in (3.13), this λ-term defines the function ADD by specifying that it sends every number y to the function $\lambda x_n.y + x$: the function sending every number x to $y + x$. When describing the result of applying the function ADD to the values 1 and 5, we get the following simplifications:

(3.28) $((\lambda y_n.\lambda x_n.y + x)(1))(5) = (\lambda x_n.1 + x)(5) = 1 + 5$

The simplification in (3.28) involves two steps. First, when the function ADD takes the argument 1, this value is substituted for 'y'. The result is the function $\lambda x_n.1 + x$. This function applies to 5. When 5 is substituted for 'x', we get the result $1 + 5$.

In (3.24), (3.27) and (3.28) above we use λ-terms for function application. In all of these cases, when a function $\lambda x.\varphi$ applies to an argument a, the result $(\lambda x.\varphi)(a)$ was displayed in a simplified notation, by substituting a for x's occurrences in φ. This substitution technique is based on common mathematical intuitions about the workings of functions. However, as usual, we should be careful when formalizing intuitions. There are some cases where naively using substitution as described above fails to derive the correct results. When using λ-terms for actual calculations, we need a more general rule for simplifying λ-terms under function application. This rule is known as *beta-reduction*, and it constitutes part of the rule system for computing λ-term equivalences, known as the *lambda calculus*. For our purposes in this book we will not need the full lambda calculus. Rather, the informal notational conventions above for writing and simplifying λ-terms will be sufficient. The reader is assured that none of our examples involve the formal complications that motivated the more intricate rule of beta-reduction in the lambda calculus. For more on this point, see the further reading at the end of this chapter.

REFLEXIVE PRONOUNS

In order to get a better feel for the value of lambda notation, let us now see how it works in a more complicated example: the case of *reflexive pronouns* like *herself* or *himself*. Consider the following sentence:

(3.29) Tina [praised herself]

Intuitively, this sentence should be treated as having the following truth-value:

(3.30) **praise**$_{e(et)}$(**tina**)(**tina**)

In words, (3.30) is the truth-value that results from applying the denotation of *praise* twice to the entity denotation of *Tina*. What denotation of the pronoun *herself* can guarantee that this truth-value is derived for sentence (3.29)? One obvious way to derive (3.30) from (3.29) is to let the pronoun *herself* denote the entity **tina**. This would be a correct treatment of sentence (3.29), but it definitely could not work as a general account of reflexive pronouns. To see why, let us consider the sentence *Mary praised herself*. Here, we must guarantee that the entity for *Mary* is given twice to the function **praise**. More generally, for any entity x denoted by the subject, we must guarantee that *that same entity* is given twice as an argument to the function **praise**. This "sameness" cannot be described by treating the pronoun *herself* as denoting an entity of type e. For instance, if we analyzed *herself* as denoting the entity **tina**, the unwelcome result would be that the sentence *Mary praised herself* would be analyzed as having the same truth-value as *Mary praised Tina*. Similar problems would appear for any analysis of the pronoun *herself* as an entity-denoting noun phrase.

Let us see how we solve the problem. First, following our previous analyses, we let the verb phrase *praised herself* in (3.29) denote a function of type et. In this way we can treat it on a par with verb phrases like *praised Mary*. Thus, we want to solve the following type equation for the verb phrase *praised herself*, where X is the type for *herself*:

$$e(et) + X = et$$

Letting X be e was fine type-theoretically, but it did not allow us to respect the semantic properties of reflexive pronouns. Fortunately, there is another solution: $X = (e(et))(et)$. Thus, we will let the pronoun *herself* denote a function that takes the $e(et)$ denotation **praise** as an argument, and returns a function of type et: the denotation of the phrase *praised herself*. These type-theoretical ideas about the analysis of sentence (3.29) are summarized in Figure 3.5.

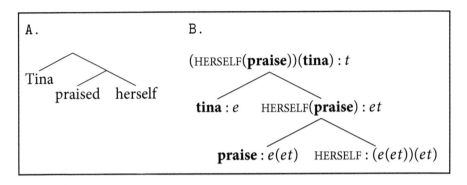

Figure 3.5 Syntactic structure and semantic interpretation for Tina praised herself.

The analysis in Figure 3.5 does not yet define the $(e(et))(et)$ function that the pronoun HERSELF should denote. To define it correctly, we rely on our intuition that sentence (3.29) has to have the same truth-value as (3.30). Thus, what we want to achieve is the following identity:

(3.31) $[\![$*praised herself*$]\!]$ (**tina**) $=$ **praise(tina)(tina)**

In words: the one-place predicate for *praised herself* holds of the entity **tina** if and only if the two-place predicate **praise** holds of the pair $\langle$**tina, tina**$\rangle$.

The denotation $[\![$*praised herself*$]\!]$ in (3.31) is obtained by applying the denotation of *herself* to the function **praise**. Thus, by spelling out the denotation $[\![$*praised herself*$]\!]$, we restate (3.31) as the following identity:

(3.32) $(\text{HERSELF}_{(e(et))(et)}(\textbf{praise}_{e(et)}))$ (**tina**)
   $= [\![$*praised herself*$]\!]$ (**tina**)
   $=$ **praise(tina)(tina)**

In words: when the function HERSELF applies to the denotation **praise**, the result is the *et* function $[\![$*praised herself*$]\!]$ in (3.31) above. As we saw, this resulting *et* function sends the entity **tina** to 1 if and only if the two-place predicate **praise** holds of the pair $\langle$**tina, tina**$\rangle$.

Since the denotations of the verb *praise* and the name *Tina* are arbitrary, we want the function HERSELF to satisfy the identity in (3.32) for all possible $e(et)$ and e denotations. We therefore conclude:

(3.33) For all functions R of type $e(et)$, for all entities x:

$$(\text{HERSELF}_{(e(et))(et)}(R))(x) = R(x)(x)$$

This generalization defines the result of the function HERSELF for every argument of type $e(et)$. Thus, we get:

(3.34) HERSELF$_{(e(et))(et)}$ is

the function sending every function R of type $e(et)$ to the et function sending every entity x to $R(x)(x)$.

This definition is rather long. Let us save space and use a λ-term for rewriting it:

(3.35) HERSELF$_{(e(et))(et)}$

$= \lambda R_{e(et)}.$the et function sending every entity x to $R(x)(x)$

But behold: we can save more space! The et function that HERSELF returns can also be written as a lambda term: $\lambda x_e.R(x)(x)$. Here is what we get when we use it in (3.35):

(3.36) HERSELF$_{(e(et))(et)}$

$= \lambda R_{e(et)}.(\lambda x_e.R(x)(x))$

Since we don't like unnecessary parentheses, we will write instead:

(3.37) $\lambda R_{e(et)}.\lambda x_e.R(x)(x)$

And this is as much as we get by abbreviating our definition for the function HERSELF.

We can now write our analysis of the truth-value of sentence (3.29) using λ-terms alone, with some notes for clarification, but without any description of functions in natural language:

(3.38) a. $(\text{HERSELF}_{(e(et))(et)}(\textbf{praise}_{e(et)}))(\textbf{tina}_e)$

$\quad\qquad\qquad\qquad\qquad\quad\triangleright$ compositional analysis (Figure 3.5)

$\qquad$ b. $= ((\lambda R_{e(et)}.\lambda x_e.\,R(x)(x))(\textbf{praise}))(\textbf{tina})$

$\quad\qquad\qquad\qquad\qquad\qquad\triangleright$ definition (3.37) of HERSELF

$\qquad$ c. $= (\lambda x_e.\textbf{praise}(x)(x))(\textbf{tina})$

$\quad\qquad\qquad\qquad\qquad\qquad\triangleright$ application to **praise**

$\qquad$ d. $= \textbf{praise(tina)(tina)}\quad\triangleright$ application to **tina**

Our compositional analysis assigns the verb phrase *praised herself* the denotation HERSELF(**praise**), of type *et*. This is the same type we assigned to the intransitive verb *smiled* and to the verb phrase *praised Mary*. As we see in (3.38b–c), with our definition of the function HERSELF, the denotation we get for *praised herself* is the *et* function $\lambda x_e.\textbf{praise}(x)(x)$, which characterizes the set of self-praisers, as intuitively required by sentence (3.29). By letting all verb phrases denote *et* functions we obtain pleasing uniformity in our system. This uniformity will prove useful later on in this chapter, when we analyze verb phrase conjunctions like *smiled and praised herself*, as we will do in (3.53)–(3.54) below, and in Exercise 12c.

You are now advised to solve Exercises 8, 9, 10 and 11 at the end of this chapter.

PART 4: RESTRICTING DENOTATIONS

In Chapter 2 we introduced the distinction between constant and arbitrary denotations. This distinction is also instrumental with our new type system. For words like *Tina, smile, tall* and *praise*, we assume arbitrary denotations of the type we assign. By contrast, when analyzing functional words like *is, not* and *herself*, we focus on one denotation of the relevant type. In this part we study more examples where denotations are restricted in this way. This will lead us to some general conclusions about the relations between formal semantics and the specification of lexical meanings.

PROPOSITIONAL NEGATION AND PREDICATE NEGATION

Let us now get back to the negation in sentence (3.18) (*Tina is not tall*). We analyzed this sentence using definition (3.19), which describes the set complement operation using characteristic functions. Using λ-terms we restate this definition as follows:

$$(3.39) \quad \text{NOT} = \lambda g_{et}.\lambda x_e. \begin{cases} 1 & \text{if } g(x) = 0 \\ 0 & \text{if } g(x) = 1 \end{cases}$$

In words: the function NOT sends every et function g to the function that sends every entity x to 1 in case $g(x) = 0$, and to 0 in case $g(x) = 1$. Driven by our wish to save space, we can shorten up the "piece-wise" definition in (3.39) by using *propositional negation*: the function from truth-values to truth-values that sends 0 to 1, and 1 to 0. We denote this tt function '$\sim$'. For its formal definition we can use subtraction, as stated in (3.40) below:

$$(3.40) \quad \sim = \lambda x_t.1 - x$$

Using this definition of propositional negation, we can rewrite definition (3.39) above more concisely as:

$$(3.41) \quad \text{NOT} = \lambda g_{et}.\lambda x_e.\sim(g(x))$$

The three definitions (3.19), (3.39) and (3.41) are equivalent, and they all boil down to the analysis of the word *not* as set complementation. However, since we now work with characteristic functions, our use of propositional negation in (3.41) has some presentational advantages. Given the structure in (3.18) (page 62), we analyze the sentence *Tina is not tall* as in (3.42) below.

(3.42) a. $(\text{IS}_{(et)(et)}(\text{NOT}_{(et)(et)}(\textbf{tall}_{et})))(\textbf{tina}_e)$
   $\triangleright$ compositional analysis of structure (3.18)

   b. $= ((\lambda g_{et}.g)(\text{NOT}(\textbf{tall})))(\textbf{tina})$
   $\triangleright$ definition of IS as identity function

   c. $= (\text{NOT}(\textbf{tall}))(\textbf{tina})$
   $\triangleright$ application to NOT(**tall**)

   d. $= ((\lambda g_{et}.\lambda x_e.\sim(g(x)))(\textbf{tall}))(\textbf{tina})$
   $\triangleright$ definition (3.41) of NOT

   e. $= ((\lambda x_e.\sim(\textbf{tall}(x))))(\textbf{tina})$
   $\triangleright$ application to **tall**

   f. $= \sim(\textbf{tall}(\textbf{tina}))$ $\triangleright$ application to **tina**

In (3.42) we see two different representations of the same truth-value that our model assigns to sentence (3.18). In (3.42a–c) it is easy to see that the truth-value assigned to the sentence is 1 if the denotation **tina** is in the complement of the set characterized by the *et* denotation **tall**. This was the view that we adopted in Chapter 2. It is also very much in line with our compositional analysis of the sentence. After simplifying the representation by employing propositional negation, (3.42d–f) makes it easier to see that the truth-value that we assign to (3.18) is 1 if the function **tall** sends **tina** to 0. In simple sentences such as (3.18) these two perspectives are equivalent. However, the general question of how we should use propositional negation when analyzing the semantics of negative sentences is more complex. Later on in this chapter, and in Exercise 12e below, we briefly touch upon this problem. See also the further reading at the end of this chapter.

PROPOSITIONAL CONJUNCTION AND PREDICATE CONJUNCTION

Another useful propositional operator is *propositional conjunction*. In Chapter 2 we focused on predicate conjunction of adjectives and simple entailments as in (3.43) below:

(3.43) Tina is tall and thin $\Rightarrow$ Tina is thin.

We also briefly noted the use of the conjunction *and* between sentences, and the very similar entailments that it often leads to. This is illustrated again in (3.44) below.

(3.44) Tina is tall and Tina is thin $\Rightarrow$ Tina is thin.

For the sentential conjunction in (3.44) we assume the following binary structure:

(3.45) [Tina [is tall]] [and [Tina [is thin]]]

In (3.45) the conjunction word *and* combines with the right-hand sentence and forms the constituent *and Tina is thin*. This expression combines with the left-hand sentential conjunct, of type *t*, and together they form a sentence of the same type. Thus, the type we assign to the constituent *and Tina is thin* in (3.45) is a function of type *tt*, from truth-values to truth-values. This function is derived by combining the conjunction word *and* with a sentence of type *t*, and hence we conclude that the word *and* in (3.45) is of type $t(tt)$: a function from truth-values to functions from truth-values to truth-values. We define this denotation as the Curried version of the classical *propositional conjunction* operator $\wedge$. Propositional conjunction is a two-place function that maps two truth-values into a single truth-value. In numeric terms, it amounts to *multiplication* between truth-values: the binary function that maps a pair of truth-values to 1 if both of them are 1, and to 0 otherwise. Formally:

(3.46) For any two truth-values x and y: the truth-value $x \wedge y$ is $x \cdot y$, the multiplication of x by y.

In (3.47) below, we define our Curried $t(tt)$ version of propositional conjunction using lambda notation. In order to distinguish this $t(tt)$ denotation of *and* from other denotations of this word, we refer to this $t(tt)$ function as 'AND^t':

(3.47) AND$^t = \lambda x_t.\lambda y_t.y \wedge x$

In words: the denotation of sentential *and* maps any truth-value x to the function mapping any truth-value y to the multiplication $y \wedge x$ of x and y. For example, for structure (3.45), we get:

(3.48) AND^t([[*Tina is thin*]])([[*Tina is tall*]])
     $=$ [[*Tina is tall*]] $\wedge$ [[*Tina is thin*]]

The denotation of the second conjunct in (3.45) is used as the first argument of the function AND^t. When AND^t sends its arguments to the $\wedge$ operator, we let it reverse their order, so that the first argument of AND^t is the second argument of $\wedge$. This is innocuous, since $y \wedge x$ is the same as $x \wedge y$. The reason we reverse the order is merely aesthetic: it is more pleasing to the eye to see a '$y \wedge x$' notation when x is the denotation of the right-hand conjunct in the sentence.

For a fuller analysis of structure (3.45), see Figure 3.6. The semantic interpretation uses the functions AND^t for *and*, and the identity function IS for *is*.

In (3.49) below we use our definition of the denotations AND^t and IS to analyze the truth-value derived in Figure 3.6.

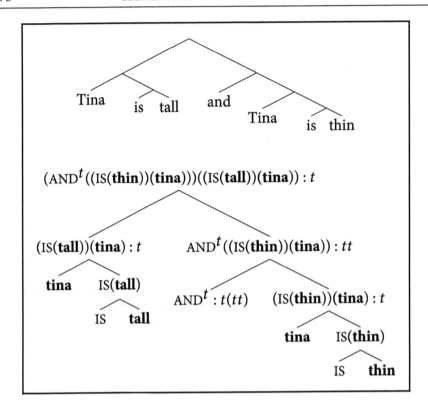

Figure 3.6 Syntactic structure and semantic interpretation for Tina is tall and Tina is thin.

(3.49) a. $(\text{AND}^t((\text{IS}(\textbf{thin}))(\textbf{tina})))((\text{IS}(\textbf{tall}))(\textbf{tina}))$

        ▷ compositional analysis in Figure 3.6

    b. $= (\text{AND}^t(\textbf{thin}(\textbf{tina})))(\textbf{tall}(\textbf{tina}))$

        ▷ applying IS (identity function)

    c. $= ((\lambda x_t.\lambda y_t.y \wedge x)(\textbf{thin}(\textbf{tina})))(\textbf{tall}(\textbf{tina}))$

        ▷ definition of AND^t

    d. $= ((\lambda y_t.y \wedge \textbf{thin}(\textbf{tina})))(\textbf{tall}(\textbf{tina}))$

        ▷ application to $\textbf{thin}(\textbf{tina})$

    e. $= \textbf{tall}(\textbf{tina}) \wedge \textbf{thin}(\textbf{tina})$

        ▷ application to $\textbf{tall}(\textbf{tina})$

As in our example of number addition, we see that lambda notation allows us to use Curried functions while reverting to traditional notation when convenient. The Curried notation in (3.49a–b) is convenient when considering the truth-value derivation from syntactic forms as in Figure 3.6. The standard notation in (3.49e) is convenient if we are interested in the relations between our results and classical logical analyses. However, the two notations are equivalent in terms of the truth-values they represent.

As noted in Chapter 2, the connections between our compositional treatment of conjunction and classical analyses become less straightforward when we consider predicate conjunction. In Chapter 2 we analyzed the conjunction between adjectives in the sentence *Tina is tall and thin* using set intersection. Given our current emphasis on the use of Curried functions, it is convenient to analyze the same sentence analogously to (3.45), using only binary structures. Thus, we now assume the structure in (3.50) below:

(3.50) Tina [is [tall [and thin]]

To mimic our intersective analysis of conjunction, here we let the word *and* denote a function of type $(et)((et)(et))$. When we read it in English, this is the type that describes *functions from characteristic functions to functions from characteristic functions to characteristic functions.* You may say gee whiz, but when replacing "characteristic functions" by "sets", we see that it is just our usual Currying practice. The functions we have just mentioned correspond to functions that map every pair of sets to a set. The intersection operator is such a function: it sends every pair of sets to their intersection. Thus, type $(et)((et)(et))$ is the proper type for defining an operator on et functions that mimics set intersection.

When we define the denotation of predicate conjunction in (3.50) as a function of type $(et)((et)(et))$, it is convenient, as we did in the case of predicate negation, to use the corresponding propositional operator. Below we give our denotation of predicate conjunction, denoted 'AND^{et}', using the operator $\wedge$ between truth-values:

(3.51) $\text{AND}^{et} = \lambda f_{et}.\lambda g_{et}.\lambda x_e.g(x) \wedge f(x)$

In words: the denotation of the predicate conjunction *and* maps any *et* function f to the function mapping any *et* function g to the function mapping any entity x to $g(x) \wedge f(x)$. This definition has the following simple property: when two *et* functions h_1 and h_2 characterize sets of entities A_1 and A_2, respectively, the result of applying the function AND^{et} to h_1 and h_2 is the function characterizing the intersection of A_1 and A_2 (see Exercise 12). Thus, treating predicate conjunction using $(et)((et)(et))$ functions encodes the same analysis of (3.50) as in Chapter 2, where we used set intersection.

To see in more detail how definition (3.51) works, consider the analysis of structure (3.50) in (3.52) below:

(3.52) a. $(\text{IS}((\text{AND}^{et}(\textbf{thin}))(\textbf{tall})))(\textbf{tina})$
$\qquad\qquad\qquad\qquad\qquad\qquad\quad \triangleright$ compositional analysis of (3.50)

$\qquad$ b. $= ((\text{AND}^{et}(\textbf{thin}))(\textbf{tall}))(\textbf{tina})$
$\qquad\qquad\qquad\qquad\qquad\qquad\quad \triangleright$ applying IS (identity function)

$\qquad$ c. $= (((\lambda f_{et}.\lambda g_{et}.\lambda x_e.g(x) \wedge f(x))(\textbf{thin}))(\textbf{tall}))(\textbf{tina})$
$\qquad\qquad\qquad\qquad\qquad\qquad\quad \triangleright$ definition of AND^{et}

$\qquad$ d. $= (((\lambda g_{et}.\lambda x_e.g(x) \wedge \textbf{thin}(x)))(\textbf{tall}))(\textbf{tina})$
$\qquad\qquad\qquad\qquad\qquad\qquad\quad \triangleright$ application to **thin**

$\qquad$ e. $= (((\lambda x_e.\textbf{tall}(x) \wedge \textbf{thin}(x))))(\textbf{tina})$
$\qquad\qquad\qquad\qquad\qquad\qquad\quad \triangleright$ application to **tall**

$\qquad$ f. $= \textbf{tall}(\textbf{tina}) \wedge \textbf{thin}(\textbf{tina}) \;\; \triangleright$ application to **tina**

The truth-value that we end up deriving for sentence (3.50) (*Tina is tall and thin*) is the same as the one we got for (3.45) (*Tina is tall and Tina is thin*). Thus, we have captured the intuitive semantic equivalence between these sentences. However, note that simplifications as in (3.49) and (3.52) are only one way of explaining this equivalence, and sometimes they can obscure insights about denotations of constituents. Specifically, in (3.52f) we no longer see that our compositional analysis of predicate conjunction is equivalent to the set intersection of Chapter 2. The direct compositional analysis in (3.49a) highlights this fact more clearly. More generally, we analyze the equivalence between (3.50) and (3.45) as following from elementary considerations about the relationships between set intersection (in (3.50)) and multiplication of truth-values (in (3.45)). In formula, let χ_A and χ_B be *et* functions that characterize the sets of entities A and B, respectively. For every entity x, we have:

$$x \in A \cap B \text{ if and only if } \chi_A(x) \cdot \chi_B(x) = 1$$

For instance, the entity **tina** is in the intersection of the sets characterized by the *et* functions **tall** and **thin** if and only if both functions send **tina** to 1. Thus, we can see that we account for the equivalence already in the interpreted structures (3.52a) and (3.49a), without any simplification of λ-terms. This point is of some historical interest: unlike early analyses of conjunction in the 1960s, our compositional semantics directly interprets the structures of both sentences (3.50) and (3.45). Neither of these structures is assumed to be "deeper" or "more basic" than the other.

Our treatment of adjective conjunction can now be directly used for other predicates, especially verb phrases as in the examples below:

(3.53) Tina smiled and danced. Tina smiled and praised Mary. Tina praised Mary and smiled. Tina praised Mary and thanked John.

(3.54) Tina smiled and praised herself. Tina thanked Mary and praised herself.

These sentences with verb phrase conjunctions also demonstrate an equivalence with sentential conjunction. Consider for instance the following equivalence:

Tina thanked Mary and praised herself $\leftrightarrow$ Tina thanked Mary and Tina praised herself

Such equivalences are immediately explained by our analysis of propositional conjunction and predicate conjunction. However, it should be noted that the equivalence scheme is not valid in general: it does not necessarily hold with more complex subjects. For instance, the sentence *someone is smiling and someone is dancing* does not entail *someone is smiling and dancing*: the existence of people doing two different things does not mean that someone is doing both. We will return to this point in Chapter 4.

As with our treatment of negation, the lambda notation exposes the semantic relation between a propositional operator ($\wedge$) and a set-theoretical operator (intersection), where the latter is presented by means of characteristic functions. However, in contrast to our treatment of negation, where propositional negation was not directly used in our compositional analysis, now it becomes clear that *both* propositional conjunction and set intersection are useful as denotations of conjunction: the first has a straightforward use with sentential conjunctions, the latter with predicate conjunction. To conclude, our type system requires the use of two denotations for conjunction: AND^t for sentential conjunction and AND^{et} for predicate conjunction. Although the two functions are of different types, namely $t(tt)$ and $(et)((et)(et))$, they are logically related. In fact, the parallelism we have observed only reflects a small part of the semantic relations between *and* conjunctions of different categories in natural language. Similar relations exist between *disjunctive* coordinations with *or* in different categories, and, to a lesser extent, between negation in different categories. These relations are often analyzed as revealing *Boolean structures* in natural language semantics. Relevant details can be found in the further reading at the end of this chapter.

INTERSECTIVE ADJECTIVES AND SUBSECTIVE ADJECTIVES

Let us move on to another example where set intersection and propositional conjunction play a major role: the different usages of adjectives. So far we have only considered adjectives in sentences like *Tina is tall*, where they appear in *predicative* positions, following the copula *is*. However, English also allows adjectives to precede nouns, as in the following sentences:

(3.55) Tina is a *tall* woman; the *tall* engineer visited us; I met five *tall* astronomers.

Occurrences of adjectives before the noun as in (3.55) are often referred to as 'attributive', or *modificational*. In many cases, we find strong semantic relations between these modificational occurrences and the predicative use. Consider for instance the following equivalences:

(3.56) a. Tina is a *Chinese* pianist ⇔ Tina is *Chinese* and Tina is a pianist.

b. My doctor wears no *white* shirts ⇔ No shirts that my doctor wears are *white*.

c. Dan saw six *carnivorous* animals ⇔ Six animals that Dan saw are *carnivorous*.

In each of these examples, we see an equivalence between a sentence with a modificational adjective, and another sentence with the same adjective in a predicative position. When analyzing such equivalences, we will concentrate on (3.56a) as a representative example. Before further analyzing the sentence *Tina is a Chinese pianist* in (3.56a), let us first consider the following simpler sentence:

(3.57) Tina [is [a pianist]]

Given the constituency that we assume in (3.57), we analyze the noun *pianist* as denoting a function **pianist** of type *et*. This is similar to our treatment of intransitive verbs and predicative adjectives. The indefinite article *a* is analyzed, similarly to the copula *is*, as denoting the identity function of type (*et*)(*et*). Formally:

(3.58) $A_{(et)(et)} = \text{IS} = \lambda g_{et}.g$

With these assumptions, structure (3.57) is analyzed as denoting the following truth-value.

(3.59) $(\text{IS}(A(\textbf{pianist})))(\textbf{tina})$
      $= \textbf{pianist}(\textbf{tina})$

This truth-value is 1 when the entity **tina** is in the set characterized by the function **pianist**, and 0 otherwise. As for the modificational construction in (3.56a), we now assume the following structure:

(3.60) Tina [is [a [Chinese pianist]]]

We already know how to analyze sentences with predicative adjectives like *Tina is Chinese*, where we let the adjective denote an *et* function. It might be tempting to let the modificational occurrence of the adjective *Chinese* in (3.60) denote the same *et* function. However, with such an analysis, we would have a problem when treating the constituent *Chinese pianist* in (3.60). If both the adjective and the noun are assigned the type *et*, function application would not be able to combine their denotations. Our solution to this problem is to assume that there are two different denotations of the adjective *Chinese*. One denotation is the arbitrary *et* function **chinese** that we use for the predicative use, e.g. in *Tina is Chinese*. The other denotation is used for modificational occurrences as in (3.60). The modificational denotation is a function of type $(et)(et)$, from characteristic functions to characteristic functions. This will allow the adjective to combine with nouns like *pianist*, as in (3.60). To highlight its use, we refer to this function as '**chinese**^{mod}'. Now, since there is a semantic connection between the two usages of the adjective *Chinese*, we define the $(et)(et)$ denotation **chinese**^{mod} on the basis of the *et* function **chinese**. Specifically, we associate **chinese**^{mod} with the function mapping any set A to the *intersection of A with the Chinese entities*. In this way, the expression *Chinese pianist* is associated with the set of pianists who are also Chinese. In lambda notation we define the function **chinese**^{mod} as follows:

(3.61) $\mathbf{chinese}^{mod}_{(et)(et)} = \lambda f_{et}.\lambda x_e.\mathbf{chinese}(x) \wedge f(x)$

The function **chinese**^{mod} maps any *et* function f to the function that maps an entity x to 1 if and only if x is in both sets that are characterized by the *et* functions f and **chinese**. Treating the constituent *Chinese pianist* using this denotation, we get the following analysis of sentence (3.60):

(3.62) $(\text{IS}(\text{A}(\mathbf{chinese}^{mod}(\mathbf{pianist}))))(\mathbf{tina})$
$\qquad\qquad\qquad\qquad$ ▷ compositional analysis of (3.60)

$= (\mathbf{chinese}^{mod}(\mathbf{pianist}))(\mathbf{tina})$
$\qquad\qquad\qquad\qquad$ ▷ applying IS and A (identity functions)

$= ((\lambda f_{et}.\lambda x_e.\mathbf{chinese}(x) \wedge f(x))(\mathbf{pianist}))(\mathbf{tina})$
$\qquad\qquad\qquad\qquad$ ▷ definition (3.61) of **chinese**^{mod}

$= (\lambda x_e.\mathbf{chinese}(x) \wedge \mathbf{pianist}(x))(\mathbf{tina})$
$\qquad\qquad\qquad\qquad$ ▷ application to **pianist**

$= \mathbf{chinese}(\mathbf{tina}) \wedge \mathbf{pianist}(\mathbf{tina})$
$\qquad\qquad\qquad\qquad$ ▷ application to **tina**

The analysis in (3.62) immediately accounts for the equivalence we observed in (3.56a). Similar analyses of the modificational usage of adjectives also account for the equivalences in (3.56b) and (3.56c) with the adjectives *white* and *carnivorous*. Because their analysis as modifiers involves intersecting the noun denotation with the predicative adjective's denotation, adjectives like *Chinese, white* and *carnivorous* are referred to as intersective.

Intersective adjectives also support equivalences like the one between (3.63a) and (3.63b) below:

(3.63) a. Tina is a Chinese pianist and a biologist.

  b. Tina is a Chinese biologist and a pianist.

We can now easily account for such equivalences as well. Our analysis of the pre-nominal usage of the adjective *Chinese* is based on set intersection. The occurrences of *Chinese* in (3.63a) and (3.63b) are interpreted by intersecting the set C of Chinese entities with another set: the set P of pianists, and the set B of biologists, respectively. With these notations, let us consider the following set-theoretical equality:

(3.64) $(C \cap P) \cap B = (C \cap B) \cap P$

In words: the intersection of the set B with the intersection of C and P is the same as the intersection of P with the intersection of C and B. Having observed this equality, we see that the equivalence in (3.63) follows directly from our analysis of intersective adjectives.

It is important to note that, although intersective interpretations are pretty common, adjectives may also show non-intersective behavior in their modificational use. Unlike what we saw with the adjective *Chinese*, there are other adjectives that do not support the equivalence pattern in (3.63). Consider for instance the adjective *skillful* in (3.65) below:

(3.65) a. Tina is a skillful pianist and a biologist.

  b. Tina is a skillful biologist and a pianist.

Sentence (3.65a) can be true if Tina is competent as a pianist but amateurish as a biologist. Thus, (3.65a) does not entail (3.65b). For a similar reason, (3.65b) does not entail (3.65a). This lack of equivalence shows that we cannot analyze constructions like *skillful pianist* or *skillful biologist* by intersecting the set of pianists/biologists with some set of "skillful entities". Such an analysis, together with the set-theoretical equality we saw in (3.64), would lead us to incorrectly expect equivalence in (3.65). Intuitively, we say that the adjective *skillful* shows a *non-intersective* behavior in (3.65). How can we describe this usage?

To solve this problem, we assume that the <u>basic</u> denotation of the adjective *skillful* is of type $(et)(et)$. This immediately allows us to construct models where one of the sentences in (3.65a–b) denotes 1 and the other denotes 0. The reason is that, when the $(et)(et)$ function associated with *skillful* is arbitrary, we no longer assume that the denotations of *skillful pianist* and *skillful biologist* are formed by intersection. Specifically, let us look at a model with the following denotations:

pianist$_{et}$:	characterizes the singleton set {**tina**}
biologist$_{et}$:	characterizes the set {**tina**, **mary**}
$[\![skillful]\!]_{(et)(et)}$(**pianist**):	characterizes the singleton set {**tina**}
$[\![skillful]\!]_{(et)(et)}$(**biologist**):	characterizes the singleton set {**mary**}

In words: the only pianist is Tina, the only biologists are Tina and Mary, the only skillful pianist is Tina, and the only skillful biologist is Mary.

In this model, we use the $(et)(et)$ denotation for *skillful*, and not an *et* function denotation. Thus, we consider Tina skillful relative to the denotation of *pianist*, but not relative to the denotation of *biologist*. Because our analysis does not use any set of "skillful entities", the fact that Tina is a biologist in the model does not entail that she is considered a skillful biologist. Thus, sentence (3.65a) denotes 1 whereas (3.65b) denotes 0. This agrees with our intuitions about the lack of entailment between these sentences.

But now we have to treat another property of the adjective *skillful*. Let us consider the following entailment:

(3.66) Tina is a skillful pianist $\Rightarrow$ Tina is a pianist.

This entailment reflects the obvious intuition that every skillful pianist is a pianist. Adjectives like *skillful* that show this behavior are often called *subsective adjectives*. An alternative name for these adjectives is 'restrictive' or 'restricting'. The judgment about the validity of (3.66) must lead us to think a little more about the $(et)(et)$ denotation of the adjective *skillful*. This denotation cannot be allowed to be any $(et)(et)$ function. If such arbitrariness were allowed, models might let the denotation of *skillful pianist* be any set of entities they contain, not necessarily a subset of the set of pianists. For instance, a function from sets to set can send the set $\{a, b\}$ to the set $\{c, d\}$. To avoid such situations, we require that the denotation of *skillful* sends any set P to a *subset* of P. More formally, we define this general restriction as follows:

(3.67) For any model M, the denotation of *skillful* in M is an $(et)(et)$ function **skillful**^{mod} that satisfies the following: for every et function f in M, the set characterized by **skillful**$^{mod}(f)$ is a *subset* of the set characterized by f.

Another possible way to state the restriction, which is elegant though harder to grasp, is to define **skillful**^{mod} so that it satisfies (3.67) by relying on another, arbitrary, function of type $(et)(et)$. When we denote this function **skillful**^{arb}, the definition of **skillful**^{mod} reads as follows:

(3.68) **skillful**$^{mod} = \lambda f_{et}.\lambda x_e.(\textbf{skillful}^{arb}(f))(x) \wedge f(x)$

In words: the function **skillful**^{mod} sends every et function f to the characteristic function of the (arbitrary) set characterized by **skillful**$^{arb}(f)$, intersected with the set characterized by f. If the restriction (3.67) is all that we want our models to specify about the denotation of the adjective *skillful*, then it is equivalent to the definition in (3.68). The $(et)(et)$ function **skillful**^{arb} is free to vary from one model to another like the other arbitrary denotations we have assumed. The superscript arb is a reminder that we assume that the function **skillful**^{arb} is arbitrary, although it is not the denotation of the word *skillful*.

With the denotation in (3.68), the sentence *Tina is a skillful pianist* is analyzed as follows:

(3.69) $(\text{IS}(\text{A}(\textbf{skillful}^{\text{mod}}(\textbf{pianist}))))(\textbf{tina})$

$\qquad\qquad\qquad\qquad\qquad\qquad \triangleright$ compositional analysis

$= (\textbf{skillful}^{\text{mod}}(\textbf{pianist}))(\textbf{tina})$

$\qquad\qquad\qquad\qquad\qquad\qquad \triangleright$ applying IS and A

$= (\lambda f_{et}.\lambda x_e.(\textbf{skillful}^{\text{arb}}(f))(x) \wedge f(x))(\textbf{pianist})(\textbf{tina})$

$\qquad\qquad\qquad\qquad\qquad\qquad \triangleright$ definition (3.68)

$= \textbf{skillful}^{\text{arb}}(\textbf{pianist})(\textbf{tina}) \wedge \textbf{pianist}(\textbf{tina})$

$\qquad\qquad\qquad\qquad\qquad\qquad \triangleright$ application to **pianist** and **tina**

The analysis in (3.69) immediately accounts for the entailment in (3.66). At the same time, it also accounts for the lack of entailment in the opposite direction: when Tina is a pianist, it does not follow that she is a skillful pianist. This is easily explained, since when Tina is a pianist the truth-value derived in (3.69) may still be 0. This happens in models where the entity **tina** is not in the set characterized by **skillful**^{arb}(**pianist**).

We should note that intersective adjectives also show entailments as in (3.66). This is directly accounted for in our analysis. In other words, our treatment of intersective adjectives correctly expects them to be a sub-class of the adjectives we classified as subsective. Below we summarize the concepts of intersective and subsective adjective, and intersective and subsective adjective functions. For convenience, we look at functions from sets of entities to sets of entities.

The following entailments define an adjective **A** *as being intersective/subsective, where* **X** *is a proper name and* **N** *is a common noun:*

A is **intersective** – **X** *is a* **A** **N** $\Leftrightarrow$ **X** *is* **A** *and* **X** *is a* **N**

                   e.g. *Dan is a Dutch man*

                   $\Leftrightarrow$ *Dan is Dutch and Dan is a man*

A is **subsective**   – **X** *is a* **A** **N** $\Rightarrow$ **X** *is* **N**

                   e.g. *Dan is a skillful pianist* $\Rightarrow$ *Dan is a pianist*

For a function F *from* $\wp(E)$ *to* $\wp(E)$ *we define:*

F is **intersective** – *There is a set A, s.t. for every set B:*

                   $F(B) = A \cap B.$

F is **subsective**   – *For every set B:* $F(B) \subseteq B.$

By treating the denotations of adjectives as intersective and subsective functions of type $(et)(et)$, we have been able to analyze the behavior of intersective and subsective adjectives.

The examples above show some cases of intersective adjectives like *Chinese*, as well as one example of a non-intersective, subsective adjective, *skillful*. Classifying adjectives into intersective and non-intersective is a highly complex problem, both empirically and theoretically. To see one example of the difficulty, let us reconsider our favorite adjectives *tall* and *thin*. So far, we have assumed that these adjectives denote arbitrary *et* functions. Therefore, in their modificational usages, e.g. in *tall woman* and *thin woman*, we may like to use the intersective analysis. However, this would be questionable: tall children are not necessarily tall; thin hippos are not necessarily thin. On the other hand, treating *tall* and *thin* as subsective adjectives may also lead to complications. For instance, when saying that *Tina is a child and she is tall*, our assertion that Tina is a child affects our understanding of the adjective *tall* in much the same way as it does in the sentence *Tina is a tall child*. Following this kind of observation, many researchers propose that adjectives like *tall* and *thin* should be treated as intersective, while paying more attention to the way they are affected by the context of the sentence. This and other questions about the semantics of adjectives constitute a large body of current research. For some of these problems, see the further reading at the end of this chapter.

The semantic concepts of subsective and intersective functions are useful for other categories besides adjectives. Consider for instance the following entailments:

(3.70) a. Tina [smiled [charmingly]] $\Rightarrow$ Tina smiled.

　　　　b. Tina [ran [with John]] $\Rightarrow$ Tina ran.

(3.71) a. Tina [is [a [pianist [from Rome]]]]
　　　　　 $\Leftrightarrow$ Tina is a pianist and Tina is from Rome.

　　　　b. Tina [is [a [pianist [who [praised herself]]]]]
　　　　　 $\Leftrightarrow$ Tina is a pianist and Tina praised herself.

In sentences (3.70a–b), we see that the adverbial modifiers *charmingly* and *with John* give rise to 'subsective' entailments. Furthermore, the adnominal prepositional modifier *from Rome* in (3.71a) and the relative clause *who praised herself* in (3.71b) show 'intersective' equivalences. A simple analysis of the adverb *charmingly* may assign it a subsective denotation of type $(et)(et)$. Similarly, the prepositional phrases *with John* and *from Rome* can be analyzed as subsective, or even intersective, $(et)(et)$ functions. The relative clause *who praised herself* can also be analyzed as an intersective $(et)(et)$ function. By solving Exercise 13, you may analyze these constructions in more detail.

SUMMARY: LEXICAL DENOTATIONS

By way of recapitulation, let us take stock of the variety of lexical denotations that we have so far assumed. First, for some words like *is* and *not* we assigned denotations on the basis of a *definition*. The denotations of these words are fully specified by our analysis, with little freedom left for models to change them. These denotations are subdivided into two classes:

1. Denotations like IS and HERSELF: functions that are exclusively defined by means of their workings on other functions, without further definitions or assumptions. Such denotations are functions that can be expressed as 'pure' λ-terms, and they are also referred to as *combinators*.
2. Denotations like NOT, AND^t and AND^{et}: functions that are defined by means of some additional concepts, e.g. the functions of propositional negation and propositional conjunction. Because these constant denotations rely on truth-values, they are often referred to as *logical*.

Most words whose denotations are combinatorially or logically defined belong in the class that linguists call *function words* or *functional words*. These words are contrasted with *content words*, which are the bulk of the lexicon in all natural languages. We have seen two kinds of denotations for content words:

3. *Arbitrary* denotations, for which no restrictions hold in our models besides those following from their types. We gave such denotations to proper names (*Tina*), common nouns (*pianist*), verbs (*smile, praise*) and predicative usages of adjectives.
4. Denotations that are logically or combinatorially defined on the basis of other, arbitrary denotations. This is how we accounted for modificational adjectives, when deriving their denotations from arbitrary denotations.

Table 3.2: Lexical denotations and their restrictions.

Denotation	Type	Restrictions	Category
tina	e	-	proper name
smile	et	-	intransitive verb
praise	$e(et)$	-	transitive verb
pianist	et	-	common noun
chinese	et	-	predicative adjective
chinese^{mod}	$(et)(et)$	intersective: $\lambda f_{et}.\lambda x_e.$ $\mathbf{chinese}(x) \wedge f(x)$	modificational adjective
skillful^{mod}	$(et)(et)$	subsective: $\lambda f_{et}.\lambda x_e.$ $(\mathbf{skillful}^{arb}(f))(x) \wedge f(x)$	modificational adjective
IS	$(et)(et)$	combinator: $\lambda g_{et}.g$	copula (auxiliary verb)
A	$(et)(et)$	combinator: $\lambda g_{et}.g$	indefinite article
HERSELF	$(e(et))(et)$	combinator: $\lambda R_{e(et)}.\lambda x_e.R(x)(x)$	reflexive pronoun
NOT	$(et)(et)$	logical: $\lambda g_{et}.\lambda x_e.{\sim}(g(x))$	predicate negation
AND^t	$t(tt)$	logical: $\lambda x_t.\lambda y_t.y \wedge x$	sentential conjunction
AND^{et}	$(et)((et)(et))$	logical: $\lambda f_{et}.\lambda g_{et}.\lambda x_e.g(x) \wedge f(x)$	predicate conjunction

The lexical denotations that we assumed, together with their restrictions, are summarized in Table 3.2.

This summary of our restrictions on lexical denotations only scratches the surface of a vast topic: the organization of lexical meanings. Let us briefly mention some of the questions that we have left untreated. Restrictions on lexical meanings that affect entailments do not only involve restricting the possible denotations of single entries. There are also many strong semantic relations between different lexical entries. Consider for instance the following examples:

(3.72) a. Tina danced $\Rightarrow$ Tina moved.
b. John is a bachelor $\Rightarrow$ John is a man and John is not married.

The entailments in (3.72) illustrate that theories of entailment should also constrain the relations between lexical denotations. Entailment (3.72a) can be explained if the set associated with the verb *dance* is contained in the set for *move*; (3.72b) is explained when the set for *bachelor* is contained in the intersection between the set of men and the complement set of the married entities. Our theory should include an architecture that allows encoding such lexical restrictions on denotations more systematically than we have attempted to do here.

The role of *syntactic theory* in analyzing lexical meanings is another issue that should be further emphasized. For instance, consider the constituent structure *Tina* [*is* [*not thin*]] that we assumed for sentences with predicate negation. This structure made us adopt the $(et)(et)$ type for the word *not*. Now, suppose that for syntactic reasons we used the structure *not* [*Tina* [*is thin*]]. A treatment of the word *not* as propositional negation of type tt would then be forthcoming. We conclude that the choice between the types $(et)(et)$ and tt hinges heavily on theoretical syntactic questions about the structure of negation.

Such puzzles are highly challenging for theories about the relations between formal semantics and other parts of grammar, especially lexical semantics and syntactic theory. They constitute a fascinating and very active area of research in linguistics. Some references for works in this area can be found in the further reading below.

You are now advised to solve Exercises 12 and 13 at the end of this chapter.

FURTHER READING

Introductory: For introductions of the lambda calculus from a linguistic perspective see Dowty et al. (1981); Gamut (1982). The treatment we used for reflexive pronouns is based on the variable-free approach to anaphora, introduced in Jacobson (2014). For an overview of other treatments of reflexives and other anaphors see Büring (2005). On various problems of negation and relevant references see Horn and Kato (2003). On coordination see Haspelmath (2004); Zamparelli (2011). On adjectives see McNally and Kennedy (2008).

Advanced: For more on type theory and higher-order logics see Thompson (1991); Kamareddine et al. (2004). The Ajdukiewicz Calculus is from Ajdukiewicz (1935). The original idea of Currying appeared in Schönfinkel (1924). Solving type equations is part of the more general problem of *type inference* in programming languages (Gunter 1992), especially in relation to *functional programming* (Hutton 2007; Van Eijck and Unger 2010). For an early semantic treatment of reflexive pronouns see Keenan (1989). For more on variable-free semantics, see Jacobson (1999); Keenan (2007); Hendriks (1993); Steedman (1997); Szabolcsi (1987). On the λ-calculus see Barendregt et al. (2013), and, in relation to combinators, Hindley and Seldin (1986). On the Boolean approach to coordination and negation phenomena see Keenan and Faltz (1985); Winter (2001). For a survey on adjectives and modification see Lassiter (2015).

EXERCISES (ADVANCED: 7, 9, **10**, **11**, 12, 13)

1. For $D_e = \{u, v, w, m\}$:

   a. Give the functions in D_{et} that characterize: (i) the set $\{u, w\}$; (ii) the empty set; (iii) the complement set of $\{u, w\}$, i.e. $\overline{\{u, w\}}$, or $D_e - \{u, w\}$.

   b. Give the set that is characterized by the function that sends every element of D_e to 1.

2. a. Give the types for the following English descriptions (cf. (3.5)):

   (i) functions from functions from entities to entities to functions from entities to truth-values;

   (ii) functions from functions from entities to truth-values to entities;

   (iii) functions from functions from entities to truth-values to functions from truth-values to entities;

   (iv) functions from entities to functions from truth-values to functions from entities to entities;

   (v) functions from functions from entities to truth-values to functions from entities to functions from entities to entities;

   (vi) functions from entities to functions from functions from entities to truth-values to functions from truth-values to entities;

   (vii) functions from functions from functions from truth-values to truth-values to functions from truth-values to entities to functions from entities to functions from entities to entities.

   b. Give English descriptions (cf. (3.5)) for the following types: $(et)t$, $t(te)$, $(tt)e$, $(e(et))t$, $e((et)t)$, $(e(et))(e(tt))$.

3. a. Give the functions in D_{tt}.

   b. For $D_e = \{u, v, w, m\}$, give the functions in D_{te} and D_{et}.

   c. For $D_e = \{l, n\}$, give the functions in $D_{(ee)t}$.

4. For each of the following pairs of types say if our function application tion rule holds. If that's the case, write the resulting type:

$e + e(et)$,　　　　　　$(et)t + et$,
$tt + (ee)(tt)$,　　　　　$et + e(tt)$,
$(e(et))(et) + ee$,　　　　$e(et) + (e(et))(et)$,
$(e(et))(et) + e$,　　　　$(e((et)t))(tt) + e((et)t)$,
$(e((et)t))(tt) + e$,　　　$(ee)(et) + e$,
$e((et)(et)) + e(et)$,　　$(et)(et) + ((et)(et))(e(e(et)))$.

5. a. In a model with $D_e = \{t, j, m\}$, suppose that Tina, John and Mary praised Mary, that Tina and Mary praised John, and that nobody else praised anybody else. What should the denotation of the verb *praise* be in this model?

   b. Consider sentences of the form *John [[read Mary] Moby Dick]*. We let the ditransitive verb *read* be of type $e(e(et))$. Assume that John read Mary *Moby Dick*, Tina read Mary *Lolita*, and nobody else read anything else to anybody else. In such a model, give the *et* denotation of the expression *read Mary Moby Dick* and the *e(et)* denotation of the expression *read Mary*.

6. a. Solve the following type equations:

   $$tt + X = t(tt), \quad Y + e = ee, \quad Z + t = et, \quad (et)t + M = e((et)t).$$

   b. Each of the following type equations has <u>two</u> solutions. Find them:

   $$t(tt) + X = tt, \quad Y + ee = e, \quad Z + et = t, \quad e((et)t) + M = (et)t.$$

   c. Complete the general conclusions from your answers to 6*a* and 6*b*:

   (i) Equations of the form $X + y = z$ always have the solution $X =$ ___.

   (ii) Equations of the form $X + yz = z$ always have the solutions $X =$ ___ and $X =$ ___.

7. a. The sentence structures below introduce "typing puzzles" similar to (3.15). Solve these puzzles and find appropriate types for the underlined words.

   (i) $[\,\text{Mary}_e\ [\text{walked}_{et}\ \underline{\text{quickly}}_X]_Y\,]_t$

   (ii) $[\,\text{Mary}_e\ [\text{walked}_{et}\ [\underline{\text{in}}_X\text{Utrecht}_e]_Z]_Y\,]_t$

   (iii) $[[\,\underline{\text{the}}_X\text{pianist}_{et}\,]_e\ [\,\text{smiled}_{et}\,]_{et}\,]_t$

   (iv) $[[\,\text{the}_X\ [\,\underline{\text{skillful}}_Y\ \text{pianist}_{et}\,]_{et}]_e\ \text{smiled}_{et}\,]_t$

(v) $[[\text{Walk}_{et}\text{ing}\underline{\hspace{0.2em}}_X]_e\,[\text{is}_{(et)(et)}\,\text{fun}_{et}]_{et}]_t$

(vi) $[[\text{the}_X\,[\text{man}_{et}\,[\underline{\text{who}}_Y\,\text{walked}_{et}]_Z]_M]_e\,\text{smiled}_{et}]_t$

(vii) $[[\underline{\text{if}}_X[\text{you}_e\,\text{smile}_{et}]_t]_Y\,[\text{you}_e\,\text{win}_{et}]_t]_t$

(viii) $[\,\text{I}_e\,[[\text{love}_{e(et)}\,\text{it}_e]_Y\,[\underline{\text{when}}_X\,[\text{you}_e\,\text{smile}_{et}]_t]_Z]_M]_t$

b. Now consider the following puzzle: $[[\underline{\text{no}}_X\,\text{man}_{et}]_Y\,\text{smiled}_{et}]_t$. Give two solutions for Y. For each solution give the corresponding solution for X.

c. Based on your answers to 7a and 7b, find at least one solution for X, Y and Z in the following puzzle:
$[\underline{\text{There}}_X\,[\text{is}_{(et)(et)}\,[\text{trouble}_{et}\,[\underline{\text{in}}_Y\,\text{Paradise}_e]_Z]]]_t$.
Can you find any more solutions?

8. a. Give English descriptions (cf. (3.34)) for the following λ-terms:

   (i) $\lambda f_{(et)t}.\lambda y_t.f(\lambda z_e.y)$

   (ii) $\lambda x_e.\lambda f_{et}.f(x)$

   (iii) $\lambda f_{et}.\lambda g_{tt}.\lambda x_e.g(f(x))$

   (iv) $\lambda f_{ee}.\lambda g_{(ee)t}.\lambda x_e.g(\lambda y_e.f(x))$

   b. Give λ-terms for the following English descriptions:
      (i) the function sending every function f_{ee} to the function sending every entity x to the result of applying f to $f(x)$;
      (ii) the function sending every function of type $(ee)e$ to its value on the identity function of type ee;
      (iii) the function sending every function R of type $e(et)$ to its inverse, i.e. the function R^{-1} of type $e(et)$ that satisfies for every two entities x and y: $(R^{-1}(x))(y) = (R(y))(x)$.

9. a. Simplify the following λ-terms as much as possible using function application:

   (i) $((\lambda x_e.\lambda f_{et}.f(x))(\textbf{tina}_e))(\textbf{smile}_{et})$

   (ii) $((\lambda f_{et}.\lambda g_{tt}.\lambda x_e.g(f(x)))(\textbf{smile}_{et}))(\lambda y_t.y)$

   (iii) $(((\lambda g_{e(et)}.\lambda x_e.\lambda y_e.(g(y))(x))(\textbf{praise}_{e(et)}))(\textbf{tina}_e))(\textbf{mary}_e)$

   b. We analyze sentences like *Mary is Tina* by letting the word *is* denote an $e(et)$ function F, which is different from the identity function of type $(et)(et)$. Define F as a λ-term, basing your definition on the equality formula $x = y$, which has the truth-value 1 iff x and y are equal. Write the λ-term for the structure *Lewis Carroll [is [C. L. Dodgson]]*, and then simplify it as much as possible.

c. We analyze the sentence [*Tina* [*praised* [*her mother*]]] using the following denotations:

$\text{HER} = \lambda f_{ee}.\lambda g_{e(et)}.\lambda x_e.(g(f(x)))(x)$ and $\textbf{mother}_{ee}$ = the function sending each entity x to x's mother.

Assuming these denotations, give the λ-term we derive for the sentence. Then simplify the λ-term you got as much as possible using function application.

10. a. Give English descriptions for the λ-terms:

(i) $\lambda y_n.(\text{DOUBLER})(y)$ (see (3.25))
(ii) $\lambda y_e.(\lambda x_e.x)(y)$

b. Write simpler descriptions for the functions you described in 10*a*.

c. Complete the following conclusion:
for any function $f_{\tau\sigma}$, the function _____ equals f.
In the λ-calculus, the simplification rule that this conclusion supports is known as *eta-reduction*.

d. Simplify the following λ-term as much as possible using function application and eta-reductions:

$((\lambda f_{e(et)}.\lambda g_{tt}.\lambda x_e.\lambda y_e.g(f(x)(y)))(\lambda u_e.\lambda z_e.\textbf{praise}(z)(u)))(\lambda w_t.w)$

11. Consider the equivalence between the active sentence *Mary* [*praised Tina*] and its *passive* form *Tina* [[*was praised by*] *Mary*]. In this structure, we unrealistically assume that the string *was praised by* is a constituent. Express the denotation of this constituent in terms of the denotation **praise**, in a way that captures the equivalence between the active and passive sentences.

12. a. Simplify the following λ-term as much as possible using function application and the definition of AND^t:

$(\lambda f_{e(et)}.\lambda x_e.\lambda y_e.(\text{AND}^t((f(x))(y)))((f(y))(x)))(\textbf{praise}_{e(et)})$.

Describe in words the $e(et)$ function that you got.

b. (i) Give the two binary structures for the sentence *Tina is not tall and thin*.

(ii) For each of these structures, give the semantic interpretation derived using the lexical denotations $\text{NOT}_{(et)(et)}$ and AND^{et}.

(iii) Simplify the resulting λ-terms as much as possible using function application and the definitions of $\text{NOT}_{(et)(et)}$ and AND^{et}.

c. (i) Give binary structures for the sentences in (3.53) and (3.54).

(ii) For each of these structures, give the semantic interpretation derived using the lexical denotations AND^{et} and HERSELF.

(iii) Simplify the resulting λ-terms as much as possible using function application and the definitions of AND^{et} and HERSELF.

d. For every function f of type et, we use the notation f^* to denote the set of entities $\{x \in D_e : f(x) = 1\}$ that f characterizes. For instance, for the function X_S in (3.2) we denote: $X_S{}^* = S = \{a, c\}$. Show that for all functions h_1, h_2 of type et, the following holds:

$$(\text{AND}^{et}(h_2)(h_1))^* = h_1{}^* \cap h_2{}^*.$$

In words: the function $\text{AND}^{et}(h_2)(h_1)$ characterizes the intersection of the sets that are characterized by h_1 and h_2.

e. Assume that the sentence *Tina is not tall* has the structure *not [Tina is tall]*. What should the type and denotation of *not* be under this analysis? How would you account for the ambiguity of *Tina is not tall and thin*? Explain all your structural assumptions.

13. a. Account for the entailment (3.70a) with the adverb *charmingly*: describe the restriction on the adverb's denotation by completing the following sentence:

the function **charmingly** of type ___ maps any set A characterized by ___ to ___.

b. Account for the same entailment by postulating a λ-term for **charmingly** in terms of an arbitrary function **charmingly**^{arb}. Simplify the λ-terms for the two sentences in (3.70a), and explain why the $\leq$ relation must hold between them in every model.

c. (i) Repeat your analysis in 13a, but now for the entailment (3.70b) and the preposition *with*. Complete the following sentence:

the function **with** of type ___ maps any entity (e.g. for *John*), to a function mapping any characteristic function X_A (e.g. for *ran*) to ___.

(ii) Repeat your analysis in b, but now for (3.70b). Postulate a λ-term for **with** in terms of an arbitrary function **with**^{arb}. Simplify the λ-terms you get for the sentences in (3.70b).

d. Account for the equivalence (3.71a) by defining the denotation **from** (of which type?) on the basis of an arbitrary function **from**^{arb} of type $e(et)$. Show that after simplifications, the truth-values you get for the two sentences in (3.71a) are the same.

e. Account for the entailments (i) *Tina is very tall* ⇒ *Tina is tall*, and (ii) *Tina is a [[very tall] student]* ⇒ *Tina is a tall student*: postulate proper restrictions on the denotation of the word *very* in (i) and (ii), of types $(et)(et)$ and $((et)(et))((et)(et))$ respectively.

f. Account for the equivalence in (3.71b) by postulating a proper type and a proper restriction on the denotation of the word *who*. Give it a λ-term. Show that after simplifications, the truth-values you get for the two sentences in (3.71b) are the same.

SOLUTIONS TO SELECTED EXERCISES

1. a. $[u \mapsto 1, v \mapsto 0, w \mapsto 1, m \mapsto 0]$; $[u \mapsto 0, v \mapsto 0, w \mapsto 0, m \mapsto 0]$; $[u \mapsto 0, v \mapsto 1, w \mapsto 0, m \mapsto 1]$.   b. $\{u, v, w, m\}$, i.e. the whole domain D_e.

2. a. (i) $(ee)(et)$,   (ii) $(et)e$,
   (iii) $(et)(te)$,   (iv) $e(t(ee))$,
   (v) $(et)(e(ee))$,   (vi) $(e(et))(te)$,
   (vii) $((tt)(te))(e(ee))$.

3. a. $D_{tt} = \{[0 \mapsto 0, 1 \mapsto 0], [0 \mapsto 0, 1 \mapsto 1], [0 \mapsto 1, 1 \mapsto 0], [0 \mapsto 1, 1 \mapsto 1]\}$.

   b. $D_{et} = \{$
   $[u \mapsto 0, v \mapsto 0, w \mapsto 0, m \mapsto 0], [u \mapsto 0, v \mapsto 0, w \mapsto 0, m \mapsto 1]$,
   $[u \mapsto 0, v \mapsto 0, w \mapsto 1, m \mapsto 0], [u \mapsto 0, v \mapsto 0, w \mapsto 1, m \mapsto 1]$,
   $[u \mapsto 0, v \mapsto 1, w \mapsto 0, m \mapsto 0], [u \mapsto 0, v \mapsto 1, w \mapsto 0, m \mapsto 1]$,
   $[u \mapsto 0, v \mapsto 1, w \mapsto 1, m \mapsto 0], [u \mapsto 0, v \mapsto 1, w \mapsto 1, m \mapsto 1]$,
   $[u \mapsto 1, v \mapsto 0, w \mapsto 0, m \mapsto 0], [u \mapsto 1, v \mapsto 0, w \mapsto 0, m \mapsto 1]$,
   $[u \mapsto 1, v \mapsto 0, w \mapsto 1, m \mapsto 0], [u \mapsto 1, v \mapsto 0, w \mapsto 1, m \mapsto 1]$,
   $[u \mapsto 1, v \mapsto 1, w \mapsto 0, m \mapsto 0], [u \mapsto 1, v \mapsto 1, w \mapsto 0, m \mapsto 1]$,
   $[u \mapsto 1, v \mapsto 1, w \mapsto 1, m \mapsto 0], [u \mapsto 1, v \mapsto 1, w \mapsto 1, m \mapsto 1]\}$.
   The solution for D_{te} is along similar lines.

   c. For $D_e = \{l, n\}$, there are four functions in D_{ee}: $[l \mapsto l, n \mapsto l]$, $[l \mapsto l, n \mapsto n], [l \mapsto n, n \mapsto l]$ and $[l \mapsto n, n \mapsto n]$. If we substitute these four functions for u, v, w and m in the answer to *3b*, we get the sixteen functions in $D_{(ee)t}$.

4. et, t, −, −, −, et, −, tt, −, −, −, $e(e(et))$.

5. a. **praise** $= t \mapsto [t \mapsto 0 \quad j \mapsto 0 \quad m \mapsto 0] \quad j \mapsto [t \mapsto 1 \quad j \mapsto 0 \quad m \mapsto 1]$
   $m \mapsto [t \mapsto 1 \, j \mapsto 1 \, m \mapsto 1]$

  b. $[\![read\ Mary\ Moby\ Dick]\!] = [t \mapsto 1\ j \mapsto 0\ m \mapsto 0\ md \mapsto 0\ lo \mapsto 0]$
    $[\![read\ Mary]\!] = t \mapsto [t \mapsto 0\ j \mapsto 0\ m \mapsto 0\ md \mapsto 0\ lo \mapsto 0]$,
       $j \mapsto [t \mapsto 0\ j \mapsto 0\ m \mapsto 0\ md \mapsto 0\ lo \mapsto 0]$,
       $m \mapsto [t \mapsto 0\ j \mapsto 0\ m \mapsto 0\ md \mapsto 0\ lo \mapsto 0]$,
       $md \mapsto [t \mapsto 0\ j \mapsto 1\ m \mapsto 0\ md \mapsto 0\ lo \mapsto 0]$,
       $lo \mapsto [t \mapsto 1\ j \mapsto 0\ m \mapsto 0\ md \mapsto 0\ lo \mapsto 0]]$.

6. a. $(tt)(t(tt))$; $e(ee)$; $t(et)$; $((et)t)(e((et)t))$.
  b. t and $(t(tt))(tt)$; e and $(ee)e$; e and $(et)t$; e and $(e((et)t))((et)t)$.
  c. the solution $X = yz$; the solutions $X = y$ and $X = (yz)z$.

7. a. (i) $X=(et)(et)$ (ii) $X=e((et)(et))$,
    (iii) $X=(et)e$ (iv) $Y=(et)(et)$,
    (v) $X=(et)e$ (vi) $Y=(et)((et)(et))$,
    (vii) $X=t(tt)$ (viii) $X=t((et)(et))$.
  b. $Y=e$ and $X=(et)e$; $Y=(et)t$ and $X=(et)((et)t)$.
  c. $X=e$ or $(et)t$; $Y=e((et)(et))$; $Z=(et)(et)$.
    Additional solutions for 7c:
    $X=et$, $Y=e((et)(((et)(et))e))$, $Z=(et)(((et)(et))e)$; $X=e$,
    $Y=e((et)(((et)(et))(et)))$, $Z=(et)(((et)(et))(et))$.

8. a. (i) the function sending every function f of type $(et)t$ to the function sending every truth-value y to the result of applying f to the constant et function sending every entity to y.
  (ii) the function I sending every entity x to the function sending every et function f to the truth-value result of applying f to x (I sends every x to the characteristic function of the set of functions characterizing subsets of D_e containing x).
  (iii) the function C sending every et function f to the function sending every tt function g to the function from entities x to the result of applying g to $f(x)$ (C returns the *function composition* of g_{tt} on f_{et}).
  (iv) the function sending every ee function f to the function sending every $(ee)t$ function g to the function from entities x to the result of applying g to the constant function sending every entity to $f(x)$.
  b. (i) $\lambda f_{ee}.\lambda x_e.f(f(x))$;
  (ii) $\lambda f_{(ee)e}.f(\lambda x_e.x)$;
  (iii) $\lambda R_{e(et)}.\lambda x_e.\lambda y_e.(R(y))(x)$.

9. a. (i) **smile(tina)**; (ii) $\lambda x_e.\textbf{smile}(x)$; (iii) $(\textbf{praise(mary)})(\textbf{tina})$
  b. $F = \lambda y_e.\lambda x_e.x = y$; $(F(\textbf{cld}))(\textbf{lc}) = (\textbf{lc}=\textbf{cld})$

   c. $((\text{HER}(\textbf{mother}))(\textbf{praise}_{e(et)}))(\textbf{tina}_e) =$
     $(\textbf{praise}(\textbf{mother}(\textbf{tina})))(\textbf{tina})$

10. a. (i) the function sending every number y to DOUBLER(y)
     (ii) the function sending every entity y to the result that the
     function sending every entity x to x returns for y
  b. (i) DOUBLER
     (ii) the function sending every entity y to y, a.k.a. the function
     sending every entity x to x
  c. the function $\lambda x_\tau . f(x)$ equals f
  d. **praise**.

11. $[\![\textit{was praised by}]\!] = \lambda x_e . \lambda y_e . \textbf{praise}(y)(x)$

12. a. $\lambda x_e . \lambda y_e . (\textbf{praise}(y))(x) \wedge (\textbf{praise}(x))(y)$ – the function sending
     x to the function sending y to 1 iff x and y praised each other.
  b. (i) Tina [is [not [tall [and thin]]]]; Tina [is [[not tall] [and thin]]]
     (ii) $(\text{IS}(\text{NOT}((\text{AND}^{et}(\textbf{thin}))(\textbf{tall}))))(\textbf{tina})$;
     $(\text{IS}((\text{AND}^{et}(\textbf{thin}))(\text{NOT}(\textbf{tall}))))(\textbf{tina})$
     (iii) $\sim(\textbf{tall}(\textbf{tina}) \wedge \textbf{thin}(\textbf{tina}))$; $(\sim(\textbf{tall}(\textbf{tina}))) \wedge \textbf{thin}(\textbf{tina})$.
  d. Suppose $h_1{}^* = A_1$, $h_2{}^* = A_2$.   By   def.   of   AND^{et}:
     $(\text{AND}^{et}(h_2)(h_1))^* = (\lambda x_e . h_1(x) \wedge h_2(x))^*$, i.e. the set $A = \{x \in$
     $E : (h_1(x) \wedge h_2(x)) = 1\}$. By def. of $\wedge$, for every $y \in E$: $y \in A$
     iff $h_1(y) = 1$ and $h_2(y) = 1$, i.e. $y \in A_1$ and $y \in A_2$, i.e.
     $y \in A_1 \cap A_2$.

13. c. **with** of type $e((et)(et))$ maps any entity x (e.g. for *John*), to a
     function mapping any characteristic function X_A (e.g. for *ran*)
     to a function characterizing subsets of A;
     $\textbf{with} = \lambda x_e . \lambda f_{et} . \lambda y_e . ((\textbf{with}^{\text{arb}}_{e((et)(et))}(x))(f))(y) \wedge f(y)$.
  d. $\textbf{from}_{e((et)(et))} = \lambda x_e . \lambda f_{et} . \lambda y_e . (\textbf{from}^{\text{arb}}_{e(et)}(x))(y) \wedge f(y)$.
  f. WHO is assigned type $(et)(et)$, which leads to the term:
     $(\text{IS}(\text{A}(\text{WHO}(\text{HERSELF}(\textbf{praise}))(\textbf{pianist}))))(\textbf{tina})$.   With   the
     assumption   WHO=AND^{et},   this   term   is   simplified   to:
     $\textbf{pianist}(\textbf{tina}) \wedge \textbf{praise}(\textbf{tina})(\textbf{tina})$. We get the same term
     when simplifying the term for the sentence *Tina is a pianist and*
     Tina praised herself.

CHAPTER 4

QUANTIFIED NOUN PHRASES

*This chapter addresses noun phrases (NPs) that involve counting and
other statements about quantity. We compositionally analyze
complex NP structures by letting them denote (et)t functions, or
generalized quantifiers. Quantificational elements within the noun
phrase are analyzed as denoting (et)((et)t) functions, or determiner
relations. This analysis accounts for many entailments with
quantified NPs: monotonicity-based entailments, entailments with
various coordinations, and a possibly universal entailment pattern
in natural language, known as* conservativity. *When studying NP
coordinations, we reveal new facts about the behavior of proper
names. To deal with these facts, we reanalyze proper names using
generalized quantifiers, so that they end up being treated similarly to
quantified NPs.*

Many expressions intuitively involve processes of counting or measuring. Consider for instance the italicized expressions in the following
sentences:

(4.1) John *rarely/usually* eats meat.

(4.2) We are *close to/far from* Beijing.

(4.3) There is *little/a lot of* work to do today.

(4.4) *Many/few* people admire Richard Wagner.

We refer to such items as *quantificational expressions*. Intuitively, in
sentence (4.1) the adverbs refer to the frequency of John's carnivorousness; in (4.2) the prepositional phrases estimate the distance to
Beijing; in (4.3) the mass term expressions evaluate an amount of
work. Similarly, in (4.4) the quantificational expressions *many* and *few*
evaluate the number of Wagner's admirers.

Table 4.1: Count noun phrases.

	Singular	Plural	Plural
I	every/each astronaut	all astronauts	between six and eleven historians
	some architect	some architects	most barbers
	no vegetarian	no vegetarians	many spies
	one analyst	three analysts	few columnists
	more than one reviewer	more than three reviewers	at least three reviewers
	at most one archeologist	at most five archeologists	fewer than five archeologists
	exactly one troublemaker	exactly nine troublemakers	at least half the managers
II	a thief	thieves	
	the thief	the thieves	

In general, words like *many* and *few* combine with count nouns, such as *tables* or *people* in (4.4). In the previous chapter, we have described the denotations of such nouns using sets of entities from the domain E. The members of the E domain are assumed to be distinct, separated objects, without any smooth variation from one to the other. For instance, in our entity domain, we have no entity that "lies between", say, different entity denotations for *Tina* and *Mary*. This is unlike the situation in sets of real numbers, geometrical shapes etc., where there are endless variations between any two different entities. Because the E domain has this property, we refer to it as being discrete. In this book we only study quantification with count nominals as in (4.4), which are analyzed using discrete domains. More quantificational expressions of this kind are given in Table 4.1. Theories of adverbial quantification as in (4.1), spatial quantification as in (4.2) and mass quantification as in (4.3) often rely on non-discrete, continuous domains for analyzing measurement of time, space and substance. For some work on these quantificational expressions, see the further reading at the end of this chapter.

The noun phrases (NPs) in Table 4.1 are linguistically divided into two classes. The NPs in part I of the table are constructed from a quantificational expression like *many*, *every* or *at most five* and a singular or plural common noun. The syntactic and semantic behavior of the NPs in part II of the table is different in many respects, due to the special properties of the articles *a* and *the* and the English bare plural. We set these NPs aside and concentrate on those NPs in part I of Table 4.1. We refer to these NPs as quantified NPs. For work on definite and indefinite NPs as in part II of Table 4.1, see the further reading at the end of this chapter.

GENERALIZED QUANTIFIERS AND THE DENOTATION
OF QUANTIFIED NPs

To analyze quantified NPs, let us first consider the maximally simple sentence below:

(4.5) [Every man] ran.

Following our assumptions in Chapter 3, we let the noun *man* and the intransitive verb *ran* in (4.5) denote the *et* functions **man** and **run**, respectively. We introduce the notations **man*** and **run*** for the sets of entities that these functions characterize. More generally, we adopt the following convention:

> *For every function f of type et, the notation 'f^*' refers to the set of entities $\{x \in D_e : f(x) = 1\}$ that f characterizes.*

A simple way to analyze the semantics of sentence (4.5) is as requiring that the set of men is contained in the set of runners. Thus, we assume that sentence (4.5) denotes 1 if and only if the following requirement holds:

(4.6) $\mathbf{man}^* \subseteq \mathbf{run}^*$

To derive the subset requirement in (4.6) using our compositional treatment of sentence (4.5), we need to find a proper denotation for the noun phrase *every man*. Given the type *et* for the predicate *ran* and the type *t* of sentence (4.5), we first need to solve the following type equation, where X is the type of the noun phrase *every man*:

(4.7) $X + et = t$

One solution for X is of course type e, the same type that we have assigned to simple NPs like *Tina* in sentences like *Tina ran*. However, assigning type e to the noun phrase *every man* would not allow us to capture the subset requirement in (4.6) without serious complications: under our semantic framework in Chapter 3, there is no entity x in the D_e domain that would make the truth-value $\mathbf{run}(x)$ be 1 if and only if the subset relation in (4.6) holds. Similar difficulties would show up if we tried to assign type e to other NPs in Table 4.1. For instance, imagine the problems that we would encounter if we wanted to analyze the NP in the sentence *no man ran* as denoting an entity. Entities are simply not fine-grained enough for describing the complex meaning of NPs as in Table 4.1.

Readers who want to look at a formal expression of this claim may now solve the advanced Exercise 16 at the end of this chapter.

Fortunately, there are other types of denotations besides entities that we can use for treating quantified NPs. In addition to type e, there is another solution for the type equation in (4.7). Another type X that solves this equation is $(et)t$: the type of functions that map et-functions to truth-values. Thus, instead of letting the denotation of *every man* be the e-type argument of the verbal et-function, we can let it be a *function* that takes the verbal meaning as its argument. When using type $(et)t$ for our analysis of sentence (4.5), we can compositionally derive the subset requirement in (4.6). For our denotation of *every man*, we are interested in the $(et)t$ function Q that satisfies the following requirement:

(4.8) $Q_{(et)t}(\mathbf{run}_{et}) = 1$ iff $\mathbf{man}^* \subseteq \mathbf{run}^*$

In words, the function Q sends the et function **run** to 'true' iff the set of men is contained in the set of runners.

The function Q encodes a specific requirement that is suitable for sentence (4.5), where the main VP denotation is the function **run**. However, the $(et)t$ denotation for the noun phrase *every man* must be defined for all possible VP denotations of type et. Based on the subset requirement, this function should map any et function to a truth-value. Therefore, for every model, we define the denotation Q of the noun phrase *every man* as follows, for every et function P:

(4.9) $Q_{(et)t}(P_{et}) = 1$ iff $\mathbf{man}^* \subseteq P^*$

In lambda notation, we write the definition of the function Q as follows:

(4.10) $\lambda P_{et}.\mathbf{man}^* \subseteq P^*$

When we assume this denotation for *every man*, we get the following compositional analysis of sentence (4.5), which gives us the desired result:

(4.11) $[\![$ [every man] ran $]\!] = 1$

   $\Leftrightarrow [\![every\ man]\!]([\![ran]\!]) = 1$

   $\quad\quad\quad \triangleright$ applying subject denotation to verb denotation

   $\Leftrightarrow (\lambda P_{et}.\mathbf{man}^* \subseteq P^*)(\mathbf{run}_{et}) = 1$

   $\quad\quad\quad \triangleright$ denotation (4.10) of *every man*

   $\Leftrightarrow \mathbf{man}^* \subseteq \mathbf{run}^*$

   $\quad\quad\quad \triangleright$ application

In this analysis, we use the function in (4.10) as the denotation of the noun phrase *every man*. Such functions, of type $(et)t$, characterize sets of functions of type et. Each such et function itself characterizes a set of entities. Therefore, we can view a denotation of type $(et)t$ as a *set of sets of entities*. For example, we can describe the function in (4.10) using the following set of sets:

(4.12) $\{B \subseteq E : \mathbf{man}^* \subseteq B\}$

In words, (4.12) describes the set of subsets of E that contain the set of men. These are precisely the sets characterized by et functions that the function in (4.10) sends to 1. Sets of sets of entities as in (4.12) will occur frequently in our $(et)t$ analysis of NPs. We refer to them as *generalized quantifiers* (GQs) over E. Formally:

> Let E be a set of entities. Every set of subsets of E is referred to as a **generalized quantifier** over E.

In (4.11), we let the $(et)t$ function in (4.10) apply to the et denotation of the verb *run*. Subsequently, (4.11) specifies the conditions under which the resulting truth-value of this application is 1. These conditions amount to requiring that the set $\mathbf{run}^*$ is in the GQ in

(4.12). Using this GQ, we can reach the same conclusion as in (4.11), as follows:

(4.13) $[\![$ [every man] ran $]\!] = 1$

  $\Leftrightarrow$ $\mathbf{run}^* \in \{B \subseteq E : \mathbf{man}^* \subseteq B\}$

    $\triangleright$ the set of runners is in the set of supersets of the set of men (4.12)

  $\Leftrightarrow$ $\mathbf{man}^* \subseteq \mathbf{run}^*$

    $\triangleright$ the set of runners is a superset of the set of men = the set of men is contained in the set of runners

The same method that we used for analyzing sentence (4.5) is useful for analyzing many other sentences with quantified NPs. As another simple example, let us consider the following sentence:

(4.14) [Some man] ran.

Intuitively, we want sentence (4.14) to be true when the set of men contains an entity that ran. This is the same as requiring that the intersection of the sets $\mathbf{man}^*$ and $\mathbf{run}^*$ is not empty. We analyze the sentence in this way, by adopting the following GQ analysis for the noun phrase *some man* in (4.14):

(4.15) $\{B \subseteq E : \mathbf{man}^* \cap B \neq \emptyset\}$

In words, this is the set of sets whose intersection with the set of men is not empty. As a result, we get the following analysis of sentence (4.14):

(4.16) $[\![$ [some man] ran $]\!] = 1$

  $\Leftrightarrow$ $\mathbf{run}^* \in \{B \subseteq E : \mathbf{man}^* \cap B \neq \emptyset\}$

    $\triangleright$ the set of runners is in the set of sets whose intersection with the set of men is not empty

  $\Leftrightarrow$ $\mathbf{man}^* \cap \mathbf{run}^* \neq \emptyset$

    $\triangleright$ the intersection of the set of men with the set of runners is not empty

In a similar way, we require that sentence (4.17) below denotes 1 if and only if the set of men and the set of runners have an empty

Table 4.2:   Some NPs and their corresponding GQs.

Noun phrase	Generalized quantifier	Monotonicity (*see page 110*)
I *every man*	$\{B \subseteq E : \mathbf{man}^* \subseteq B\}$	MON↑
II *some man*	$\{B \subseteq E : \mathbf{man}^* \cap B \neq \emptyset\}$	MON↑
no man	$\{B \subseteq E : \mathbf{man}^* \cap B = \emptyset\}$	MON↓
exactly one man	$\{B \subseteq E : \mid \mathbf{man}^* \cap B \mid = 1\}$	MON¬
at least three men	$\{B \subseteq E : \mid \mathbf{man}^* \cap B \mid \geq 3\}$	MON↑
fewer than five men	$\{B \subseteq E : \mid \mathbf{man}^* \cap B \mid < 5\}$	MON↓
between six and eleven men	$\{B \subseteq E : 6 \leq \mid \mathbf{man}^* \cap B \mid \leq 11\}$	MON¬
III *at least half the men*	$\{B \subseteq E : \mid \mathbf{man}^* \cap B \mid \geq 1/2 \cdot \mid \mathbf{man}^* \mid\}$	MON↑

intersection. Thus, we assume the GQ analysis in (4.18) for the noun phrase *no man*:

(4.17) [No man] ran.

(4.18) $\{B \subseteq E : \mathbf{man}^* \cap B = \emptyset\}$

In words, (4.18) describes the set of sets whose intersection with the set of men is empty. As a result, we get the following analysis of sentence (4.17):

(4.19) $[\![\; [no\ man]\ ran \;]\!] = 1$

     $\Leftrightarrow \mathbf{run}^* \in \{B \subseteq E : \mathbf{man}^* \cap B = \emptyset\}$

     ▷ the set of runners is in the set of sets whose intersection with

       the set of men is empty

     $\Leftrightarrow \mathbf{man}^* \cap \mathbf{run}^* \neq \emptyset$

     ▷ the intersection of the set of men with the set of runners

       is empty

We have seen how to analyze different sentences with quantified NPs by letting these NPs denote $(et)t$ functions, or, equivalently, GQs. Table 4.2 summarizes some more examples for the GQ analysis of different NPs.

The GQs that we have associated above with the noun phrases *some man* and *no man* impose a requirement on the intersection set $\mathbf{man}^* \cap B$. The *some* NP requires that this set is not empty, whereas the *no* NP requires that it is empty. Thus, both NPs put a requirement on the *cardinality* of the set **man*** ∩ B: non-zero cardinality and zero cardinality, respectively. Standardly, we denote the cardinality of a set A by '$|A|$'. More examples for quantified NPs that put cardinality restrictions on the relevant intersection set are given in part II of Table 4.2. The GQs corresponding to such NPs are called *intersective*. NPs that are associated with such GQs appear easily in existential *there* sentences. For instance: *there is some/no man in the garden*. Such NPs are also referred to as *weak NPs*. Other NPs, which do not denote intersective GQs, are sometimes referred to as *strong*. Strong NPs are often unacceptable in *there* sentences, as in #*there is every man in the garden*. For more on intersective GQs, the weak/strong distinction and *there* sentences, see the further reading at the end of this chapter. The noun phrase *at least half the men*, in part III of Table 4.2, also puts a requirement on the cardinality of the set **man*** ∩ B, but this requirement is more complex: the cardinality $|$**man*** ∩ B$|$ is required to stand in a numeric *proportion* to the cardinality $|$**man***$|$ of the set **man***. Intuitively, a sentence like *at least half of the men ran* is true if and only if the number of men who ran, i.e. the cardinality of the set **man*** ∩ **run***, is not smaller than half the number of men, i.e. the cardinality $|$**man***$|$. Quantifier denotations for such NPs, which put a condition on the proportion between two or more cardinalities, are often referred to as *proportional quantifiers*.

You are now advised to solve Exercise 1 at the end of this chapter.

LOOKING AT GENERALIZED QUANTIFIERS IN MODELS

When viewing NP denotations as sets of sets, we can quite easily look at specific models. Let us consider a model where the domain E is {a, b, c, d}, and the denotations of the noun *man* and the verb *run* satisfy:

$$\textbf{man}^* = \{a, b\} \qquad \textbf{run}^* = \{a, b, c\}.$$

In this model, the set **man*** is obviously a subset of the set **run***, and the sentence *every man ran* is intuitively true. Let us see how this is compositionally derived by our analysis in (4.13). First, by our assumptions E = {a, b, c, d} and **man*** = {a, b} we conclude that the GQ associated with *every man* in our model is:

$$\{B \subseteq E : \textbf{man}^* \subseteq B\} = \{B \subseteq \{a, b, c, d\} : \{a, b\} \subseteq B\}$$

$$\{a, b, c, d\}$$

$$\{a, b, c\} \ \{a, b, d\} \ \{a, c, d\} \ \{b, c, d\}$$

$$\{a, b\} \quad \{a, c\} \quad \{b, c\} \quad \{a, d\} \quad \{b, d\} \quad \{c, d\}$$

$$\{a\} \qquad \{b\} \qquad \{c\} \qquad \{d\}$$

$$\emptyset$$

Figure 4.1   The gray area depicts the GQ for the noun phrase every
man, *in a model over a domain* $E = \{a, b, c, d\}$, *where the men are*
a *and* b.

In words, this is the collection of subsets of the domain $\{a, b, c, d\}$ that
are supersets of the set $\{a, b\}$. There are four such sets:

$\{a, b\}, \{a, b, c\}, \{a, b, d\}$ and $\{a, b, c, d\}$.

We conclude:

(4.20) $\{B \subseteq E : \mathbf{man}^* \subseteq B\} = \{\{a, b\}, \{a, b, c\}, \{a, b, d\}, \{a, b, c, d\}\}$

This conclusion is graphically depicted in Figure 4.1.

In the model we assumed, the set denotation $\mathbf{run}^*$ equals $\{a, b, c\}$.
This set is among the four sets we found in the generalized quantifier
$\{B \subseteq E : \mathbf{man}^* \subseteq B\}$. Thus, we conclude:

$\mathbf{run}^* \in \{B \subseteq E : \mathbf{man}^* \subseteq B\}$

Accordingly, the sentence *every man ran* is intuitively analyzed as true
in the given model. It is important to note that, in this model, the
set denotation of the verb *ran* includes an element that is not in the
denotation of the noun *man*: the entity c. This fact has little effect
on our intuition that the sentence must be true in this model. In a
situation where all the men ran, the set of runners may also include
entities that are not men, like the entity c in our example. For this
reason, sets like $\{a, b, c\}, \{a, b, d\}$ and $\{a, b, c, d\}$ must be in the GQ
associated with *every man* in our model, even though some – and
potentially, many – of the entities in them are not classified as men.

Let us now also consider the denotations of the noun phrases
some man and *no man* in our model. The GQ that is associated with

some man:		no man:	
{a, b, c, d}		{a, b, c, d}	
{a, b, c} {a, b, d} {a, c, d} {b, c, d}		{a, b, c} {a, b, d} {a, c, d}{b, c, d}	
{a, b} {a, c} {b, c} {a, d} {b, d} {c, d}	{a, b} {a, c} {b, c} {a, d} {b, d} {c, d}
{a} {b} {c} {d}	{a} {b} {c} {d}
Ø		Ø	

Figure 4.2   The two gray areas depict the GQs for the noun phrases some man and no man, with $E = \{a, b, c, d\}$, and $\mathbf{man}^* = \{a, b\}$.

some man is the following:

$$(4.21) \quad \{B \subseteq E : \mathbf{man}^* \cap B \neq \emptyset\} \qquad\qquad (=(4.15))$$
$$= \{B \subseteq \{a, b, c, d\} : \{a, b\} \cap B \neq \emptyset\} \quad (E = \{a, b, c, d\} \text{ and } \mathbf{man}^* = \{a, b\})$$

This is the set of subsets of the domain $\{a, b, c, d\}$ whose intersection with the set $\{a, b\}$ is not empty. There are twelve such sets, which constitute the GQ associated with some man in the given model:

$$\{\{a\}, \{b\}, \{a, b\}, \{a, c\}, \{a, d\}, \{b, c\}, \{b, d\}, \{a, b, c\}, \{a, b, d\},$$
$$\{a, c, d\}, \{b, c, d\}, \{a, b, c, d\}\}$$

Similarly, the GQ that is associated with no man is the following:

$$(4.22) \quad \{B \subseteq E : \mathbf{man}^* \cap B = \emptyset\} \qquad\qquad (=(4.18))$$
$$= \{B \subseteq \{a, b, c, d\} : \{a, b\} \cap B = \emptyset\} \quad (E = \{a, b, c, d\} \text{ and } \mathbf{man}^* = \{a, b\})$$

This is the set of subsets of the domain $\{a, b, c, d\}$ whose intersection with the set $\{a, b\}$ is empty. There are four such sets, which constitute the GQ associated with no man in the given model:

$$\{\emptyset, \{c\}, \{d\}, \{c, d\}\}$$

The GQs that are associated with the noun phrases some man and no man in our model are graphically illustrated in Figure 4.2. We can see here that these two GQs complement each other: any set A of entities in the model is in the GQ for the former NP, if it is not in the GQ for the latter, and vice versa. This is desirable, since the sentence some man ran is true in precisely those situations where no man ran is false, and vice versa.

You are now advised to solve Exercise 2 and 3 at the end of this chapter.

QUANTIFIER MONOTONICITY

Having seen some quantifier denotations, let us see how GQs allow us to account for simple entailments with quantified NPs. Consider the following entailment:

(4.23) [Every man] [ran quickly] $\Rightarrow$ [Every man] ran.

To account for this entailment, we use the following notation:

$R_1 = [\![ran\ quickly]\!]^*$ = the set of entities that ran quickly

$R_2 = [\![ran]\!]^* = \mathbf{run}^*$ = the set of entities that ran

In Chapter 3, we observed that adverbs like *quickly* are subsective modifiers. With the sentences in (4.23), the subsectivity of *quickly* guarantees that R_1 is a subset of R_2. With this in mind, let us note the following reasoning about the GQ for the noun phrase *every man*:

(4.24) a. Suppose that the set R_1 is in the generalized quantifier $\{B \subseteq E : \mathbf{man}^* \subseteq B\}$.

   b. Then $\mathbf{man}^* \subseteq R_1$.

   c. By our assumption $R_1 \subseteq R_2$, we also have $\mathbf{man}^* \subseteq R_2$.

   d. Thus, the set R_2 is also a member of the generalized quantifier $\{B \subseteq E : \mathbf{man}^* \subseteq B\}$.

The crucial step is the conclusion in (4.24c), which relies on the fact that the subset relation is *transitive*: since $R_1 \subseteq R_2$ holds, any subset of R_1 is also a subset of R_2. From (4.24) we conclude that in every model where the set for *ran quickly* is in the GQ for *every man*, the set for *ran* is also in that GQ. This accounts for the entailment (4.23) on the basis of our GQ-based analysis and the TCC.

Entailments similar to (4.23) appear with many NPs. For instance, let us consider the noun phrase *some man* in the following entailment:

(4.25) [Some man] [ran quickly] $\Rightarrow$ [Some man] ran.

Using our GQ for *some man*, we account for the entailment in (4.25) along similar lines to our analysis in (4.24). This is shown below, where R_1 and R_2 are again any sets of entities such that R_1 is a subset of R_2:

(4.26) a. Suppose that the set R_1 is in $\{B \subseteq E : \mathbf{man}^* \cap B \neq \emptyset\}$.

b. Then $\mathbf{man}^* \cap R_1 \neq \emptyset$.

c. By our assumption $R_1 \subseteq R_2$, we also have $\mathbf{man}^* \cap R_2 \neq \emptyset$.

d. Thus, the set R_2 is also a member of $\{B \subseteq E : \mathbf{man}^* \cap B \neq \emptyset\}$.

Here, the main point is in (4.26c), which relies on the fact that when a set A has a non-empty intersection with some set, any superset of A also has a non-empty intersection with that set. This shows that our GQ-based analysis accounts for the entailment in (4.25) above.

The entailment pattern in (4.23) and (4.25) is referred to as *upward monotonicity*. Accordingly, we say that the NPs "every man" and "some man" are *upward monotone*. In correlation with this observation about entailments, analyses (4.24) and (4.26) show a property that holds of the GQs that we assigned to these NPs: whenever a certain set R_1 is in these GQs, any superset of R_1 is in it as well. In more general terms, we define upward monotonicity of GQs as follows:

> *A generalized quantifier over E is* **upward monotone** (MON↑) *if and only if for all sets $A \subseteq B \subseteq E$: if $A \in Q$ then $B \in Q$.*

Upward monotone NPs and GQs are also referred to as *monotone increasing*.

Although upward monotonicity is quite common with noun phrases, it does not hold for all quantified NPs. For instance, let us consider the following non-entailment:

(4.27) No man ran quickly $\nRightarrow$ No man ran.

Intuitively, it may of course happen that one man or several men ran slowly, but no man ran quickly. In such situations the antecedent of entailment (4.27) is intuitively true but the consequent is false. This means that the noun phrase *no man* is not upward monotone. The GQ that we associated with this NP captures this lack of monotonicity. For instance, in Figure 4.2 above we considered a model with three entities, where the men are a and b. This led to the following GQ for *no man*:

(4.28) $\{B \subseteq E : \mathbf{man}^* \cap B = \emptyset\} = \{\emptyset, \{c\}, \{d\}, \{c, d\}\}$

Suppose that the runners in our model are a and c, but of these two runners, only c ran quickly. Intuitively, the sentence *no man ran quickly* is true in this situation, as c is not a man. This truth is modeled by the fact that the singleton $R_1 = \{c\}$ is in the generalized quantifier (4.28). By contrast, the sentence *no man ran* is intuitively false in this situation, which is modeled by the fact that the set $R_2 = \{a, c\}$ is not in the generalized quantifier (4.28). We have seen a model in which a set R_1 is in the GQ for *no man*, but a set R_2 that contains it is not. Thus, the GQ for *no man* is not upward monotone, in agreement with the behavior of that NP.

Now we should also observe that the noun phrase *no man* shows an entailment in the opposite direction to upward monotonicity. This is illustrated below:

(4.29) No man ran $\Rightarrow$ No man ran quickly.

Intuitively, this entailment is again very clear: if no man ran, then of course there cannot be any man who ran quickly. Our treatment of the noun phrase *no man* accounts for this behavior too. This is shown by the following consideration about the GQ that we associated with the noun phrase *no man* in (4.18). Again we assume the subset relation $R_1 \subseteq R_2$.

(4.30) a. Suppose that the set R_2 is in $\{B \subseteq E : \mathbf{man}^* \cap B = \emptyset\}$.
  b. Then $\mathbf{man}^* \cap R_2 = \emptyset$.
  c. By our assumption $R_1 \subseteq R_2$, we have $\mathbf{man}^* \cap R_1 = \emptyset$.
  d. Thus, the set R_1 is also a member of $\{B \subseteq E : \mathbf{man}^* \cap B = \emptyset\}$.

This analysis relies on property (4.30c): when a set A has an empty intersection with some set, any subset of A also has a non-empty intersection with that set. This shows that our GQ-based account describes the entailment in (4.29). Whenever a certain set R_2 is in the GQ for *no man*, any subset of R_2 is in that GQ as well. This property is called *downward monotonicity*, and is formally defined below:

> *A generalized quantifier over E is* **downward monotone** (MON↓) *if and only if for all sets $A \subseteq B \subseteq E$: if $B \in Q$ then $A \in Q$.*

Downward monotone NPs and GQs are also referred to as *monotone decreasing*. We will refer to quantifiers that are upward or downward monotone as *monotone quantifiers*. Accordingly, we talk about *monotonicity* when referring to the general property of upward/downward monotonicity with NPs and GQs.

Let us note that the upward monotone noun phrases *every man* and *some man* are not downward monotone. This is illustrated by the following non-entailments:

(4.31)   a.   Every man ran $\not\Rightarrow$ Every man ran quickly.

        b.   Some man ran $\not\Rightarrow$ Some man ran quickly.

We can verify that our GQ treatment captures these properties as well by looking at a model where $[\![man]\!]^* = \{a, b\}$, $[\![ran]\!]^* = \{a, b, c\}$, and $[\![ran\ quickly]\!]^* = \{c\}$. In this model, both antecedents in (4.31) denote 1 and both consequents denote 0.

Some NPs do not show any monotonicity entailments. Consider for instance the following non-entailments with the noun phrase *exactly one man*:

(4.32)   a.   Exactly one man ran quickly $\not\Rightarrow$ Exactly one man ran.

        b.   Exactly one man ran $\not\Rightarrow$ Exactly one man ran quickly.

Intuitively, it is possible that many men ran, but only one man ran quickly. This shows the lack of entailment in (4.32a). It is also possible that exactly one man ran, but no man ran quickly. This shows the lack of entailment in (4.32b). As we shall see in Exercise 4, this lack of entailment is reflected in our analysis of the noun phrase *exactly one man* as a GQ that is neither upward nor downward monotone. We refer to such NPs and GQs as *non-monotone* (MON¬). In Table 4.2 above we summarize more (non-)monotonicity properties of the GQs we have defined for some representative NPs.

You are now advised to solve Exercise 4 and 5 at the end of this chapter.

QUANTIFIED NPs AND VERB PHRASE COORDINATION

Let us now consider sentences with verb phrase coordinations like *sang and danced* or *praised Mary and thanked Tina* (cf. Chapter 3, page 79). When quantified NPs appear in such sentences, they display a rather heterogenous pattern of entailments. Consider for instance the following (non-)entailments:

(4.33) a. At least one man sang *and* danced

$\not\rightleftarrows$ At least one man sang *and* at least one man danced.

   b. At least one man sang *or* danced
       $\Leftrightarrow$ At least one man sang *or* at least one man danced.

(4.34) a. Every man sang *and* danced
            $\Leftrightarrow$ Every man sang *and* every man danced.

   b. Every man sang *or* danced

       $\not\rightleftarrows$ Every man sang *or* every man danced.

(4.35) a. Exactly one man sang *and* danced

       $\not\rightleftarrows$ Exactly one man sang *and* exactly one man danced.

   b. Exactly one man sang *or* danced

       $\not\rightleftarrows$ Exactly one man sang *or* exactly one man danced.

In all these cases, the *and* or *or* coordination is between intransitive verbs, and the subject of the sentence is a quantified NP. As these examples illustrate, entailments may or may not show up between the sentential coordination and the sentence with the phrasal coordination, depending on the subject NP. Our GQ-based analysis naturally accounts for this complex pattern of (non-)entailments.

As one example, let us analyze the uni-directional entailment in (4.33a) in some detail. The entailment intuitively asserts that any situation with at least one man who sang and danced must have at least one man who sang and at least one man who danced. However, the opposite direction in (4.33a) does not hold: a situation that contains one man who sang and one man who danced may contain no man who did both. This asymmetry is directly accounted for by our analysis of GQs and predicate conjunction. Let us see how, by considering the analyses below:

(4.36) [[at least one] man] [sang [and danced]]

$$\text{AT\_LEAST\_1}(\mathbf{man})(\text{AND}^{et}(\mathbf{dance})(\mathbf{sing})) = 1$$

$$\Leftrightarrow \mathbf{sing}^* \cap \mathbf{dance}^* \in \{A \subseteq E : |\,\mathbf{man}^* \cap A\,| \geq 1\}$$

$$\Leftrightarrow |\,\mathbf{man}^* \cap (\mathbf{sing}^* \cap \mathbf{dance}^*)\,| \geq 1$$

(4.37) [[[at least one] man] sang] [and [[[at least one] man] danced]]

$$\text{AND}^t(\text{AT\_LEAST\_1}(\mathbf{man})(\mathbf{dance}))(\text{AT\_LEAST\_1}(\mathbf{man})(\mathbf{sing})) = 1$$

$$\Leftrightarrow \mathbf{sing}^* \in \{A \subseteq E : |\,\mathbf{man}^* \cap A\,| \geq 1\}$$
$$\wedge\ \mathbf{dance}^* \in \{A \subseteq E : |\,\mathbf{man}^* \cap A\,| \geq 1\}$$

$$\Leftrightarrow |\,\mathbf{man}^* \cap \mathbf{sing}^*\,| \geq 1 \ \wedge \ |\,\mathbf{man}^* \cap \mathbf{dance}^*\,| \geq 1$$

In (4.36) we analyze the denotation of the left-hand sentence in (4.33a). The verb phrase *sang and danced* is analyzed by intersecting the two sets $\mathbf{sing}^*$ and $\mathbf{dance}^*$. As in Chapter 3, this is achieved by the predicate conjunction operator AND^{et}. The noun phrase *at least one man* is analyzed using the quantifier $\{A \subseteq E : |\,\mathbf{man}^* \cap A\,| \geq 1\}$, i.e. the set of sets whose intersection with the set of men is of cardinality 1 or more. The resulting assertion $|\,\mathbf{man}^* \cap (\mathbf{sing}^* \cap \mathbf{dance}^*)\,| \geq 1$ in (4.36) can only be true if both intersections $\mathbf{man}^* \cap \mathbf{sing}^*$ and $\mathbf{man}^* \cap \mathbf{dance}^*$ are of cardinality 1 or more, which is asserted by our analysis in (4.37). This accounts for the left-to-right entailment in (4.33a). The right-to-left *non*-entailment in (4.33a) is also accounted for. For instance, in a model where $\mathbf{man}^* = \{a, b\}$, $\mathbf{sing}^* = \{a\}$ and $\mathbf{dance}^* = \{b\}$, the sentence in (4.37) denotes 1 but the sentence in (4.36) denotes 0. This is immediately described by our GQ analyses in (4.36) and (4.37). In Exercise 6 we will see that our GQ-based account also naturally extends to many other (non-)entailments of the sort that is illustrated in (4.33)–(4.35).

You are now advised to solve Exercise 6 at the end of this chapter. The advanced Exercise 7 will give you more insight into GQs and 'or' coordinations as in (4.33)–(4.35).

DETERMINER EXPRESSIONS

So far we have analyzed complex quantified NPs like *every man* and *exactly one man*, ignoring their internal structure. However, we would also like to explain how GQs are compositionally derived from the denotations of the words within the NP. This is important for analyzing NPs where the nominal is more complex than just the noun *man*, e.g. *every tall man, some tall man from Japan, exactly one tall man from Japan who sings the blues*, etc. In order to analyze such NPs, we should look into the semantics of determiner expressions like *every* and *exactly one* in isolation from the quantified NPs in which they appear. Let us reconsider our analysis for the noun phrase *every man*:

(4.38) $[\![every\ man]\!] = \lambda P_{et}.\mathbf{man}^* \subseteq P^* = \lambda P_{et}.[\![man]\!]^* \subseteq P^*$

If we were to replace the noun *man* with another noun or with a complex nominal, we would like to analyze the NP denotation using the same principles that we employed in (4.38). For instance, in the quantified noun phrase *every boy* we would like to use a similar analysis to (4.38), where the *et* denotation $[\![man]\!]$ is replaced by the *et* denotation $[\![boy]\!]$. Obviously, the *et* denotations of the nouns *man* and *boy* are similarly used within the $(et)t$ denotations of the NPs *every man* and *every boy*. More generally, the determiner *every* should combine with *any* denotation of type *et*, to give a function of type $(et)t$. What type should such determiners have? To answer this question, let us solve the following type equation:

(4.39) $X + et = (et)t$

In this equation, X is the type of the determiner expression, *et* is the type of the noun, and $(et)t$ is the type of the derived quantified NP. The solution for X in (4.39) is $(et)((et)t)$: the type of functions from *et* functions to $(et)t$ functions. Defining the denotation of the determiner *every* as being of this type, we generalize over the definition in (4.38), and get the following definition:

(4.40) EVERY $= \lambda A_{et}.\lambda B_{et}.A^* \subseteq B^*$

This $(et)((et)t)$ function is our Curried rendition of the subset relation between sets of entities: essentially, it takes two sets and returns 0 or 1 depending on whether the subset relation holds between them. More accurately, the Curried function EVERY sends every *et* function A to an $(et)t$ function, which sends every *et* function B to the truth-value 1 if and only if the set of entities characterized by A is a subset of the set characterized by B.

Using our definition of the determiner function EVERY we now compositionally derive the NP denotation in (4.38), as shown below:

(4.41) $[\![every\ man]\!]$
  $= \text{EVERY}(\mathbf{man})$
  $= (\lambda A_{et}.\lambda B_{et}.A^* \subseteq B^*)(\mathbf{man})$ (by (4.40))
  $= \lambda B_{et}.\mathbf{man}^* \subseteq B^*$

Since we got the desired $(et)t$ analysis of the NP, the denotation for the sentence *every man ran* remains intact:

(4.42) $[\![[every\ man]\ ran]\!] = 1$
  $\Leftrightarrow (\text{EVERY}(\mathbf{man}))(\mathbf{run}) = 1$
  $\Leftrightarrow (\lambda B_{et}.\mathbf{man}^* \subseteq B^*)(\mathbf{run}) = 1$ (by (4.41))
  $\Leftrightarrow \mathbf{man}^* \subseteq \mathbf{run}^*$

We refer to functions of type $(et)((et)t)$, like the function EVERY above, as *determiner functions*. Using such functions, we can systematically treat other determiner expressions, and hence quantified NPs. For instance, the determiners *some* and *no* are treated using the following determiner functions:

(4.43) SOME $= \lambda A_{et}.\lambda B_{et}.A^* \cap B^* \neq \emptyset$
  NO $= \lambda A_{et}.\lambda B_{et}.A^* \cap B^* = \emptyset$

In words, the denotation SOME is the Curried rendition of the relation that holds between any two non-disjoint sets of entities. Similarly, the denotation NO is a Curried relation holding between disjoint sets of entities.

From a compositional perspective, it is very convenient to use Curried functions of type $(et)((et)t)$. Such functions allow us to use the same compositional principles as we did in Chapter 3. However, to get a better feel of what such denotations do, it is also useful to deCurry them and speak in terms of sets and relations. Thus, for every determiner function f of type $(et)((et)t)$, we define the corresponding *determiner relation* $\mathbf{D}_f$. This is a *binary relation between sets of entities*, i.e. a set of pairs $\langle A, B \rangle$, where A and B are subsets of E. For instance, the following identity makes a connection between the determiner function EVERY and the corresponding determiner relation $\mathbf{D}_{\text{EVERY}}$:

(4.44) For all functions $A, B \in D_{et}$: EVERY$(A)(B) = 1 \Leftrightarrow \langle A^*, B^* \rangle \in \mathbf{D}_{\text{EVERY}}$.

The relation $\mathbf{D}_{\text{EVERY}}$ is simply the subset relation. More generally, for every determiner function f of type $(et)((et)t)$, we define:

(4.45) For all functions $A, B \in D_{et}$: $f(A)(B) = 1 \Leftrightarrow \langle A^*, B^* \rangle \in \mathbf{D}_f$.

In words: for every determiner function f, the corresponding relation holds of the pairs of sets $\langle A, B \rangle$ whose characteristic functions are sent by f to 1. When $\mathbf{D}$ is a determiner relation and $A, B \subseteq E$ are sets of entities, we standardly write "$\mathbf{D}(A, B)$" as an abbreviation for "$\langle A, B \rangle \in \mathbf{D}$". We refer to the set A as the *left argument* of $\mathbf{D}$, and to B as its *right argument*. For instance, in the sentence *every tall man ran quickly*, the left argument of EVERY corresponds to the nominal *tall man* and its right argument corresponds to the verb phrase *ran quickly*.

Because of the natural correspondence in (4.45) between determiner functions and determiner relations, we can freely move back and forth between the two perspectives. To avoid notational complications, we use the same notations for determiner functions and determiner relations. For instance, instead of defining determiner functions directly using λ-terms as in (4.40) and (4.43), we can define the corresponding determiner relations, using the same notation. Specifically, for every domain E of entities, for all sets $A, B \subseteq E$, we define:

(4.46) EVERY$(A, B) \Leftrightarrow A \subseteq B$
       SOME$(A, B) \Leftrightarrow A \cap B \neq \emptyset$
       NO$(A, B) \Leftrightarrow A \cap B = \emptyset$

Here we use the notation EVERY, SOME and NO ambiguously for determiner functions and the corresponding determiner relations. Accordingly, for instance, the derivation of the GQ in (4.12) for the noun phrase *every man* may be written in two different but equivalent

Table 4.3:   Some determiner relations.

	Determiner relations			Monotonicity
I	EVERY (A, B)	$\Leftrightarrow$	$A \subseteq B$	$\downarrow$MON$\uparrow$
II	SOME (A, B)	$\Leftrightarrow$	$A \cap B \neq \emptyset$	$\uparrow$MON$\uparrow$
	NO (A, B)	$\Leftrightarrow$	$A \cap B = \emptyset$	$\downarrow$MON$\downarrow$
	EXACTLY_1 (A, B)	$\Leftrightarrow$	$\lvert A \cap B \rvert = 1$	$\neg$MON$\neg$
	AT_LEAST_3 (A, B)	$\Leftrightarrow$	$\lvert A \cap B \rvert \geq 3$	$\uparrow$MON$\uparrow$
	FEWER_THAN_5 (A, B)	$\Leftrightarrow$	$\lvert A \cap B \rvert < 5$	$\downarrow$MON$\downarrow$
	BETWEEN_6_AND_11 (A, B)	$\Leftrightarrow$	$6 \leq \lvert A \cap B \rvert \leq 11$	$\neg$MON$\neg$
III	AT_LEAST_HALF (A, B)	$\Leftrightarrow$	$\lvert A \cap B \rvert \geq \frac{1}{2} \cdot \lvert A \rvert$	$\neg$MON$\uparrow$

ways, as in (4.47) below:

(4.47)   a. $\{B^* \subseteq E : \text{EVERY}(\mathbf{man})(B) = 1\}$

the set of sets B^* whose characteristic functions B are mapped to 1 by the $(et)t$ function EVERY(**man**)

b. $\{B \subseteq E : \text{EVERY}(\mathbf{man}^*, B)\}$

the set of sets B that are in the relation EVERY to the set **man***

Table 4.3 shows some more definitions of determiner relations. When the left argument of these relations is the set **man***, these definitions derive the GQs in Table 4.2 similarly to the derivations of the GQ for *every man* in (4.47).

The correspondence between Tables 4.2 and 4.3 highlights the deep connection between GQ denotations and the determiner functions (or relations) from which they are derived. Specifically, the monotonicity properties of complex NPs are systematically related to the properties of the determiners within them. For instance, the upward monotonicity of *every man* that we saw in the simple entailment (4.23) reappears with all nominals and verb phrases, as long as the quantified NP is headed by *every*. For instance:

(4.48)   [Every [tall man]] [ran quickly] $\Rightarrow$ [Every [tall man]] ran

[Every [tall man from Japan]] [ran quickly]
$\Rightarrow$ [Every [tall man from Japan]] ran

[Every [tall man from Japan who sings the blues]] [ran quickly]
$\Rightarrow$ [Every [tall man from Japan who sings the blues]] ran

In these entailments, we see that the pattern in (4.23) remains stable for all nominals substituted for *man*. In a schematic form, we conclude that the following entailment holds for all nominals N:

(4.49) [Every N] [ran quickly] $\Rightarrow$ [Every N] ran

This reflects a general property of the determiner *every*: when holding the nominal constant, replacing one verb phrase VP_1 (e.g. *ran quickly*) with another verb phrase VP_2 (e.g. *ran*) leads to an entailment, provided that the latter VP denotes a superset of the former. This property of the determiner *every* guarantees that all NPs that it forms are upward monotone. Because we hold the left argument (the nominal) constant, and modify the right argument (the VP), we refer to this property of *every* as *right monotonicity*. This property is formally defined below, for both upward and downward monotonicity:

A determiner relation **D** *over E is called* **right upward monotone** (MON↑) *if and only if for all* $A \subseteq E$ *and* $B_1 \subseteq B_2 \subseteq E$: $\mathbf{D}(A, B_1) \Rightarrow \mathbf{D}(A, B_2)$.

A determiner relation **D** *over E is called* **right downward monotone** (MON↓) *if and only if for all* $A \subseteq E$ *and* $B_1 \subseteq B_2 \subseteq E$: $\mathbf{D}(A, B_2) \Rightarrow \mathbf{D}(A, B_1)$.

In words: a determiner D is upward (downward) monotone in its right argument if it preserves truth when its right argument is replaced by a superset (subset) thereof, while holding the left argument unchanged.

Above, we have observed that the right upward monotonicity of *every* corresponds to the upward monotonicity of the NPs that it forms. More generally, any determiner D that is upward/downward monotone in its right argument derives upward/downward monotone GQs for any set that is provided as a left argument. Formally:

(4.50) For every set $A \subseteq E$, the generalized quantifier $\{B \subseteq E : \mathbf{D}(A, B)\}$ is MON↑ (MON↓) if the determiner relation **D** is MON↑ (MON↓, respectively).

We conclude that the monotonicity properties we have seen with quantified NPs stem from the right-monotonicity properties of the determiners they contain.

It is also instructive to examine the monotonicity entailments of determiners when changing their left, nominal argument. For instance, let us consider the following entailment:

(4.51) [Every man] ran $\Rightarrow$ [Every [tall man]] ran.

Here, we replace the nominal argument *man* of the determiner *every* with the complex nominal *tall man*. In Chapter 3, we treated modificational adjectives like *tall* in (4.51) as subsective functions of type $(et)(et)$. This means that the set for *tall man* is a subset of the set for *man*. The entailment in (4.51) reflects a general property of the determiner EVERY: because a set (the men) is replaced by its subset (the tall men), we say that the entailment in (4.51) illustrates a *downward monotonicity* of the determiner *every* on its nominal arguments. In other words: *every* is *left downward monotone*. This is instructive, since, as we saw, "every" is *upward* monotone on its verb phrase argument, i.e. it is also *right upward monotone*. In sum: we see that *every* has different monotonicity properties in its two arguments.

To account for the downward-monotonicity entailment in (4.51), let us suppose that A_1 and A_2 are any sets associated with the nominals *man* and *tall man*, respectively, where A_2 is a subset of A_1. Now for any set of entities B, we note the following reasoning about the determiner relation for *every*:

(4.52)   a.   Suppose that the relation EVERY(A_1, B) holds.

          b.   Then $A_1 \subseteq B$.

          c.   By our assumption $A_2 \subseteq A_1$, we also have $A_2 \subseteq B$.

          d.   Thus, the relation EVERY(A_2, B) holds.

This accounts for the entailment (4.51) on the basis of our determiner analysis of *every* and the Truth-Conditionality Criterion.

Further, the (non-)entailments in (4.53) and (4.54) below illustrate the upward (rather than downward) monotonicity of the determiner *some* on its nominal argument, and the non-monotonicity of *exactly one* on its nominal argument:

(4.53)   a.   Some man ran $\nRightarrow$ Some tall man ran.

          b.   Some tall man ran $\Rightarrow$ Some man ran.

(4.54)   a. Exactly one man ran $\not\Rightarrow$ Exactly one tall man ran.

b. Exactly one tall man ran $\not\Rightarrow$ Exactly one man ran.

In general, we refer to this type of determiner monotonicity, on the nominal argument, as *left monotonicity*. As we have seen, left monotonicity of determiners is naturally characterized by properties of determiner relations. This is formally summarized below:

A determiner relation **D** *over E is called* **left upward monotone** *($\uparrow$MON) if and only if for all $A_1 \subseteq A_2 \subseteq E$ and $B \subseteq E$:* $\mathbf{D}(A_1, B)$ $\Rightarrow \mathbf{D}(A_2, B)$.

A determiner relation **D** *over E is called* **left downward monotone** *($\downarrow$MON) if and only if for all $A_1 \subseteq A_2 \subseteq E$ and $B \subseteq E$:* $\mathbf{D}(A_2, B)$ $\Rightarrow \mathbf{D}(A_1, B)$.

Determiner relations that are neither $\uparrow$MON nor $\downarrow$MON are referred to as *non-monotone in their left argument* ($\neg$MON). We combine the two notations we use for the left monotonicity and right monotonicity of determiners, and write, for instance, that the determiner *every* is "$\downarrow$MON$\uparrow$", as an abbreviation for "$\downarrow$MON and MON$\uparrow$". The two monotonicity properties of determiners are further illustrated in Table 4.3 above.

We have seen that formal properties of determiner expressions are at the core of the behavior of quantified NPs. We accounted for this fact by looking at determiner relations and the GQs they give rise to. Because of these close connections between determiner relations and GQs, it is also instructive to look at determiner denotations in specific models. Any determiner relation – and equivalently, any determiner function – specifies pairs of subsets of the domain E. For instance, for the domain $E = \{a, b\}$ we get the following sets of pairs:

(4.55)   EVERY: $\langle \emptyset, \emptyset \rangle, \langle \emptyset, \{a\} \rangle, \langle \emptyset, \{b\} \rangle, \langle \emptyset, \{a, b\} \rangle, \langle \{a\}, \{a\} \rangle, \langle \{a\}, \{a, b\} \rangle,$
$\langle \{b\}, \{b\} \rangle, \langle \{b\}, \{a, b\} \rangle, \langle \{a, b\}, \{a, b\} \rangle$

SOME: $\langle \{a\}, \{a\} \rangle, \langle \{a\}, \{a, b\} \rangle, \langle \{b\}, \{b\} \rangle, \langle \{b\}, \{a, b\} \rangle, \langle \{a, b\}, \{a\} \rangle,$
$\langle \{a, b\}, \{b\} \rangle, \langle \{a, b\}, \{a, b\} \rangle$

NO: $\langle \emptyset, \emptyset \rangle, \langle \emptyset, \{a\} \rangle, \langle \emptyset, \{b\} \rangle, \langle \emptyset, \{a, b\} \rangle, \langle \{a\}, \emptyset \rangle, \langle \{a\}, \{b\} \rangle,$
$\langle \{b\}, \emptyset \rangle, \langle \{b\}, \{a\} \rangle, \langle \{a, b\}, \emptyset \rangle$

The relation for EVERY collects all the pairs of subsets within the powerset of {a, b}. The relation SOME collects all the pairs of sets within this powerset whose intersection is not empty. Conversely, NO collects those pairs of sets whose intersection is empty.

Many other intricate phenomena with quantified NPs are studied in the large body of literature on generalized quantifiers and natural language. Some further reading is suggested at the end of this chapter.

You are now advised to solve Exercise 8 and 9 at the end of this chapter.

A NOTE ON MONOTONICITY AND NEGATIVE POLARITY ITEMS

A syntactic phenomenon that is closely related to monotonicity concerns words like *any* or *ever*, which are collectively referred to as *negative polarity items* (NPIs). These words often reveal differences between sentences which, on the surface, look very similar. For example, let us consider the triplets of sentences in (4.56a) and (4.56b) below. The only difference between the sentences in each triplet is the identity of the determiner: *no*, *every* or *some*. However, some of these sentences are clearly worse than others, as indicated by the asterisk '*'.

(4.56) a. *No* man saw *any* boy. *Every* man saw *any* boy. *Some* man saw *any* boy.

   b. *No* man who saw *any* boy ran. *Every* man who saw *any* boy ran. *Some* man who saw *any* boy ran.

In the three sentences in (4.56a), the word *any* appears within the main verb phrase *saw any boy*. The subjects in all of these sentences are quantified NPs with different determiners. As we see, the word *any* is OK when the subject determiner is *no*, but not when it is *every* or *some*. Interestingly, this behavior correlates with the MON↓ property of *no*. The other two determiners in (4.56a), *every* or *some*, are MON↑. Thus, roughly speaking, we may say that the NPI is "licensed" by the negative meaning of *no*.

However, in (4.56b) we see that this intuition about NPIs must be refined. In these examples, the word *any* is again OK when the subject determiner is *no*, and unacceptable when it is *some*. However, with the determiner *every*, the word *any* is now OK, in contrast to its behavior in (4.56a). Does this mean that "negative meanings" have nothing to do with the behavior of NPIs? Quite the contrary! Indeed, in (4.56b), we again see the word *any* with the same three determiners as in (4.56a). However, the instances of *any* in (4.56b) now appear *embedded within the subjects*. The acceptability of the sentences in (4.56b) again correlates with the monotonicity properties of the determiners, but this time, it is the *left*-downward-monotonicity property ($\downarrow$MON) of *no* and *every* – and its absence with *some* – that is in correlation with the behavior of *any*. To see that, we should note that the determiner *every* is upward right monotone but downward left monotone. And when moving from (4.56a) to (4.56b), we have changed the position of *any* from the right argument to the left argument of *every*. For the determiners *no* and *some*, moving from right to left does not change monotonicity: *no* is $\downarrow$MON$\downarrow$, and *some* is $\uparrow$MON$\uparrow$. Accordingly, the correlation between monotonicity and acceptability is only strengthened by the behavior of the NPIs in (4.56b).

We conclude that the NPI may indeed be licensed by the downward monotonicity of the determiner, but *only in the determiner's argument in which it appears*. This conclusion strengthens our intuition that NPIs are sensitive to "negative meanings". The notion of downward monotonicity, and our compositionality principle, give us a more precise definition of "negative meanings", and how NPIs are sensitive to them within the syntactic structure. The sentences in (4.57a–b) below illustrate a similar point with respect to the word *ever*:

(4.57)   a. *No* man has *ever* run. **Every* man has *ever* run. **Some* man has *ever* run.

   b. *No* man who has *ever* run smiled. *Every* man who has *ever* run smiled. **Some* man who has *ever* run smiled.

In both (4.56) and (4.57), we find an elegant correlation between our analysis of determiner monotonicity and the complex acceptability pattern that determiners show with NPIs. Solving the advanced assignment in Exercise 18 will allow you to further analyze the relations between NPIs and monotonicity.

MORE ENTAILMENTS, AND DETERMINER CONSERVATIVITY

With our treatment of determiner denotations, we can now easily analyze entailments like the following, which illustrate some of the classical inferences known as *syllogisms*:

(4.58) Every cook ran and every man is a cook $\Rightarrow$ Every man ran.

(4.59) Every cook ran and some man is a cook $\Rightarrow$ Some man ran.

(4.60) No cook ran and every man is a cook $\Rightarrow$ No man ran.

We can also analyze many other entailments and equivalences, like the following ones:

(4.61) Every cook who is not a tall man ran
        $\Rightarrow$ Every cook who is not a man ran.

(4.62) Some man is a cook who ran $\Leftrightarrow$ Some man who ran is a cook.

(4.63) More than half of the cooks ran and more than half of the cooks smiled $\Rightarrow$ Some cook ran and smiled.

(4.64) Between one-third and two-thirds of the men ran
        $\Leftrightarrow$ Between one-third and two-thirds of the men did not ran.

You are now advised to solve Exercise 10 at the end of this chapter. Solving the more advanced assignment in Exercise 11 will help you to see further how entailments like (4.58)–(4.64) are analyzed.

Another important inferential property of quantificational sentences is illustrated by the following equivalences:

(4.65) a. Every man ran $\Leftrightarrow$ Every man is a man who ran.
        b. Some man ran $\Leftrightarrow$ Some man is a man who ran.
        c. Exactly one man ran $\Leftrightarrow$ Exactly one man is a man who ran.
        d. Exactly half of the men ran
            $\Leftrightarrow$ Exactly half of the men are men who ran.

As it turns out, similar equivalences hold for most expressions that are classified as natural language determiners. Intuitively, this means that when quantifying over a set of objects – in (4.65), the set of *men* – and checking how many of them have some property – in (4.65), the property *ran* – it is only necessary to consider the elements that satisfy the property *ran* that are also *men*. More formally, the equivalences in (4.65) suggest the following general equivalence with determiner relations **D**:

(4.66) $\mathbf{D}(A, B) \Leftrightarrow \mathbf{D}(A, B \cap A)$.

We refer to determiner relations that satisfy this equivalence as *conservative determiners*. A well-known hypothesis proposes that conservativity is a *universal* about all determiner expressions in natural language. Formally:

A determiner relation **D** *over E is called* **conservative** *if and only if for all A, B $\subseteq$ E:* $\mathbf{D}(A, B) \Leftrightarrow \mathbf{D}(A, B \cap A)$.

Hypothesis: *All determiner expressions in natural language denote conservative determiner relations.*

Indeed, all of our analyses of different determiner expressions have something in common: they are all conservative. The hypothesis above expects this to be the case for all determiner expressions, in all languages. This is not a trivial hypothesis: as we shall see in Exercise 12, we can quite easily define determiner relations that are not conservative. Within current semantic theories, the pervasiveness of conservativity in natural language quantification has received different explanations. For work on this topic, see the further reading at the end of this chapter.

You are now advised to solve Exercise 12 at the end of this chapter. This advanced exercise will help you work further with the notion of determiner conservativity.

COORDINATION OF QUANTIFIED NPs

So far, our treatment of quantified NPs has only concentrated on single NP structures containing a determiner and a possibly complex nominal constituent like *man, tall man* or *man who smiled*. Another common NP structure involves conjunctive, disjunctive and negative coordination between NPs. This is illustrated below:

(4.67) every woman and/or every man, most women and most men, many students but/and few teachers, one student and five teachers, some teacher and every student, neither more than five years nor fewer than two years, neither every action nor every passion, neither many women nor many men.

One inferential property that such coordinations demonstrate is illustrated by the following equivalence:

(4.68) Every woman and every man ran
      $\Leftrightarrow$ Every woman ran and every man ran.

The treatment of the NPs in (4.67) as denoting $(et)t$ functions, or equivalently the corresponding GQs, allows us to give a simple analysis of such equivalences. For instance, sentences like *every woman and every man ran* are simply analyzed by extending our treatment of sentence and predicate conjunction in Chapter 3 to the conjunction *and* over the $(et)t$ domain. As an operator on $(et)t$ functions, this analysis leads to the following function as the denotation of *and*:

(4.69) $\text{AND}^{(et)t} = \lambda F_{(et)t}.\lambda G_{(et)t}.\lambda P_{et}.G(P) \wedge F(P)$

In words: the $\text{AND}^{(et)t}$ operator sends any two $(et)t$ functions F and G to the $(et)t$ function sending any et function P to 1 iff both F and G send P to 1, This definition of $\text{AND}^{(et)t}$ extends our definitions (3.47) and (3.51) in Chapter 3. It is part of the general *Boolean* behavior of this conjunction that was mentioned there. When describing the function $\text{AND}^{(et)t}$ as an operator on GQs, we observe the following fact:

(4.70) Let f_1 and f_2 be any $(et)t$ functions with the corresponding generalized quantifiers Q_1 and Q_2. For every et function g characterizing a set g^* of entities, we have:
$$((\text{AND}^{(et)t}(f_1))(f_2))(g) = 1 \Leftrightarrow g^* \in Q_1 \cap Q_2$$

In words: our conjunction operator $\text{AND}^{(et)t}$ on $(et)t$ functions is equivalent to set intersection between the corresponding GQs. This observation immediately explains equivalences as in (4.68). Consider the analysis in (4.71) of our sentential structures for the sentences in (4.68):

(4.71) $[\![[every\ woman\ [and\ [every\ man]]]\ ran]\!] = 1$

$\Leftrightarrow (\text{AND}^{(et)t}(\text{EVERY}(\textbf{man}))(\text{EVERY}(\textbf{woman})))(\textbf{run}) = 1$

$\triangleright$ lexical denotations

$\Leftrightarrow \textbf{run}^* \in \{A \subseteq E : \textbf{woman}^* \subseteq A\} \cap \{A \subseteq E : \textbf{man}^* \subseteq A\}$

$\triangleright$ (4.70) and def. EVERY

$\Leftrightarrow \textbf{run}^* \in \{A \subseteq E : \textbf{woman}^* \subseteq A\} \wedge \textbf{run}^* \in \{A \subseteq E : \textbf{man}^* \subseteq A\}$

$\triangleright$ def. set intersection

$\Leftrightarrow \textbf{woman}^* \subseteq \textbf{run}^* \wedge \textbf{man}^* \subseteq \textbf{run}^*$ $\triangleright$ directly

$\Leftrightarrow \text{AND}^{t}(\text{EVERY}(\textbf{man})(\textbf{run}))(\text{EVERY}(\textbf{woman})(\textbf{run})) = 1$

$\triangleright$ def. AND^t & EVERY

$= [\![[[[every\ woman]\ ran]\ [and\ [every\ man]\ [ran]]]]\!] = 1$

$\triangleright$ lexical denotations

In this derivation we see how the analysis that uses the conjunction operator AND$^{(et)t}$ is equivalent to a statement with a sentential conjunction. This analysis relies on a simple fact: when a set of entities like **run*** is in the intersection of two GQs (e.g. for *every woman* and *every man*), it is in each of those GQs. Similar equivalences hold for extensions of this analysis with the other NP coordinations in (4.67). This naturally accounts for equivalences like the ones below:

(4.72) a. Every woman or every man ran
        $\Leftrightarrow$ Every woman ran or every man ran.
     b. Many students and few teachers ran
        $\Leftrightarrow$ Many students ran and few teachers ran.
     c. Neither every action nor every decision shows a reason
        $\Leftrightarrow$ Neither every action shows a reason nor does every decision show a reason.

You are now advised to solve Exercise 13 at the end of this chapter.

PROPER NAMES AND GENERALIZED QUANTIFIERS

So far in this chapter, we have considered quantified NPs as a class of their own. Implicitly, we have distinguished quantified NPs from proper names, which in previous chapters we treated using *e*-type entities. We have not given any formal semantic motivation for this distinction between NPs. In fact, quantified NPs and proper names have more in common than appears at first glance. NP coordination is an area where some of the similarities between quantified NPs and proper names are especially clear. To begin with, as the examples below illustrate, proper names are as acceptable in NP coordinations as other NPs are:

(4.73) a. Tina and/or Mary, neither Tina nor Mary

         b. Tina but no other student, Mary and every other cook, John or some other doctor

With our e-type analysis of proper names, we cannot easily extend our analysis of NP coordination to cases like (4.73). To solve this problem, let us look more closely at GQs and the possibilities they open up for our analysis. Let us first reconsider the type we assign to proper names. Consider for instance the simple sentence *Tina ran*. Given the type et of the predicate, and the type t of the sentence, we get the same type equation as in (4.7), where X is the type of the noun phrase *Tina*. This equation is repeated below:

(4.74) $X + et = t$

Now, in the same way as we assigned the type $X = (et)t$ to quantified NPs, we can assign this type to proper names. But what, then, should the denotations of proper names be? To answer this question, let us first make a formal observation: some GQs work in a way that resembles e-type individuals. For instance, suppose that **tina** $\in E$ is the entity denotation of the proper name *Tina*. We consider the following GQ, which we call I_{tina}. We consider this GQ to be the "individual substitute" for the entity **tina**.

(4.75) $I_{\text{tina}} = \{A \subseteq E : \textbf{tina} \in A\}$

In words: the generalized quantifier I_{tina} is the set of sets of entities that have **tina** as one of their members. Now for the sentence *Tina ran*, we observe the following equivalence, for any set of entities **run**$^* \subseteq E$:

(4.76) **run**$^* \in I_{\text{tina}}$

      $\Leftrightarrow$ **run**$^* \in \{A \subseteq E : \textbf{tina} \in A\}$

      $\Leftrightarrow$ **tina** $\in$ **run***

$$\{a, b, c, t\}$$
$$\{a, b, c\} \quad \{a, b, t\} \quad \{a, c, t\} \quad \{b, c, t\}$$
$$\{a, b\} \quad \{a, c\} \quad \{b, c\} \quad \{a, t\} \quad \{b, t\} \quad \{c, t\}$$
$$\{a\} \quad \{b\} \quad \{c\} \quad \{t\}$$
$$\emptyset \qquad .$$

Figure 4.3   The gray area depicts the individual substitute $I_t \subseteq \wp(E)$ for the entity t over a domain $E = \{a, b, c, t\}$

In words: the set **run*** is in the set of sets having the entity **tina** as a member if and only if **tina** is a member of **run***.

In more general terms, below we define those GQs that function as *individual substitutes*:

> Let E be a set of entities, and let x be an entity in E. The **individual substitute** for the entity x over E is the generalized quantifier $I_x = \{A \subseteq E : x \in A\}$.

In words, the generalized quantifier I_x is defined as the set of subsets of E that have x as a member. In work on Boolean algebras, individual substitutes are referred to as *principal ultrafilters*. To see a concrete example, let us consider a model where the domain of entities E is $\{a, b, c, t\}$ and the entity corresponding to the proper name *Tina* is t. In this model, the individual substitute for the entity t is the GQ depicted in Figure 4.3.

Individual substitutes, being GQs, can also be mimicked in the $(et)t$ domain. In lambda notation we obtain the type-theoretical substitutes for e-type entities using the following *type lifting* operator:

(4.77) $L = \lambda x_e . \lambda P_{et} . P(x)$

In words, the L operator maps every e-type entity x to the function mapping any et-function P to the value $P(x)$. If as usual we take **tina** to be the e-type denotation of the proper name *Tina*, then the $(et)t$ function $L(\textbf{tina})$ is $\lambda P_{et} . P(\textbf{tina})$. Using this lambda notation, our analysis in (4.76) of the simple sentence *Tina ran* is rewritten as follows:

(4.78) Tina ran.

$$(L(\textbf{tina}_e))(\textbf{run}_{et})$$
$$\Leftrightarrow ((\lambda x_e.\lambda P_{et}.P(x))(\textbf{tina}))(\textbf{run})$$
$$\Leftrightarrow (\lambda P_{et}.P(\textbf{tina}))(\textbf{run})$$
$$\Leftrightarrow \textbf{run}(\textbf{tina})$$

In order to obtain full generality in our treatment of NPs, we replace our convention of assigning type e to proper names by the following convention:

> *Any proper name* Blik *denotes the function* $\lambda P_{et}.P(\textbf{blik})$ *of type* $(et)t$, *where* **blik** *is an arbitrary entity in the model.*

Since the function $L(\textbf{tina})$ corresponds to the individual substitute $I_{\textbf{tina}}$, this convention amounts to treating proper names using GQs.

Individual substitutes are quite useful for the general theory of quantification in natural language. Proper names, as well as NPs like *the man, this pet, my dog* and their corresponding plural forms, have all been treated as entity denoting. These NPs are often called *referential*. Using individual substitutes, all referential NPs can be treated as GQs. For convenience, we may resort back to the e type for referential NPs whenever it is needed. However, as soon as we start generalizing our theory to more NPs and more constructions, the GQ-based analysis of referential NPs often comes in handy.

In particular, with $(et)t$ type/GQ denotations for proper names, we can analyze coordinations with proper names as in (4.73) using simple set-theoretical operations on GQs. This is done very much in the same way as we analyzed coordinations of quantified NPs in (4.71). For instance, consider the following sentences and their analyses:

(4.79) [Tina [and Mary]] ran.

$$(\text{AND}^{(et)t}(L(\textbf{mary}_e))(L(\textbf{tina}_e)))(\textbf{run}_{et})$$
$$\Leftrightarrow \textbf{run}^* \in I_{\textbf{tina}} \cap I_{\textbf{mary}}$$
$$\Leftrightarrow \textbf{run}^* \in I_{\textbf{tina}} \wedge \textbf{run}^* \in I_{\textbf{mary}}$$
$$\Leftrightarrow \textbf{tina} \in \textbf{run}^* \wedge \textbf{mary} \in \textbf{run}^*$$

(4.80) [Tina [and every man]] ran.

$(\text{AND}(\text{EVERY}(\mathbf{man})))(L(\mathbf{tina}_e)))(\mathbf{run}_{et})$

$\Leftrightarrow \mathbf{run}^* \in I_{\mathbf{tina}} \cap \{A \subseteq E : \mathbf{man}^* \subseteq A\}$

$\Leftrightarrow \mathbf{run}^* \in I_{\mathbf{tina}} \wedge \mathbf{run}^* \in \{A \subseteq E : \mathbf{man}^* \subseteq A\}$

$\Leftrightarrow \mathbf{tina} \in \mathbf{run}^* \wedge \mathbf{man}^* \subseteq \mathbf{run}^*$

In both examples above, *and* conjunctions with proper names are analyzed by intersecting two GQs, in conformity with our general treatment of conjunction and other NPs. In both sentences the analysis immediately accounts for their equivalence with sentential conjunctions, like the analysis in (4.71). Similar analyses correctly capture equivalences as in (4.72) with disjunctive and negative NP coordinations, as Exercise 14 illustrates.

You are now advised to solve Exercise 14 at the end of this chapter. Exercises 15–18 are more advanced exercises that will help you better grasp the materials of this chapter.

FURTHER READING

Introductory: For further linguistic perspectives on GQs see Keenan (1996, 2006, 2011); Szabolcsi (2010).

Advanced: GQs were introduced into linguistics in Montague (1973), and, more thoroughly, in Keenan and Faltz (1978); Barwise and Cooper (1981). For an up-to-date survey on the usages of GQ theory in linguistics and philosophy of language, see the monograph Peters and Westerståhl (2006). Survey articles from a logical semantic perspective include Keenan and Westerståhl (2011); Westerståhl (2015). For NP coordinations and their quantificational analysis, see Keenan and Faltz (1985); Winter (2001); Zamparelli (2011). Other linguistic phenomena that interact with the interpretation of quantified NPs include: plurality (Winter and Scha 2015), definiteness (Heim 2011), genericity (Carlson 2011), mass terms (Lasersohn, 2011), polarity (Penka and Zeijlstra 2010) and existential *there* sentences (Keenan 2003; McNally 2011). For further questions about quantification phenomena in different languages see the collections Bach et al. (1995); Matthewson (2008); Keenan and Paperno (2012).

EXERCISES (ADVANCED: 5, **7**, 11, 12, **15**, 16, **17**, **18**)

1. Use similar reasoning to analyses (4.13) (4.16) and (4.19) for analyzing the following sentences, both in a formula and in words:
   (i) Exactly one man ran.
   (ii) At least half of the men ran.
   (iii) All but one of the men ran.
   For instance, for (i) you need to complete the following reasoning:
   run* $\in$ ____ (GQ for *exactly one man*)   the set of runners is in the set of sets that ____ (describe GQ) $\Leftrightarrow$ ____ (requirement for **run*** and **man***)   _____ (describe requirement).
   You may like to consult Table 4.2.

2. a. Write down the GQ denotation of *exactly one man* when the domain of entities E is {a, b, c, d}, and the set denotation of *man* is {a, b}.
   b. Write down the GQ denotation of *at least half the men* for the same domain E, with the set denotation {a, b, c} for *man*.

3. With the denotation in (3.36) (Chapter 3) for the reflexive pronoun *herself*, write down a λ-term for the sentence *every woman admires herself*. Using our definitions of the denotations EVERY and HERSELF, simplify this term as much as possible.

4. a. Use reasoning similar to that in (4.24) and (4.26) to show that our GQ denotations for *at least three men* and *at least half the men* (Table 4.2) are MON↑.
   b. Similarly, show that our GQ treatment of *less than five men* is MON↓ (cf. (4.30)).
   c. The non-entailment (4.32a) characterizes the NP *exactly one man* as non-MON↑. Give two suitable sets $R_1 \subseteq R_2$ that show that the GQ denotation for this NP in Exercise 2a is not MON↑. Do the same for the non-entailment (4.32b) and non-MON↓.
   d. Show a non-entailment that characterizes the NP *at least half the men* as non-MON↓. Give two suitable sets $R_1 \subseteq R_2$ that show that the GQ denotation for this NP in Exercise 2b is not MON↓.

5. a. Assign proper GQ denotations to the NP subjects in (i)–(iii) below. Show reasoning similar to that in Exercise 1, both in a formula and in words.
   (i) [Not every man] ran.
   (ii) [Some but not every man] ran.
   (iii) [Less than one third of the men] ran.

b. For each subject NP in (i)–(iii), if it is MON↑, give an entailment that shows that. If it is not MON↑, give a non-entailment that shows that. Do the same for MON↓.

c. For each GQ you suggested in 5a, for each of the two (non-)monotonicity properties you recognized in 5b: if the GQ is MON↑ or MON↓, show reasoning similar to that in Exercise 4a–b; if the GQ is non-MON↑ or non-MON↓, show a set **man*** and two suitable sets $R_1 \subseteq R_2$ similar to 4c–d.

6. a. For the equivalence in (4.34a), show a set-theoretical consideration that explains it (cf. our analysis of (4.33a) in (4.36)–(4.37)).

b. For each of the two non-entailments in (4.35a) show a model where the antecedent denotes 1 and the consequent denotes 0 (again cf. our analysis of (4.33a)).

7. a. Similarly to the treatment of propositional *and* in Chapter 3, we define the function OR^t of type $t(tt)$. OR^t is defined as the *maximum* operator $\vee$ between truth-values: OR$^t = \lambda x_t.\lambda y_t.y \vee x$, where $0 \vee 0 = 0$, $0 \vee 1 = 1$, $1 \vee 0 = 1$, and $1 \vee 1 = 1$. Similarly to the function AND^{et}, we define OR^{et} by: AND$^{et} = \lambda f_{et}.\lambda g_{et}.\lambda x_e.g(x) \vee f(x)$. Using these two denotations, analyze the (non-)entailments in (4.33b), (4.34b) and (4.35b). Do the same for the *and* conjunctions in (4.33)–(4.35).

b. Show a set-theoretical consideration that explains the following equivalence: *every man who sang or danced smiled* ⇔ *every man who sang smiled and every man who danced smiled*.

8. a. Write the pairs in the determiner relation EXACTLY_1 (Table. 4.3) when $E = \{a, b\}$. What's the difference from SOME in (4.55)?

b. Do the same for AT_LEAST_HALF with the same E. What's the difference from EVERY in (4.55)?

c. Show that the determiner relation AT_LEAST_3 is upward *left* monotone, using reasoning similar to that in (4.52).

d. Show that AT_LEAST_HALF is neither upward nor downward left monotone, by giving sets $A_1 \subseteq A_2 \subseteq A_3$ and a set B such that AT_LEAST_HALF(A_2, B) holds but both AT_LEAST_HALF(A_1, B) and AT_LEAST_HALF(A_3, B) do not.

9. For each of the expressions *not every, some but not every* and *less than one third of the* in Exercise 5(i–iii), define a determiner relation similar to Table 4.3. Classify the left and right (non-)monotonicity properties of these determiners.

10. Assume proper denotations for the words *is* and *a* (cf. (3.58) in Chapter 3). Using these denotations, show that the syllogism *Every man is mortal and John is a man* $\Rightarrow$ *John is mortal* is explained. For *John* you may use an e or $(et)t$-type denotation.

11. a. We assume that the word *who* in (4.62) denotes the same $(et)((et)(et))$ function as *and*, i.e. the function AND^{et}, which corresponds to set intersection (see Exercise 13f, Chapter 3). Show that for the two sentences in the equivalence (4.62), the same truth-values are derived. If we replace *some* in (4.62) with another determiner from Table 4.3, with which determiners do you expect the same kind of equivalence?

    b. With the same denotations for *who*, *is* and *a*, and with the NOT denotation for *not* (Chapters 2 and 3), show that the TCC expects the entailment in (4.61). If we replace *every* in (4.61) with another determiner from Table 4.3, with which determiners do you expect the same kind of entailment?

12. For sentences like *only men ran*, propose a determiner relation ONLY, and classify its left and right (non-)monotonicity. Show set denotations for *men* and *ran* that illustrate that ONLY is not conservative.

13. Consider a model where $E = \{a, b, c, d\}$, and in which a and b are the only women, c is the only man, and d is the only child. Based on fact (4.70), write down the GQ denotations for the following noun phrases: *every woman and every man*; *some woman but no man* (assume GQ intersection); *every woman or every man* (assume GQ union).

14. We assume the denotation of the noun phrase *Tina but not John* to be $I_{\text{tina}} \cap \overline{I_{\text{john}}}$: the intersection of the individual substitute for *Tina* with the complement of the individual substitute for *John*. In a model where $E = \{t, j, a\}$, **tina** $= t$ and **john** $= j$, write down the GQs I_{tina}, $\overline{I_{\text{john}}}$ and $I_{\text{tina}} \cap \overline{I_{\text{john}}}$.

15. Consider the sentences *more/fewer men than boys ran*.

    a. Assuming that *than* denotes the identity function, give proper types and denotations to the words *more* and *fewer*. Show that your suggested denotations account for the following entailments: *More Chinese men than boys ran* $\Rightarrow$ *More men than boys ran*; *More men than boys ran* $\Rightarrow$ *More men than Chinese boys ran*.

b. How many *et* arguments do the deCurried versions of your denotations for *more* and *fewer* have? Write down the monotonicity property (upward/downward/non-monotone) for each argument, and support each answer by an entailment (for upward/downward monotonicity) or a description of a situation (for non-monotonicity).

c. Define a parallel property to determiner conservativity for the expressions *more* and *fewer* in their NP usage above. Show the relevant entailments that are accounted for by this property.

16. Suppose the NP *every man* is of type *e*. Show a model where the entailment *every man ran and John is a man and Bill is a man* $\Rightarrow$ *John ran and Bill ran* would not be respected.

17. a. A *tt* function f is *upward monotone* if, for any truth-values x and y s.t. $x \le y$: $f(x) \le f(y)$. Along similar lines, define *downward* monotone *tt* functions, and show that propositional negation ($\sim$) from Chapter 3 is downward monotone.

b. A $t(tt)$ function g is *left upward monotone* ($\uparrow$MON) if for any truth-values x and y s.t. $x \le y$, for any truth-value z, we have: $g(x)(z) \le f(y)(z)$. Define *right* upward monotonicity (MON$\uparrow$) for $t(tt)$ functions along similar lines, and show that the conjunction operator (AND^t) from Chapter 3 is MON$\uparrow$. Demonstrate this monotonicity with an entailment in English.

18. a. For each of the sentences in (4.56), mark the nominal expression that follows the determiner, as well as the verb phrase. For instance: *every man who saw any boy ran*.

b. On the basis of the monotonicity properties of determiners (Table 4.3), add an $\uparrow$ or $\downarrow$ sign for each of the constituents you marked in 18a, depending on the determiner monotonicity in that argument. For instance: since EVERY is $\downarrow$MON$\uparrow$, we mark: *every man who saw any boy$^\downarrow$ ran$^\uparrow$*.

c. On the basis of your monotonicity marking in 18b, propose a generalization that explains the circumstances in which the NPIs *any* and *ever* may and may not appear, as illustrated in (4.56)–(4.57).

d. Similarly to 17b, and the definition of left and right monotonicity for determiners, define which functions of type $t(tt)$ are left/right downward monotone. Rely on the $\le$ order between truth-values.

e. Consider the following sentence:

(i) *If John runs, Mary smiles.* Assume that the word *if* denotes the following propositional function of type $t(tt)$: IF $= \lambda x_t.\lambda y_t.{\sim}(x \wedge {\sim} y)$. Based on your answer to 18d, classify the monotonicity properties of IF in each of its two t-type arguments.

f. Consider the contrast between the following sentences:

(ii) *If John has <u>ever</u> run, (then) Mary has smiled.*
(iii) **If Mary has smiled, (then) John has <u>ever</u> run.*

Using your answer to 18e, show that the generalization you suggested in 18c explains the contrast between (ii) and (iii).

SOLUTIONS TO SELECTED EXERCISES

1. (i) $\mathbf{run}^* \in \{B \subseteq E : \,\mid \mathbf{man}^* \cap B \mid \, = 1\}$

the set of runners is in the set of sets whose intersection with the set of men is of cardinality 1

$\Leftrightarrow \,\mid \mathbf{man}^* \cap \mathbf{run}^* \mid \, = 1$

the intersection of the set of runners and the set of men is of cardinality 1

(ii) $\mathbf{run}^* \in \{B \subseteq E : \,\mid \mathbf{man}^* \cap B \mid \, \geq \, {}^1\!/\!{}_2 \cdot \mid \mathbf{man}^* \mid \}$

the set of runners is in the set of sets whose intersection with the set of men is at least half the cardinality of the set of men

$\Leftrightarrow \,\mid \mathbf{man}^* \cap \mathbf{run}^* \mid \, \geq \, {}^1\!/\!{}_2 \cdot \mid \mathbf{man}^* \mid$

the intersection of the set of runners with the set of men is at least half the cardinality of the set of men

(iii) $\mathbf{run}^* \in \{B \subseteq E : \,\mid \mathbf{man}^* \cap \overline{B} \mid \, = 1\}$

the set of runners is in the set of sets whose complement's intersection with the set of men is of cardinality 1

$\Leftrightarrow \,\mid \mathbf{man}^* \cap \overline{\mathbf{run}^*} \mid \, = 1$

the intersection of the set of men with the set of non-runners has precisely one element

2. a. {{a}, {a, c}, {a, d}, {a, c, d}, {b}, {b, c}, {b, d}, {b, c, d}}

b. {{a, b}, {a, b, d}, {a, c}, {a, c, d}, {b, c}, {b, c, d}, {a, b, c}, {a, b, c, d}}

3. EVERY($\mathbf{woman}$)(HERSELF($\mathbf{admire}$)) $= 1 \Leftrightarrow$ $\mathbf{woman}^* \subseteq \{x \in E : \mathbf{admire}(x, x) = 1\}$

4. c. $R_1 = \{a\}$, $R_2 = \{a, b\}$

   d. $R_1 = \{b, d\}$, $R_2 = \{a, b, d\}$

5. a. $\{B \subseteq E : \mathbf{man}^* \cap \overline{B} \neq \emptyset\}$, $\{B \subseteq E : \mathbf{man}^* \cap B \neq \emptyset \land \mathbf{man}^* \cap \overline{B} \neq \emptyset\}$, $\{B \subseteq E : |\, \mathbf{man}^* \cap B \,| < \frac{1}{3} \cdot |\, \mathbf{man}^* \,|\}$

   b. *not every man*: MON↓, not MON↑,   *some but not every man*: neither MON↓ nor MON↑, *less than one third of the men*: MON↓, not MON↑.

6. a. $A \subseteq B \cap C$ iff $A \subseteq B$ and $A \subseteq C$;

   b. Model 1 (for "$\not\Rightarrow$"): $\mathbf{man}^* = \{a, b\}$ $\mathbf{sing}^* = \{a\}$ $\mathbf{dance}^* = \{a, b\}$; Model 2 (for "$\not\Leftarrow$"): $\mathbf{man}^* = \{a, b\}$ $\mathbf{sing}^* = \{a\}$ $\mathbf{dance}^* = \{b\}$.

7. a. Set-theoretical considerations: for (4.33b), $|\, A \cap (B \cup C) \,| \geq 1$ iff (at least) one of the following holds: $|\, A \cap B \,| \geq 1$ or $|\, A \cap C \,| \geq 1$; for "$\Rightarrow$" in (4.34b), $A \subseteq B \cup C$ if (at least) one of the following holds: $A \subseteq B$ or $A \subseteq C$; for "$\not\Leftarrow$" in (4.34b): $\mathbf{man}^* = \{a, b\}$, $\mathbf{sing}^* = \{a\}$, $\mathbf{dance}^* = \{b\}$.

   b. $A \cap (B \cup C) \subseteq D$ iff $A \cap B \subseteq D$ and $A \cap C \subseteq D$.

8. a. $\langle\{a\}, \{a\}\rangle, \langle\{a\}, \{a, b\}\rangle, \langle\{b\}, \{b\}\rangle, \langle\{b\}, \{a, b\}\rangle, \langle\{a, b\}, \{a\}\rangle,$ $\langle\{a, b\}, \{b\}\rangle$

   b. $\langle\emptyset, \emptyset\rangle, \langle\emptyset, \{a\}\rangle, \langle\emptyset, \{b\}\rangle, \langle\emptyset, \{a, b\}\rangle, \langle\{a\}, \{a\}\rangle, \langle\{a\}, \{a, b\}\rangle,$ $\langle\{b\}, \{b\}\rangle, \langle\{b\}, \{a, b\}\rangle, \langle\{a, b\}, \{a\}\rangle, \langle\{a, b\}, \{b\}\rangle, \langle\{a, b\}, \{a, b\}\rangle$

   d. $A_1 = \{c, d\}$, $A_2 = \{a, b, c, d\}$, $A_3 = \{a, b, c, d, e\}$, $B = \{a, b\}$

9. NOT_EVERY$(A, B) \Leftrightarrow A \cap \overline{B} \neq \emptyset$ (↑MON↓); SOME_BUT_NOT_EVERY$(A, B) \Leftrightarrow A \cap B \neq \emptyset \land A \cap \overline{B} \neq \emptyset$ (↑MON¬); LESS_THAN_ONE_THIRD$(A, B) \Leftrightarrow |\, A \cap B \,| < \frac{1}{3} \cdot |\, A \,|$ (¬MON↓).

10. AND$((\text{IS}(\text{A}(\mathbf{man})))(\mathbf{john}))((\text{EVERY}(\mathbf{man}))(\text{IS}(\mathbf{mortal}))) = 1 \Leftrightarrow$ $\mathbf{man}^* \subseteq \mathbf{mortal}^* \land \mathbf{john} \in \mathbf{man}^* \Rightarrow \mathbf{john} \in \mathbf{mortal}^* \Leftrightarrow$ IS$(\mathbf{mortal})(\mathbf{john}) = 1$

11. a. $(\text{SOME}(\mathbf{man}))(\text{IS}(\text{A}((\text{WHO}(\mathbf{run}))(\mathbf{cook})))) = 1$

   $\Leftrightarrow \mathbf{man}^* \cap (\mathbf{cook}^* \cap \mathbf{run}^*) \neq \emptyset$

   $\Leftrightarrow (\mathbf{man}^* \cap \mathbf{run}^*) \cap \mathbf{cook}^* \neq \emptyset \Leftrightarrow$

   $(\text{SOME}((\text{WHO}(\mathbf{run}))(\mathbf{man})))(\text{IS}(\text{A}(\mathbf{cook}))) = 1$

12. ONLY$(A, B) \Leftrightarrow B \subseteq A$ (↑MON↓). With this definition, ONLY$(A, B \cap A)$ holds for all sets A and B, but ONLY(A, B) does not hold when B is not a subset of A, e.g. when $B = \{a, b\}$ and $A = \{a\}$.

13. $\{\{a, b, c\}, \{a, b, c, d\}\}$; $\{\{a\}, \{a, b\}, \{a, d\}, \{a, b, d\}, \{b\}, \{b, d\}\}$; $\{\{a, b\}, \{a, b, c\}, \{a, b, d\}, \{a, b, c, d\}, \{c\}, \{a, c\}, \{a, c, d\}, \{b, c\},$ $\{b, c, d\}, \{c, d\}\}$

14. $I_{\textbf{tina}} = \{\{t\}, \{t, j\}, \{t, a\}, \{t, j, a\}\};$ $\overline{I_{\textbf{john}}} = \{\emptyset, \{t\}, \{a\}, \{t, a\}\};$
$I_{\textbf{tina}} \cap \overline{I_{\textbf{john}}} = \{\{t\}, \{t, a\}\}.$

15. c.   MORE$(A, B, C) \Leftrightarrow$ MORE$(A, B, C \cap (A \cup B))$.   Similarly   for *fewer*.

16. $E = \textbf{man}^* = \{j, b\}$, $\textbf{run}^* = \{j\}$, $[\![every\,man]\!] = [\![John]\!] = j$, $[\![Bill]\!] = b$: antecedent denotes 1 but consequent 0.

17. a. f_{tt} is *downward monotone* if for any truth-values x and y s.t. $x \leq y$: $f(x) \geq f(y)$; $\sim\!0 = 1 \geq 0 = \sim\!1$.

     b. $g_{t(tt)}$ is MON↑ if for any truth-values x and y s.t. $x \leq y$, for any truth-value z: $g(z)(x) \leq f(z)(y)$;   for $z = 0$, AND$^t(0)(0) = 0 \leq 0 =$ AND$^t(0)(1)$, and for $z = 1$, AND$^t(1)(0) = 0 \leq 1 =$ AND$^t(1)(1)$; *Tina is tall and thin and Mary is rich* $\Rightarrow$ *Tina is thin and Mary is rich*.

18. c. A determiner accepts an NPI in its left/right argument if it is downward monotone in that argument (see further readings on NPIs).

     e. IF   is   ↓MON   (for   any $y \in D_t$:   IF$(1)(y) \leq$ IF$(0)(y) = \sim\!(0 \wedge \sim\!y) = 1$)   but   not   MON↓   (IF$(1)(1) = \sim\!(1 \wedge \sim\!1) = 1 \not\leq$ IF$(1)(0) = \sim\!(1 \wedge \sim\!0) = 0$).

CHAPTER 5

LONG-DISTANCE MEANING RELATIONSHIPS

This chapter addresses challenges for the composition of meanings in more complex syntactic constructions than those we have treated so far. As we will see, the framework of Chapters 3–4 systematically fails in analyzing meaning relations between expressions that are not adjacent to each other. One such case is sentences where multiple noun phrases are in semantic relations with the same verb. We solve this problem by adding to the system of Chapter 3 a compositional principle of hypothetical reasoning, or function abstraction, which acts as a dual to function application. Our use of hypothetical reasoning motivates a revision of one of our foundational assumptions in Chapter 3. Instead of interpreting pre-generated binary trees over strings, as we have done so far, our revised grammar architecture derives semantic denotations simultaneously with the derivation of syntactic forms. Forms and meanings are paired together in integrative linguistic resources called linguistic signs. *In the ensuing grammatical framework,* Abstract Categorial Grammar, *the composition of meanings is only one of the two dimensions within the derivation of complex linguistic signs.*

In the framework laid out in Chapter 3 we have interpreted binary syntactic structures by using functional types and denotations. Function application was our semantic tool for deriving denotations of complex expressions from the denotations of their parts. The semantic system only allowed denotations of constituents to combine when they are analyzed as sisters in the syntactic structure. Sisters in the binary tree correspond to two strings that are linearly adjacent to each other. Consequently, only denotations of adjacent expressions could be glued together. For instance, consider the generalized quantifier for the noun phrase *every tall student*. Under our assumptions so far, when deriving a meaning for this expression, we first combine the denotation of the adjective *tall* with the denotation of the noun *student*, and then combine the result with the denotation of the determiner *every*. In an alternative analysis, which is syntactically dubious but analytically possible, we might let *every* and *tall* be sisters. In that case the determiner would first need to combine with the adjective denotation before the result combines with the denotation of the noun. The two options for bracketing a three-word expression like *every tall student* govern the possibilities for function–argument relations. Specifically, we have no possibility of using function application directly on the denotations of the two non-adjacent words *every* and *student* in this phrase. More generally, our compositional semantic mechanism can only operate on denotations of sub-expressions that are linearly adjacent to each other. This restriction of the semantic mechanism has so far proved useful and powerful enough, and all our compositional analyses have so far relied on it.

However, as we shall see in this chapter, formal semantics must also involve grammatical relations that are more complex than linear adjacency. Especially, verbs often need to have "long-distance" relationships with NPs that are not linearly adjacent. The simple binary structures that we have used do not describe such relations. Accordingly our semantics systematically fails in explaining entailments that rely on them. In this chapter we start out by studying the problem of long-distance relationships in simple clauses with transitive verbs. We show how the problem is solved by introducing a 'place-holder', or a 'variable', into the compositional semantic derivation. The general principle responsible for introducing such place-holders is known as *hypothetical reasoning* (or function 'abstraction'). When properly embedded in our revised grammatical framework, this principle allows us to establish meaning relationships between elements in the sentence that are not phonologically adjacent. The resulting architecture is a version of a relatively recent formal framework, known as *Abstract Categorial Grammar* (ACG).

The chapter is organized as follows. We start by reviewing problematic meaning relationships between verbs and their NP arguments. These relationships reveal challenges for compositionality that we treat by extending our system with hypothetical reasoning. Then, the resulting *Lambek-Van Benthem Calculus* will be applied to linguistic *signs* – pairs of functions over strings and denotations – in a way that is shown to respect syntax–semantics correspondences.

CLAUSES WITH MULTIPLE NOUN PHRASES

Intransitive verbs like *smile* only have a subject argument, and accordingly are assumed to denote *et* functions. Transitive verbs like *praise* require two NPs, a subject and an object, and are accordingly treated as denoting *e(et)* functions. Let us repeat our analysis from Chapter 3 of simple transitive sentences, where both subject and object were assumed to denote *e*-type entities. Our analysis (3.6) (page 54) of the sentence *Tina praised Mary* is repeated below.

(5.1) a. Tina [praised Mary]

b. $(\mathbf{praise}_{e(et)}(\mathbf{mary}_e))(\mathbf{tina}_e)$

In words: the VP constituent *praised Mary* denotes the *et* function **praise(mary)**. This function applies to the entity **tina**. Here it is instructive to also present the same analysis in set-theoretical terms. To do that, we readopt the conventions of Chapter 4, and use the notation **praise(mary)*** for the set characterized by the *et* function **praise(mary)**. In a formula:

(5.2) $\mathbf{praise(mary)}^* = \{y \in E : \mathbf{praise(mary)}(y) = 1\}$

Now let us note the following simple equivalence.

(5.3) $(\mathbf{praise}_{e(et)}(\mathbf{mary}_e))(\mathbf{tina}_e) = 1 \iff \mathbf{tina} \in \mathbf{praise(mary)}^*$

In words: the denotation of sentence (5.1a) is 1 if and only if the entity **tina** is in the set of elements that the function **praise(mary)** characterizes. This simple observation gives us some insight into the set-theoretical correlate of the Curried analysis in (5.1), and we use it as we go along.

Despite this intuitive analysis, in Chapter 4 we noted that many NPs cannot correctly be analyzed as denoting *e*-type entities. Our treatment of quantified NPs allowed us to also analyze sentences like *every student ran* or *every student praised Tina*, by applying the quantified subject's *(et)t* denotation to the *et* denotation of the VP. However, we should also like to analyze transitive sentences where the object is quantificational. Consider for instance the following sentence.

(5.4) Tina [praised [every student]]

Similarly to the noun phrase *every student* in (5.4), all NPs in Table 4.1 (page 100) can naturally appear as objects in transitive sentences. However, a short look at the $(et)t$ type of quantified NPs and the $e(et)$ type of transitive verbs will show us that function application alone does not allow these types to combine: neither of these types describes arguments for functions of the other type. Under our current assumptions, simple transitive sentences with a quantified object cannot be treated.

  Similar problems re-occur in many other sentences with multiple NPs. We can appreciate the realm of this problem better by looking at another kind of sentences with multiple NPs: sentences containing *relative clauses* (cf. Exercise 13, Chapter 3). Let us first consider sentence (5.5) with the binary structure in (5.6) below.

(5.5) Some teacher that ran smiled.

(5.6) [some [teacher [that ran]]] smiled

The constituent *that ran* in (5.6) is standardly referred to as a *relative clause*, or in short a 'relative'. Words like *that, who(m)* and *which*, when appearing as heads of relatives, are referred to as *relative pronouns*. Semantically, relative pronouns as in sentence (5.5) are similar to conjunctive elements between *et* predicates. When saying that *John is a teacher that ran*, we say that John is a teacher and that he ran. This semantic similarity between relative clauses and conjunction is further exemplified by the equivalence between sentence (5.5) and the following conjunctive sentence.

(5.7) Some teacher ran and smiled.

The complex subject in sentence (5.5) contains the determiner *some*. The denotation we assigned to the determiner *some* (cf. Chapter 4) leads here to the equivalence (5.5)⇔(5.7), which reveals the conjunctive behavior of the relative in (5.5). To capture the conjunctive meaning of relatives we let them denote predicate conjunctions between *et* functions, identical to the $(et)((et)(et))$ use of the function

AND in (5.7). Formally:

$$(5.8) \quad \text{THAT}_{(et)((et)(et))} = \text{AND}_{(et)((et)(et))} = \lambda f_{et}.\lambda g_{et}.\lambda x_e.g(x) \wedge f(x)$$

Using the lexical denotations of the words in it, we analyze the structure in (5.6) in (5.9) below.

$$(5.9) \quad \text{SOME}(\text{THAT}(\mathbf{run})(\mathbf{teacher}))(\mathbf{smile})$$

As in Chapter 4, we use the abbreviations **teacher***, **run*** and **smile*** for the sets of entities characterized by the respective *et* functions. Using these abbreviations, and by elaborating the definitions of the determiner function SOME and the intersection function THAT, we get the following simplification of the analysis in (5.9).

$$(5.10) \quad \text{SOME}(\text{THAT}(\mathbf{run})(\mathbf{teacher}))(\mathbf{smile}) = 1 \qquad \triangleright \text{ analysis (5.9)}$$
$$\Leftrightarrow (\text{THAT}(\mathbf{run})(\mathbf{teacher}))^* \cap \mathbf{smile}^* \neq \emptyset \qquad \triangleright \text{ definition SOME}$$
$$\Leftrightarrow (\mathbf{teacher}^* \cap \mathbf{run}^*) \cap \mathbf{smile}^* \neq \emptyset \qquad \triangleright \text{ definition THAT}$$

In words: sentence (5.5) is analyzed as denoting 1 if the set of teachers, the set of runners and the set of smilers have a non-empty intersection. This accounts for the intersective interpretation of sentence (5.5), and for its equivalence with (5.7).

We can use a similar analysis for sentence (5.11) below. In this sentence, unlike (5.5), the verb is transitive. Accordingly, the verb phrase *praised Mary* has an object within it. This leads to the binary structure in (5.12).

(5.11) Some teacher that praised Mary smiled.

(5.12) [some [teacher [that [praised Mary]]]] smiled

The constituent *that praised Mary* in (5.12) is analyzed similarly to the constituent *that ran* in (5.6) above. Since it will not affect the generality of our conclusions, we keep this analysis as simple as possible and assume that the name *Mary* denotes an *e*-type entity. This leads to the following analysis (cf. (5.9) and (5.10)).

(5.13) SOME(THAT(**praise(mary)**)(**teacher**))(**smile**) $= 1$

$\qquad\qquad\qquad\qquad\qquad\qquad$ ▷ analysis of (5.12)

$\Leftrightarrow$ (THAT(**praise(mary)**)(**teacher**))$^* \cap$ **smile**$^* \neq \emptyset$

$\qquad\qquad\qquad\qquad\qquad\qquad$ ▷ definition SOME

$\Leftrightarrow$ (**teacher**$^* \cap$ **praise(mary)***)$\cap$ **smile**$^* \neq \emptyset$

$\qquad\qquad\qquad\qquad\qquad\qquad$ ▷ definition THAT

$\Leftrightarrow$ **teacher**$^* \cap \{y \in E : \textbf{praise(mary)}(y) = 1\} \cap$ **smile**$^* \neq \emptyset$

$\qquad\qquad\qquad\qquad\qquad\qquad$ ▷ by (5.2)

In words, this analysis means that there exists an entity that is a teacher, that praised Mary, and that smiled. This correctly captures the intuitive meaning of sentence (5.11).

Deriving these felicitous analyses of the relative clauses as in (5.5) and (5.11) is straightforward under our assumptions so far. However, some equally simple relatives exhibit remarkable challenges for our current framework. Consider the following sentence.

(5.14) Some teacher that Mary praised smiled.

Sentence (5.14) is similar to sentence (5.11), but there is an important syntactic-semantic difference between the two sentences. In (5.11), the name *Mary* is the object of the verb within the relative clause. In (5.14), *Mary* is the subject within the relative. To see how this structural difference is manifested in terms of entailments, we note that unlike (5.11), sentence (5.14) is not equivalent to the sentence *some teacher praised Mary and smiled*. Rather, sentence (5.14) is equivalent to the following conjunctive sentence.

(5.15) Some teacher *was praised by Mary* and smiled.

While sentence (5.11) entails that some teacher praised Mary, sentence (5.14) entails that it was Mary who praised some teacher. This semantic difference between sentences (5.14) and (5.11) reveals a shortcoming of our system in Chapter 3, which relies on function application under adjacency. To see the problem, suppose that we tried to use a simple binary structure as a basis for interpreting sentence (5.14), as we did above for sentence (5.11). Without further syntactic information, we might assume the following structure for (5.14).

(5.16) [some [teacher [that [Mary praised]]]] smiled

However, once we examine the truth-value that structure (5.16) leads to, we find an unwelcome result. According to our assumptions so far, we must give structure (5.16) the same truth-value that we gave to structure (5.12) above. The only difference we assumed between the two structures is in the word order within the constituent for the relative clause: *Mary praised* in (5.16) as opposed to *praised Mary* in (5.12). The system in Chapter 3 must assign the same denotation to both constituents. In our specific analysis this denotation is the *et* function **praise(mary)**. Consequently, we are at risk of deriving the same truth-value for the two structures (5.12) and (5.16). Such a result would be highly undesired: as we have seen, the semantic analyses of sentences (5.11) and (5.14) must be distinguished.

Intuitively, the source of the problem in our putative analysis of sentence (5.14) is quite clear. As soon as we let the entity **mary** be the first argument of the *e(et)* function **praise**, we make it behave as if it had the same role as in sentence (5.11). However, when analyzing sentence (5.14), we want the entity **mary** to fill in the subject argument of the verb. Thus, under our current assumptions we must require **mary** to be the *second* argument of the *e(et)* function **praise**. But how can we do that compositionally? The equivalence between sentences (5.14) and (5.15) shows us a possible way. We need to analyze the constituent *Mary praised* in structure (5.16) as characterizing *the set of entities that were praised by Mary*. We denote this set 'pbm', and note that it is characterized by the *et* function X_{pbm} defined below.

(5.17) $X_{pbm} = \lambda x_e.\textbf{praise}(x)(\textbf{mary})$

In words: the function X_{pbm} maps every entity x to the truth-value obtained when the *et* function **praise**(x) applies to the entity **mary**. Isomorphically, the set pbm can also be described as follows.

(5.18) $pbm = X_{pbm}{}^* = \{x \in E : \textbf{praise}(x)(\textbf{mary}) = 1\}$

Let us now assume that the denotation of the constituent *Mary praised* in (5.16) is the *et* function X_{pbm} in (5.17). Thus:

(5.19) $[\![Mary\ praised]\!] = X_{pbm} = \lambda x_e.\textbf{praise}(x)(\textbf{mary})$

We can verify that this denotation is what we need for analyzing sentence (5.14) by using it in our assumed structure (5.16). Assuming the function X_{pbm} as the denotation of the constituent *Mary praised* in structure (5.16), we get the following analysis.

(5.20) SOME(THAT(X_{pbm})(**teacher**))(**smile**)

$\quad$ = SOME(THAT(λx_e.**praise**(x)(**mary**))(**teacher**))(**smile**)

With the assumed denotations of the words *some* and *that*, we get the equivalence in (5.21) below.

(5.21) SOME(THAT(λx_e.**praise**(x)(**mary**))(**teacher**))(**smile**) $= 1$
$\qquad\qquad\qquad\qquad\qquad\qquad\qquad\qquad$ $\triangleright$ analysis (5.20)

$\quad \Leftrightarrow$ (THAT(λx_e.**praise**(x)(**mary**))(**teacher**))$^* \cap$ **smile**$^* \neq \emptyset$
$\qquad\qquad\qquad\qquad\qquad\qquad\qquad\qquad$ $\triangleright$ definition SOME

$\quad \Leftrightarrow$ (**teacher**$^* \cap$ (λx_e.**praise**(x)(**mary**))*) $\cap$ **smile**$^* \neq \emptyset$
$\qquad\qquad\qquad\qquad\qquad\qquad\qquad\qquad$ $\triangleright$ definition THAT

$\quad \Leftrightarrow$ **teacher**$^* \cap \{x \in E : \textbf{praise}(x)(\textbf{mary}) = 1\} \cap$ **smile**$^* \neq \emptyset$
$\qquad\qquad\qquad\qquad\qquad\qquad\qquad\qquad$ $\triangleright$ by (5.18)

$\quad \Leftrightarrow$ **teacher**$^* \cap \{x \in E : \textit{Mary praised } x\} \cap$ **smile**$^* \neq \emptyset$
$\qquad\qquad\qquad\qquad\qquad\qquad\qquad\qquad$ $\triangleright$ informally

Sentence (5.14) is now correctly analyzed, as denoting 1 if the set of teachers, the set of entities that Mary praised and the set of smilers have a non-empty intersection. Further, using a proper analysis of the passive verb in the conjunctive sentence (5.15) (cf. Exercise 11, Chapter 3), we can account for its equivalence with sentence (5.14).

The critical assumption in our analysis is that the relative constituent *teacher that Mary praised* involves the function X_{pbm} that was defined in (5.17). Defining this function has allowed us to intersect the set pbm of entities that Mary praised with the denotation of the noun *teacher*. This implicitly establishes a semantic link between the noun *teacher* and the object argument of the verb *praise*. The link is established despite the fact that the verb and the noun *teacher* are not adjacent to each other: two other words, *that* and *Mary*, linearly separate them.

Similar semantic links within relative clauses may be established across longer distances. For instance, consider sentence (5.22) below, with the structure in (5.22a) and the informal semantic analysis in (5.22b).

(5.22) Some teacher that Tina believes Mary praised smiled.

> a. [Some [teacher [that [Tina [believes [Mary praised]]]]]] smiled
>
> b. $(\mathbf{teacher}^* \cap \{x \in D_e : \text{Tina believes Mary praised } x \})$ $\cap \mathbf{smile}^* \neq \emptyset$

In more words, sentence (5.22) is analyzed as requiring a non-empty intersection of the set of teachers, the set of entities x on which Tina has the belief "Mary praised x", and the set of smilers. We will have more to say about verbs like *believe* in Chapter 6. For the time being, let us note that intuitively, like our formal analysis (5.20) of sentence (5.14), also the informal analysis in (5.22b) establishes relationships between the noun *teacher* and the object argument of the verb *praised*: in both cases the noun *teacher* is related to the object of the verb *praised*. The linear "distance" between the words *teacher* and *praised* is longer in sentence (5.22) than in (5.14). However, the meaning relationships between these words is similar in the two sentences. Because of the way the linear distance between the related words may get quite big, such relationships are referred to as *long-distance dependencies*.

The discussion above reveals some problems for our semantic framework in Chapter 3. Let us take stock of them.

1. Example (5.4) illustrated that function application cannot compose $e(et)$ denotations of transitive verbs with generalized quantifiers.
2. Relative clauses as in sentence (5.14) also challenge function application because, even though function application *could* apply if we assumed structure (5.16), it would have led us to the wrong results.
3. Treating such clauses as in sentence (5.14) was made possible by using the function χ_{pbm} in (5.17) as the denotation for the constituent *Mary praised*. However, we have not clarified the compositional principles that allow us to derive such denotations.
4. Furthermore, we saw reason to think that, whatever those principles may be, they should also cover relative clauses with meaning dependencies over longer distances, e.g. as in sentence (5.22).

These are classical challenges for any theory of the *syntax–semantics interface*: the principles and mechanisms that guarantee that formal semantics respects syntactically informed meaning relations in language.

HYPOTHETICAL REASONING AND THE LAMBEK-VAN BENTHEM CALCULUS

Confronted with the failure of function application, we analyzed the 'object-directed' relative clause in sentence (5.14) by using the *ad hoc* denotation in (5.19), which combines the denotations of the subject with the transitive verb. However, the principles that derive this *ad hoc* denotation were not explained. We would like such principles to be embedded within a general theory of long-distance meaning relationships. The general approach that we adopt extends the compositional framework that we have used so far with a principle of *hypothetical reasoning*, or function *abstraction*. By using this principle we will obtain a general treatment of what we have informally referred to as "semantic links", like the links between a verb and its arguments. In this way we overcome the shortcomings we have observed for function application.

Let us first look in some detail at function application (FA) itself. The FA rule takes two denotations, namely a function of type $\tau\sigma$ and another denotation of type τ, and derives a denotation of type σ. We can describe this process as follows.

(5.23)   **Function Application (FA) rule**   **Interpretation**

$$\frac{\tau\sigma \quad \tau}{\sigma} \qquad\qquad \frac{A \quad B}{A(B)}$$

This presentation highlights the fact that the FA rule derives a type σ from a type $\tau\sigma$ of a function and a type τ of its argument. This rule is interpreted as deriving the result $A(B)$ of type σ by applying a function A type $\tau\sigma$ to an argument B of type τ. This presentation of the FA rule resembles the classical logical rule of *Modus Ponens* (MP). The MP rule handles reasoning with *conditional propositions*, aka 'conditionals'. Conditional propositions are the logical parallels to natural language sentences involving the *if ... then* construction.

Consider, for example, the following natural entailment, which has the conditional sentence (5.24a) in its antecedent.

(5.24)   a. If Mary is tall then Tina is tall,
         b. and Mary is tall
         c. $\Rightarrow$ Tina is tall

Modus Ponens is the general logical rule describing the pattern of entailment illustrated in (5.24). Suppose that φ and ψ are two sentences, and that the logical formula $\varphi \to \psi$ describes the conditional statement "if φ then ψ". The MP rule describes the pattern of the entailment in (5.24) as follows.

(5.25)   **Modus Ponens (MP) rule**

$$\frac{\varphi \to \psi \quad \varphi}{\psi}$$

The arrow notation '$\to$' is called the *implication* symbol. The premises in the MP rule are the conditional statement $\varphi \to \psi$ and the statement φ. Since the result ψ does not contain the implication symbol, we say that the MP rule *eliminates*, or cancels, this symbol. The FA rule in (5.23) has the same form as the MP rule in (5.25). Thus, we also view the FA rule as an elimination rule, which 'disbands' the functional connection between the two types in the complex type $\tau\sigma$. Both the MP rule and the FA rule take a complex form – a conditional or a function type – and eliminate the main syntactic operator within it: implication or the function connector. In duality to such elimination rules, logicians also consider rules that *introduce* syntactic operators. These rules define the circumstances that license a chain of reasoning where a complex item (a function type, a conditional) is derived from simpler forms. Because of the close logical relations between functions and conditionals, we will now study them in parallel.

   Let us first consider the introduction of conditionals. What principles allow us to introduce conditional statements? To get an idea, let us first look at a simple example. Consider the following intuitive entailment.

(5.26)   a. Tina is taller than Mary
         b. $\Rightarrow$ If Mary is tall then Tina is tall

This entailment has as its consequent a conditional sentence with the bare adjective *tall*. The premise of the entailment is a sentence containing the form *taller … than* of the same adjective. Such adjectival forms are known as comparative. Thus, we say that by introducing the conditional conclusion, entailment (5.26) expresses a semantic relation between the bare form of the adjective *tall* and its comparative form. Now consider the entailment in (5.27) below. This entailment also connects the two forms of the adjective *tall*, but this time without involving a conditional sentence.

(5.27)   a. Tina is taller than Mary,
             b. and Mary is tall
             c. $\Rightarrow$ Tina is tall

Despite the absence of the conditional from entailment (5.27), this entailment bears a strong relation to entailment (5.26). Let us see why. In previous chapters we have seen reasons to assume that the entailment relation between sentences is *transitive* (see Exercise 8, Chapter 2): thus, whenever a sentence S_1 entails S_2, and S_2 entails S_3, speakers also accept that sentence S_1 entails S_3. Another simple property affecting entailments is that the conjunction *and* is upward monotone in both its arguments (Exercise 17, Chapter 4). For sentential conjunction, upward monotonicity of *and* on its left argument means that when a sentence S_1 entails a sentence S_1', the conjunction S_1 *and* S_2 entails the conjunction S_1' *and* S_2. Right monotonicity means that S_1 *and* S_2 entails S_1 *and* S_2' whenever S_2 entails S_2'. Given these general properties of entailment, and the validity of the MP entailment (5.24) above, the validity of entailment (5.27) is a direct consequence from the validity of entailment (5.26). This fact is shown in (5.28) below.

(5.28)   *Tina is taller than Mary, and Mary is tall* (= premise of (5.27))
       By entailment (5.26) and left monotonicity of *and*:
       $\Rightarrow$ *If Mary is tall then Tina is tall, and Mary is tall*
       By entailment (5.24) (=MP):
       $\Rightarrow$ *Tina is tall* (= consequent of (5.27))

The chain of entailments in (5.28), together with the transitivity of entailment, means that we expect entailment (5.27) to hold too. Thus, the fact that we accept (5.27) is not at all surprising: it follows from accepting the entailment in (5.26), and on our general assumptions about transitivity, monotonicity of *and*, and the MP entailment. Loosely speaking, we say that the chain of reasoning in (5.28) "justifies" our acceptance of entailment (5.27) on the basis of entailment (5.26). We present this intuitive "justification" for entailment (5.27) using the following tree diagram.

(5.29)

$$\dfrac{\dfrac{\text{Tina is taller than Mary}}{\text{If Mary is tall then Tina is tall}} \text{(5.26)} \quad \text{Mary is tall}}{\text{Tina is tall}} \text{MP (5.24)}$$

This style of presentation is known in logic as *natural deduction* format. In this presentation we display the two sentential conjuncts in the premises of entailment (5.24) and (5.26) as separate assumptions: *Tina is taller than Mary* and *Mary is tall*. The uses of the entailments (5.24) and (5.26) are appealed to on the right of the respective steps.

In (5.28) and the tree diagram in (5.29) we justify entailment (5.27) on the basis of entailment (5.26). But this is not the end of the story, because the converse is also true: as we will now see, we can also justify entailment (5.26) on the basis of (5.27). Let us first get a feel of the kind of reasoning that we may use when doing that. Consider the following conversation.

(5.30) A: We both know that Tina is taller than Mary. But do you know whether Tina is tall?

B: I don't know, but one thing I do know: *if* Mary is tall then Tina is tall as well.

A: It doesn't seem too helpful to me, but anyway – could you explain how you reached this conclusion?

B: Sure. We agreed that Tina is taller than Mary. Now, **suppose**, for the sake of our discussion, that we knew that Mary is tall. Would you then agree that Tina is tall as well?

A: Of course I would, since Tina is the taller one. But I'd need to rely on your supposition that Mary is tall!

B: Absolutely. So far so good. Now, **forget** about my supposition. We have just agreed on one thing for sure: *if Mary is tall, then Tina is tall*. Agreed?

   A: Alright – but now you have reintroduced your supposition after the word *if* ...

   B: Of course I have! This was my only point: to show you that we must accept this conditional statement based on our knowledge that Tina is taller than Mary.

In this artificial conversation, Speaker B aims to convince Speaker A of the truth of the conditional sentence *if Mary is tall, then Tina is tall* (=(5.26b)), based on their shared assumption *Tina is taller than Mary* (=(5.26a)). To do that, Speaker B urges Speaker A to consider a hypothetical situation in which Mary is tall (witness the word '*suppose*'). Speaker A accepts entailment (5.27). Therefore, he has no problem in agreeing that in a hypothetical situation in which Mary were tall, Tina would be tall as well. From this agreement, Speaker B follows and convinces Speaker A that the conditional sentence (5.26b) is true. As the phrase '*forget about my supposition*' stresses, B's assumption that Mary is tall was only made for the sake of the argument, and does not appear in the premises that A is expected to accept. Because of this ephemeral appearance of suppositions, this kind of reasoning is called *hypothetical reasoning*. In our example, Speaker B urges Speaker A to reason about a hypothetical situation in which Mary is tall. He does that in order to support a conditional sentence, whose validity does not hinge on the validity of this hypothesis.

   Let us summarize Speaker B's reasoning in the following tree diagram (5.31), again in the style known as 'natural deduction':

(5.31) $$\cfrac{\cfrac{\text{Tina is taller than Mary} \quad [\text{Mary is tall}]^1}{\text{Tina is tall}}\text{(5.27)}}{\text{If Mary is tall then Tina is tall}}\text{discharge hypothesis 1}$$

In (5.31) we introduce two kinds of notation:

1. We put the hypothetical assumption *Tina is tall* in brackets and give it the index 1.
2. When "forgetting about" this hypothesis, we use it as a premise in a conditional sentence (*if Mary is tall then Tina is tall*), where the suffix of this conditional (*Tina is tall*) is the conclusion that

we have temporarily reached in the tree diagram. When doing that we say that we *discharge* the hypothetical assumption that we indexed as 1.

The underlying reasoning is: since we can reach the conclusion *Tina is tall* using the hypothesis *Mary is tall*, we can also reach the conditional conclusion *If Mary is tall then Tina is tall*, but this time *without* the hypothesis. Once the proof "discharges" itself of the hypothesis, we consider it a justification for entailment (5.26), since from the assumption *Tina is taller than Mary*, we have reached the conditional sentence in the conclusion of (5.26) without further hypothetical assumptions.

This motivates a general rule that describes how to introduce a conditional statement as a conclusion. The schematic form for this rule of *implication introduction* is given below.

(5.32) **Implication introduction rule**

$$\ldots \; [\varphi]^1$$
$$\vdots$$
$$\frac{\psi}{\varphi \to \psi} \quad \text{discharge hypothesis 1}$$

In words: if by hypothesizing φ we reach the conclusion ψ, then we are allowed to reach the conclusion $\varphi \to \psi$ <u>without</u> hypothesizing φ.

Let us see another example for hypothetical reasoning with conditional statements. Consider the following line of reasoning with natural language conditionals.

(5.33) From our experience we know:
    If Mary is at the party (φ_1) then if John is (also) at the party (φ_2), there is trouble (ψ).
    We discover:
    John is at the party (φ_2).
    We conclude:
    If Mary is (also) at the party (φ_1), there is trouble (ψ).

Here we suppose that we are given the conditional statement $\varphi_1 \to (\varphi_2 \to \psi)$, as well as the statement φ_2. We conclude the statement

$\varphi_1 \to \psi$. In (5.34) below we see a justification of this line of reasoning that uses the implication introduction rule in (5.32).

(5.34)
$$\dfrac{\dfrac{\varphi_1 \to (\varphi_2 \to \psi) \quad [\varphi_1]^1}{\varphi_2 \to \psi} \text{ MP} \quad \varphi_2}{\dfrac{\psi}{\varphi_1 \to \psi} \text{ discharge hypothesis 1}} \text{ MP}$$

The hypothetical reasoning in (5.34) uses our two assumptions $\varphi_1 \to (\varphi_2 \to \psi)$ and φ_2 to deduce the conditional statement $\varphi_1 \to \psi$. Note that in order to use φ_2 in a Modus Ponens step, we first need to temporarily eliminate the proposition φ_1 in the premise of the assumption $\varphi_1 \to (\varphi_2 \to \psi)$. The hypothetical assumption of φ_1 allowed us to do that. But at the end we discharge this assumption and introduce φ_1 again as the antecedent of the derived conditional.

Now that we have motivated an introduction rule for implication, we can go back to the question of the functional type constructor. Our analogy between implication and the functional constructor leads us to the following introduction rule for function types.

(5.35) **Function introduction rule**

$$\ldots \quad [\tau]^1$$
$$\vdots$$
$$\dfrac{\sigma}{\tau\sigma} \text{ discharge hypothesis 1}$$

In words, this reasoning can be stated analogically to our understanding of the implication introduction rule: suppose that by hypothesizing the type τ we reach the type σ; then, by the same style of hypothetical reasoning, we conclude that this justifies reaching the functional type $\tau\sigma$, but now without hypothesizing τ.

With the rule in (5.35), example (5.34) for reasoning with conditional propositions can be translated to reasoning with functional types. Instead of the statements φ_1, φ_2 and ψ, we write the types e, e and t, respectively.

(5.36)
$$\dfrac{\dfrac{e(et) \quad [e]^1}{et} \text{ FA} \quad e}{\dfrac{t}{et} \text{ discharge hypothesis 1}} \text{ FA}$$

This proof shows that using hypothetical reasoning over types we can reach the type et from types $e(et)$ and e. In a sense this is old news: we already know how to get this result using function application. But here, instead of one direct application, the result is obtained by two applications, plus the rule of hypothetical reasoning. As we shall now see, this makes a semantic difference.

The last step in (5.36) is an instance of the rule (5.35), which introduces a function type by discharging an assumption. This kind of function introduction is often referred to as function *abstraction*. How do we interpret such a rule? What is the function that it introduces? The idea is this: suppose that using a denotation u of type τ, we have managed to reach a denotation z of type σ. The hypothetical reasoning in (5.35) justifies introducing the function $\lambda u.z$ of type $\tau\sigma$, without having the denotation u as given. The function $\lambda u.z$ sends *any* object u of type τ to a corresponding object z of type σ. Formally, we write this interpretation of the type scheme in (5.36) as follows:

(5.37)   **Function introduction – interpretation**

$$\dots \ [u]^1$$
$$\vdots$$
$$\frac{z}{\lambda u.z} \text{ discharge hypothesis 1}$$

In words: suppose that by hypothesizing a denotation u we reach a denotation z. Then, the same reasoning justifies reaching the *function* $\lambda u.z$, this time without hypothesizing u.

Consider now our original query, where we wondered what compositional principle justifies deriving the function in (5.19) from the denotations **praise** of type $e(et)$ and **mary** of type e. Hypothetical reasoning is our candidate for such a principle. The two types in the assumptions of (5.36) are $e(et)$ and e – the types of the denotations **praise** and **mary**. Therefore, let us interpret the two types given as assumptions in (5.36) using these denotations, while interpreting the hypothetical type e in (5.36) using the hypothetical denotation u of the same type. What we get is the following derivation.

$$(5.38) \quad \frac{\dfrac{\mathbf{praise}_{e(et)} \quad [u_e]^1}{\mathbf{praise}(u)} \text{ FA} \quad \mathbf{mary}_e}{\dfrac{\mathbf{praise}(u)(\mathbf{mary})}{\lambda u_e.\mathbf{praise}(u)(\mathbf{mary})} \text{ discharge hypothesis 1}} \text{ FA}$$

In (5.38) we use hypothetical reasoning to derive the function $\lambda u_e.\mathbf{praise}(u)(\mathbf{mary})$ from the denotations **praise** and **mary**. To do that we first feed the function **praise** with a hypothetical argument u of type e. This gives us a (hypothetical) function $\mathbf{praise}(u)$ of type et. When we apply this function to the entity **mary** we get a truth-value $\mathbf{praise}(u)(\mathbf{mary})$. This value is still hypothetical, since it relies on the value of u. By discharging our hypothesis u, we get the function $\lambda u.\mathbf{praise}(u)(\mathbf{mary})$, now without any hypothetical elements. This is the same function as X_{pbm} in (5.17), which we used in our tentative analysis (5.20)–(5.21) of sentence (5.14) (= *some teacher that Mary praised smiled*). We conclude that hypothetical reasoning can be used as the basis for solving the puzzle introduced by the relative clause in sentence (5.14).

Rule (5.37) is a rule of *function introduction*. This rule, together with the elimination rule of *function application*, is the basis for a logical system known as the *Lambek-Van Benthem Calculus* (after J. Lambek and J. van Benthem). Using hypothetical reasoning in our derivation of semantic denotations can also help in accounting for the long-distance dependency in sentence (5.22), restated below.

(5.39) Some teacher that Tina believes Mary praised smiled.

Consider the meaning derivation in (5.38) before the point where the hypothesis u is discharged. We can defer discharging this hypothesis, and use the hypothetical truth-value $\mathbf{praise}(u)(\mathbf{mary})$ as the argument of the denotation **believe** of type $t(et)$. This function characterizes a relation between truth-values (of believed statements) and entities (the believers). In Chapter 6 we will see some problems with this denotation of *believe*, but here it is sufficient for illustrating our main point about the derivation of long-distance meaning relationships in the Lambek-Van Benthem Calculus. Consider derivation (5.40) below. In this derivation we let the second argument of the function **believe** be the entity **tina**, and discharge the hypothesis u long-distance, after the function **believe** applies to the truth-value **praise**(u)(**mary**) (truth-value of the belief) and to the entity **tina** (the believer). Here and henceforth, the gloss 'FA' on derivation steps that involve function application is suppressed.

(5.40)
$$\cfrac{\cfrac{\cfrac{\textbf{praise}_{e(et)} \quad [u_e]^1}{\textbf{praise}(u) \qquad \textbf{mary}_e}}{\cfrac{\textbf{believe}_{t(et)} \qquad \textbf{praise}(u)(\textbf{mary})}{\textbf{believe}(\textbf{praise}(u)(\textbf{mary})) \qquad \textbf{tina}_e}}}{\cfrac{\textbf{believe}(\textbf{praise}(u)(\textbf{mary}))(\textbf{tina})}{\lambda u.\textbf{believe}(\textbf{praise}(u)(\textbf{mary}))(\textbf{tina})} \text{ discharge hypothesis 1}}$$

The result of this derivation is the et function $\lambda u.\textbf{believe}(\textbf{praise}(u)(\textbf{mary}))(\textbf{tina})$, which characterizes the following set of entities:

(5.41) $\{u \in E : \textbf{believe}(\textbf{praise}(u)(\textbf{mary}))(\textbf{tina}) = 1\}$

Thus, with the right assumptions about the denotation of the verb *believe*, we derived the intuitively correct set of entities. In our standard analysis of sentence (5.39), this set is used for establishing a relation between the noun *teacher* and the object argument of the verb *praised*, as in the informal analysis in (5.22b). We now formalize this analysis as follows, by substituting the set (5.41) in (5.22b).

(5.42) $(\textbf{teacher}^* \cap \{u \in E : \textbf{believe}(\textbf{praise}(u)(\textbf{mary}))(\textbf{tina}) = 1\})$
$\cap \, \textbf{smile}^* \neq \emptyset$

In words: there is a teacher u such that Tina believes that Mary praised u. We conclude that, abstracting away from the issue of the correct analysis of the verb *believe*, hypothetical reasoning correctly describes long-distance meaning relationships as in sentence (5.39).

The same mechanism of hypothetical reasoning also allows us to analyze sentences with quantified objects like sentence (5.4), which is restated below.

(5.43) Tina [praised [every student]]

Consider the following derivation for the meaning of the verb phrase *praised every student*.

(5.44)

$$\dfrac{\dfrac{\dfrac{\dfrac{\textbf{praise}_{e(et)} \quad [u_e]^1}{\textbf{praise}(u) \qquad [v_e]^2}}{\dfrac{\textbf{praise}(u)(v)}{\lambda u.\textbf{praise}(u)(v)}\;\text{dis. hyp. 1} \qquad \text{EVERY}(\textbf{student})}}{\text{EVERY}(\textbf{student})(\lambda u.\textbf{praise}(u)(v))}}{\lambda v.\text{EVERY}(\textbf{student})(\lambda u.\textbf{praise}(u)(v))}\;\text{dis. hyp. 2}$$

This derivation first introduces two hypothesized entities, u and v, and lets the function **praise** apply to both of them. This derives a truth-value $\textbf{praise}(u)(v)$. The hypothesized entity u is then discharged, and the resulting et function is used as the argument of the quantifier EVERY(**student**). Discharging the second hypothesized entity, v, results in the et function in (5.45a) below, which characterizes the set of entities in (5.45b).

(5.45) a. $\lambda v.\text{EVERY}(\textbf{student})(\lambda u.\textbf{praise}(u)(v))$

   b. $\{v \in E : \text{EVERY}(\textbf{student})(\lambda u.\textbf{praise}(u)(v)) = 1\}$
      $= \{v \in E : \textbf{student}^* \subseteq (\lambda u.\textbf{praise}(u)(v))^*\}$ (def. of EVERY)
      $= \{v \in E : \textbf{student}^* \subseteq \{u \in E : \textbf{praise}(u)(v) = 1\}\}$

      (def. characteristic function)

In words: the function in (5.45a) characterizes the entities v such that the set of students is a subset of the set of entities that v praised. Thus, applying the function in (5.45a) to the entity **tina** correctly reflects the meaning of sentence (5.43): the set of students is a subset of the set of entities that Tina praised.

   These analyses are promising, and point out that hypothetical reasoning gives us a way of analyzing meaning relationships that our system of Chapter 3 failed to explain. We can now better assess the potential of the Lambek-Van Benthem Calculus as a basis for semantic composition. However, we should also note that this calculus on its own does not prevent the undesired outcomes that we saw. Quite to the contrary: without further amendments, it would generate even more undesired analyses. For instance, the constituent *Mary praised* in sentence (5.14) may still receive the faulty interpretation where the entity **mary** is the first argument of the function **praise**, and hence is incorrectly analyzed as an object. Worse still, reconsider sentence (5.11), restated below.

(5.46) Some teacher that praised Mary smiled.

Our use of the Lambek-Van Benthem Calculus is at risk of adding an undesired analysis for this sentence to the one that was correctly derived in (5.13). This is because, in our current use of hypothetical reasoning, the constituent *praised Mary* in sentence (5.46) is still treated in the same way as the constituent *Mary praised* in the object-directed relative of sentence (5.14). Thus, our tentative analysis makes no distinction between sentences (5.46) and (5.14): both sentences are now treated as ambiguous between two meanings, which is obviously incorrect. How can we use the logical strength of the Lambek-Van Benthem Calculus without this kind of overgeneration? This question leads us to a broader discussion about the grammatical analysis of natural language.

You are now advised to solve Exercises 1, 2 and 3 at the end of this chapter.

LINGUISTIC SIGNS AND ABSTRACT CATEGORIAL GRAMMAR

The framework of Chapters 3–4 assigns denotations to complex constituents by manipulating the denotations of their sub-parts, without paying attention to the syntactic relations between those subparts. For instance, in the relatives *that Mary praised* and *that praised Mary* within sentences (5.14) and (5.46) we have noted an obvious but significant difference in the relations between the NP and the verb: in one case *Mary* is the object, in the other it is the subject. Our analysis so far has ignored such differences, and as a result it has erroneously derived the same denotation (or denotations) for the two structures despite the great syntactic differences between them. How can our compositional system be synchronized with a grammatical analysis that models correctly such obvious linguistic relations?

A key for addressing this question comes from a seminal idea by a scholar of the nineteenth century: the linguist Ferdinand de Saussure

(1857–1913). In one of de Saussure's well-known works, he introduces the notion of *linguistic sign*, which he considers as a basic element in linguistic analysis. De Saussure explains:

> *The linguistic sign unites not a thing and a name, but a concept and a sound-image.*
> [Le signe linguistique unit non une chose et un nom, mais un concept et une image acoustique.]

> *Cours de Linguistique Générale* (1916)

Attacking objectivist notions like 'thing' and 'name', de Saussure defines linguistic signs as amalgamating two kinds of *mental* representations: semantic concepts on the one hand and images of auditory signals on the other. The "concept" is the understood meaning of an expression in spoken language. The "sound-image" is the *perception* of that expression's sound. Both meanings and perceived sounds are mental objects: objects that our brain represents in one way or another. For instance, using de Saussure's notion of sign, we view the word *tree* in spoken English as a pair of mental objects: the percept tree and the concept **tree**. The first object, tree, is a perceptual representation that abstracts over possible instances of English sounds for the word *tree*. The latter object, **tree**, is a concept, which abstracts over different understandings of the word *tree*, e.g. in terms of the sets that its denotations characterize.

Notions of signs are relevant for much current research in linguistics. However, we should note that since the time of de Saussure's work, linguists have discovered that there is no reason to think of human languages as exclusively related to *auditory* signals. Most notably, we must also consider the languages known as *sign languages*: languages whose expressions are articulated by manual and facial movements, rather than by speech sounds. This common term should not be confused with de Saussure's theoretical usage of the term 'sign'. As linguists have found long after de Saussure's work, sign languages show all the main properties that characterize other human languages. Taking this point into account, we adapt de Saussure's notions to modern knowledge, and also consider human languages that do not rely on speech sounds. In more general terms, we say that the perceptual unit within linguistic signs may encode a mental image of any physical signal that the language in question uses. In sum, we adopt the following terminology.

> A **linguistic sign,** *or in short a* **sign,** *is a pair* ⟨*P, C*⟩, *where P stands for a* <u>perceptual</u> *representation of sensory input and C stands for a* <u>conceptual</u> *representation of meaning.*

Upon some reflection, we see that this pairing of two mental objects underlies a foundational aspect of what we call *language*. Independently of what we think about the concepts that language evokes and the way sensory input is mentally perceived, it is clear that language *simultaneously* involves those two aspects. As any good dictionary illustrates, it is impossible to think of the English word *tree* without simultaneously considering both the concept of 'tree' and the speech sounds that English speakers perceive as associated with this word.

Looking back on Chapter 3 from this perspective, we see that our notion of semantic composition has so far been shamelessly simplistic. All along we have been assuming that the perceptual component derives simple strings. These strings, or the syntactic structures that represent them, were interpreted by denotations in the semantic apparatus. From a Saussurean perspective, this may seem to be the fallacy of studying "things" (denotations) and "names" (strings) independently of each other. Now, instead of separating the treatment of perceptual units and their meanings, we adopt a more integrative, "Saussurean" outlook. Under this view, all linguistic expressions are analyzed by signs, which have a perceptual component as well as a conceptual component. Both components are model-theoretically interpreted. Thus, in the sign ⟨tree, **tree**⟩ for the English word *tree*, the first component is interpreted as a perceptual-acoustic object in phonetic models of English. The second component is interpreted as a conceptual-semantic object in semantic models of English. These two kinds of objects may be very different mentally, but they are held together by what we refer to as "the English word *tree*".

Some readers may feel that using abstract models in order to analyze concrete things like speech sounds would be an overkill. However, from a cognitive perspective it is a very plausible move. The perceptual aspects of language are often as abstract as its meanings: think for a moment about the gross over-simplification that we make when talking about the "sound" of a word. When categorizing a sound as an instance of the word *tree* we perform a very complex task: separate this sound from other sounds, ignore many specifics of the speaker's voice, pronunciation etc. What we intuitively call the word's "sound" is no less an abstraction than its "meaning"! In this chapter, we will employ models for connecting linguistic signs with perceptual objects (related to sounds, strings etc.), in the same way as we connect linguistic signs to their semantic denotations in a model. Indeed, as formal semanticists, we will often allow ourselves to remain agnostic about the nature of perceptual objects, conceptual objects, or both. However, without some or other *pairing* of the two aspects of language, there can be no semantic theory. From now on we capitalize on the pairing that linguistic signs impose on the two mental aspects of language.

Now let us move on to the *composition* of linguistic signs. When analyzing expressions like *praised Mary* or *Mary praised* we assume that it is the signs for the words *praised* and *Mary* that our theory should deal with. Each of these two signs contains a perceptual component and a conceptual component. As the conceptual-semantic component of these signs, we keep using the typed denotations $\mathbf{praise}_{e(et)}$ and $\mathbf{mary}_e$ as we have done so far. However, as the perceptual units we no longer use strings. Rather, just like we have used abstract denotations in our semantic-conceptual model, we now assume abstract objects in a *perceptual model*. In our example we will make use of two objects, praise and mary, which describe the perception of the respective spoken English sounds. As a result, our theory will have to explain the composition of the following two signs:

$$\langle \text{praise}, \mathbf{praise}_{e(et)} \rangle \text{ and } \langle \text{mary}, \mathbf{mary}_e \rangle$$

The notations praise and mary describe perceptual objects. Since our focus is on the principles that allow combining such objects to each other, we are mostly interested in their *types*. For simplicity, we assume that all types for perceptual objects are based on one basic type: a type for *phonetic entities* that we denote 'f'. We will be rather neutral about the precise set of phonetic entities, just like we remained neutral about the nature of semantic entities of type e. Our main assumption about phonetic entities is that they can be *concatenated* to each other. To do that, we introduce an operator, denoted '$\cdot$', that concatenates phonetic entities. We assume that this concatenation operator is *associative*, i.e. it is only affected by the linear order of its arguments, not by the way they are grouped together. Further, we assume one empty phonetic entity ϵ that functions as an *identity element*: concatenating ϵ to any other phonetic entity leaves the latter intact. Formally, we define the domain of phonetic entities as follows.

Definition 3. *A **domain of phonetic entities** D_f is any set F together with a binary operator. This **concatenation operator**, which we denote '·', has the following properties.*

Closure: *for all phonetic entities x, $y \in F$, the concatenation $x \cdot y$ is also in F.*

Associativity: *for all phonetic entities $x, y, z \in F$, it holds that $x \cdot (y \cdot z) = (x \cdot y) \cdot z$.*

Identity element: *F contains an element ϵ s.t. for every phonetic entity $x \in F$, it holds that $x \cdot \epsilon = \epsilon \cdot x = x$.*

This characterizes the domain $D_f = F$ of phonetic entities as a what we in algebraic terms call a *monoid*. We freely switch between the notations 'D_f' and 'F' for this domain of phonetic entities, as we did with the notations 'D_e' and 'E' for the domain of semantic entities.

Now let us get back to the signs for the words *praise* and *Mary*. We assume that the perceptual component mary within the sign of the respective word is interpreted as a simple phonetic entity in the domain D_f. Further, we assume that the perceptual component praise is a *function* of type $f(ff)$. This function receives two phonetic entities, for the object and subject noun phrases, and returns a phonetic entity of a sentence. In English, phonetic entities of transitive sentences are in subject–verb–object word order. This means that the perceptual component for the transitive verb *praise* takes the phonetic entities for the subject and the object, and uses them to 'wrap' a phonetic entity that corresponds to the verb's sound. Accordingly, we define the $f(ff)$ function praise as follows.

> For a given phonetic entity *praised* in D_f, the function praise $\in D_{f(ff)}$ maps every phonetic entity $x \in D_f$ to the function sending every phonetic entity $y \in D_f$ to the phonetic entity $y \cdot praised \cdot x$.

In lambda notation, this perceptual representation is defined as follows:

$$\text{praise}_{f(ff)} = \lambda x_f.\lambda y_f.\; y \cdot praised \cdot x$$

Using this definition, and assuming the phonetic entities *tina* and *mary* for the perceptual descriptions tina and mary, we get the following equations:

$$\text{praise}_{f(ff)}(\text{mary}_f)(\text{tina}_f) = tina \cdot praised \cdot mary$$
$$\text{praise}_{f(ff)}(\text{tina}_f)(\text{mary}_f) = mary \cdot praised \cdot tina$$

In this way, the function $\text{praise}_{f(ff)}$ determines the sound order in a sentence. Repeating the convention we introduced for Curried semantic denotations of transitive verbs, we let this perceptual function take its object argument first, and its subject argument second. When the first argument is the phonetic entity mary and the second argument is tina, we get the phonetic entity for a sentence where Mary is the object and Tina is the subject. The converse holds for the opposite order of the arguments.

With these assumptions, let us now return to our original question. We want to combine the two signs in (5.47).

(5.47) $\langle \text{praise}_{f(ff)}, \textbf{praise}_{e(et)} \rangle$ and $\langle \text{mary}_f, \textbf{mary}_e \rangle$

To do that we again use the Lambek-Van Benthem Calculus, but now to combine signs. This is done by applying the calculus simultaneously in the two coordinates of the sign: the perceptual component as well as the conceptual component. For instance, function application works for the two signs in (5.47) as follows:

(5.48) $$\frac{\langle \text{praise}_{f(ff)}, \textbf{praise}_{e(et)} \rangle \quad \langle \text{mary}_f, \textbf{mary}_e \rangle}{\langle \text{praise}(\text{mary}), \textbf{praise}(\textbf{mary}) \rangle}\;\text{FA}$$

Given our assumptions above, we analyze the sign that is derived in (5.48) as consisting of the phonetic function in (5.49a) and the semantic function in (5.49b).

(5.49) Sign: $\langle$praise(mary), **praise(mary)**$\rangle$

    a. $\text{praise}_{f(ff)}(\text{mary}_f)$
       $= (\lambda x_f.\lambda y_f.y \cdot praised \cdot x)(mary)$
       $= \lambda y_f.y \cdot praised \cdot mary$
       = the function sending any phonetic entity y_f to the phonetic entity $y \cdot praised \cdot mary$

    b. $\textbf{praise}_{e(et)}(\textbf{mary}_e)$
       = the function sending any semantic entity y_e to the truth-value **praise(mary)**(y)

Now, since we use the Lambek-Van Benthem Calculus to derive signs, we are also free to apply hypothetical reasoning in the derivation. Thus, similarly to derivation (5.38), we also derive the following result from the signs in (5.47).

$$
(5.50)\quad \cfrac{\cfrac{\langle\text{praise}_{f(ff)}, \textbf{praise}_{e(et)}\rangle \quad [\langle u_f, u_e\rangle]^1}{\langle\text{praise}(u_f), \textbf{praise}(u_e)\rangle}\text{ FA} \quad \langle\text{mary}_f, \textbf{mary}_e\rangle}{\cfrac{\langle\text{praise}(u_f)(\text{mary}), \textbf{praise}(u_e)(\textbf{mary})\rangle}{\langle\lambda u_f.\text{praise}(u_f)(\text{mary}), \lambda u_e.\textbf{praise}(u_e)(\textbf{mary})\rangle}\text{ hyp. 1}}\substack{\text{FA}\\\text{dis.}}
$$

Comparing this derivation to derivation (5.38), we see nothing new here in terms of logical principles: we use function application and hypothetical reasoning in the same way. However, the objects that are manipulated by these rules are now pairs – signs instead of mere denotations:

- The assumptions are the signs $\langle\text{mary}_f, \textbf{mary}_e\rangle$ and $\langle\text{praise}_{f(ff)}, \textbf{praise}_{e(et)}\rangle$.
- The hypothetical assumption is the sign $\langle u_f, u_e\rangle$.
- The result derived is the sign
$\langle\lambda u_f.\text{praise}(u_f)(\text{mary}), \lambda u_e.\textbf{praise}(u_e)(\textbf{mary})\rangle$.

The phonetic function and semantic function within this derived sign are described in more detail in (5.51a–b) below.

(5.51) a. $\lambda u_f.\mathrm{praise}(u)(\mathrm{mary})$
           $= \lambda u_f.(\lambda x_f.\lambda y_f.y \cdot praised \cdot x)(u)(mary)$
           $= \lambda u_f.mary \cdot praised \cdot u$
           $=$ the function sending any phonetic entity u_f to the
              phonetic entity $mary \cdot praised \cdot u$

        b. $\lambda u_e.\mathbf{praise}(u)(\mathbf{mary})$
           $=$ the function sending any semantic entity u_e to the
              truth-value $\mathbf{praise}(u)(\mathbf{mary})$

Note the difference between the signs in (5.49) and in (5.51). The
sign in (5.49) has the phonetic entity for the name *Mary* in the post-
verbal object position, and the semantic entity for *Mary* in the first
argument of the verb denotation. The sign in (5.51) has the phonetic
entity for *Mary* in the pre-verbal subject position, and the semantic
entity in the second argument of the verb denotation. Again we see that
the Lambek-Van Benthem Calculus derives two different results given
the words *praised* and *Mary*. However, now the two results are two
different signs, which are different both in their conceptual component
and in their perceptual component. There is no overgeneration here
since the two different semantic denotations that are derived are
coupled with two different functions over phonetic entities.

The general hypothesis that emerges from the above considerations
is the following.

Hypothesis: *The Lambek-Van Benthem Calculus is a suitable logical
apparatus for manipulating the composition of signs in natural
language grammar.*

This hypothesis underlies one variant of a recently emerging framework known as *Abstract Categorial Grammar (ACG)*. ACG develops
ideas by the mathematician and logician Haskell Curry (1900–82),
whose "Currying" principle is one important ingredient of the type
system presented in Chapter 3. In his work that inspired ACG,
Curry proposed distinguishing two grammatical levels, which he called
tectogrammatics and *phenogrammatics*. These two levels nicely correspond to de Saussure's conception of linguistic signs. For Curry,
the tectogrammatical level represents the "abstract" combinatorial

structure of expressions, which interfaces a semantic component. The phenogrammatical level can be seen as representing the linguistic level that interfaces perception systems, which represent signals like sounds (in spoken language), manual signs (in sign language) or strings of alphabetical symbols (in written language). Thus, the tectogrammatical structures are semantically interpreted, whereas the phenogrammatical structures are 'phonologically' interpreted. When earlier in this book we used compositional interpretation of binary structures, we relied on one single grammatical level: that of binary trees. This level has both a semantic interpretation (through function application) and a phonological interpretation (through adjacency). Thus, the binary trees in our analysis served both as a tectogrammatical level and as a phenogrammatical level. Curry's distinction between the two levels allows us to combine his conception of grammar with de Saussure's conception of signs.

To avoid misunderstandings, it should be said that when we talk about "Abstract Categorial Grammar", we use the term "grammar" in the sense of a formal grammatical *framework*, with no pretenstions to the wide empirical coverage that we normally expect from grammatical descriptions of natural languages. Some empirical work has so far been done on the applications of ACG to natural language, but there is much more left to be done. Accordingly, at present there is no commonly accepted way of embedding ACG within linguistic theory. We will not try to do that here, but present ACG derivations as *minimal conditions* on the relations between phonetic objects and semantic denotations, which any linguistic theory should respect. With this in mind, we can move on to analyzing the way in which the ACG framework allows us to describe long-distance meaning relationships.

USING SIGNS

The assumptions above about signs and ACG are now used to solve the puzzles we saw with clauses having multiple arguments. In this framework, the lexicon consists of sign tokens, which are typed and interpreted in models similarly to the interpretation of string tokens in Chapter 3. Since our signs have two components, we assign them two different types: an *f-type* (phonetic type) and an *s-type* (semantic type). Each sign component is assigned a denotation of the right type.

Table 5.1:   Basic abstract types.

Abstract type		F-type	S-type
NP	referential noun phrase	f	e
S	sentence	f	t
A	adjective	f	et
N	noun/nominal	f	et

We refer to the denotations of the two components of the sign as its *f-denotation* and *s-denotation*. To present signs and their types more compactly, we let each sign have one "higher-level" type, which we refer to as the sign's *abstract type*. Every abstract type, or *category*, is systematically mapped to an f-type and an s-type. This mapping is viewed as a "concretization" of the type. The f-type and s-type of a sign are collectively referred to as its *concrete types*.

Like other types, abstract types are inductively defined over a small finite set of *basic abstract types*. For our purposes here, we use four basic abstract types, as specified in Table 5.1. Each of these categories is assigned an f-type and an s-type. The abstract type NP in Table 5.1 is borrowed from traditional terminology in categorial grammar, and is used for NPs that can semantically be treated in type e. These NPs are traditionally called *referential* NPs. Other NPs, which are assigned the quantificational s-type $(et)t$, will be assigned a complex abstract type. All four basic abstract types in Table 5.1 have type f (i.e. phonetic entity) as their f-type.

All complex types are defined uniformly as in Chapter 3, by inductively extending the set of basic types. This is formally specified in Definition 4 below (cf. Definition 1 in Chapter 3).

Definition 4. *Let* B *be some finite set of basic types. The set of* **types** *over* B *is the smallest set* $\mathcal{T}^{\mathsf{B}}$ *that satisfies:*

(i) $\mathsf{B} \subseteq \mathcal{T}^{\mathsf{B}}$

(ii)   *If* τ *and* σ *are types in* $\mathcal{T}^{\mathsf{B}}$ *then* $(\tau\sigma)$ *is also a type in* $\mathcal{T}^{\mathsf{B}}$.

This uniform definition derives the three sets of types we use:

$\mathcal{T}^{\{f\}}$ f-types like f, ff, $f(ff)$, $(ff)f$ etc.

$\mathcal{T}^{\{e,t\}}$ s-types like e, t, et, $e(et)$, $(et)t$ etc.

$\mathcal{T}^{\{\text{NP},\text{S},\text{N},\text{A}\}}$ abstract types like NP, S, NP$\rightarrow$S, NP$\rightarrow$(NP$\rightarrow$S), (NP$\rightarrow$S)$\rightarrow$S etc.

The arrow notation of complex abstract types is used for readability. For instance, the following two complex abstract types are used for intransitive and transitive verbs:

NP $\rightarrow$ S   abstract type for intransitive verbs, e.g. *smile*

NP $\rightarrow$ (NP $\rightarrow$ S)   abstract type for transitive verbs, e.g. *praise*

Any complex abstract type is assigned concrete types based on the concrete types of its parts. The concrete type assignment for basic abstract types in Table 5.1 allows us to do it inductively for all complex abstract types. For instance, for the two abstract types above we assign concrete types as follows.

NP $\rightarrow$ S   f-type: ff s-type: et

NP $\rightarrow$ (NP $\rightarrow$ S)   f-type: $f(ff)$ s-type: $e(et)$

In words: since the f-types of the simple types NP and S are both f, the f-type of the complex abstract type NP $\rightarrow$ S is the function type ff. Further, since the f-type of NP is f, and the f-type of NP $\rightarrow$ S is ff, the f-type of NP $\rightarrow$ (NP $\rightarrow$ S) is $f(ff)$. The s-types are similarly determined. More generally, below we define this convention of assigning concrete types to abstract types.

Definition 5. *Let τ and σ be abstract types. Suppose that τ is inductively assigned the concrete f- and s-types τ_f and τ_s, and that σ is assigned the concrete types σ_f and σ_s. Then the complex abstract type $\tau \rightarrow \sigma$ is assigned the f-type $\tau_f \sigma_f$ and the s-type $\tau_s \sigma_s$.*

Abstract types allow a compact encoding of sign derivations. For instance, instead of writing explicitly the concrete types and components of the signs for *praise* and *Mary*, as we did in the derivation (5.50), we use the following shortened notation.

(5.52)

$$\cfrac{\cfrac{\text{PRAISE}_{\text{NP}\to(\text{NP}\to\text{s})} \quad [U_{\text{NP}}]^1}{\text{PRAISE}(U_{\text{NP}})}\text{ FA} \quad \text{MARY}_{\text{NP}}}{\cfrac{\text{PRAISE}(U_{\text{NP}})(\text{MARY})}{\lambda U_{\text{NP}}.\ \text{PRAISE}(U)(\text{MARY})}\text{ discharge hypothesis 1}}\text{ FA}$$

From abstract-level derivations as in (5.52) we can immediately spell out the concrete f-component and s-component of the derived sign. For instance, for the sign derived in (5.52) we saw the two concrete components in (5.51), repeated in (5.53) below.

(5.53)   Derived sign: $\lambda U_{\text{NP}}.\ \text{PRAISE}(U)(\text{MARY})$

      a.   f-component: $\lambda u_f.\text{praise}(u)(\text{mary})$
                     $= \lambda u_f.\text{mary} \cdot \text{praised} \cdot u$
                     (by assumption on the f-function praise)

      b.   s-component: $\lambda u_e.\mathbf{praise}(u)(\mathbf{mary})$

Note that the abstract derivation in (5.52) represents one of the possibilities of combining the signs PRAISE and MARY, by using hypothetical reasoning. The concrete results in (5.53) model the use of the word *Mary* as the verb's subject. As we saw, by applying the sign PRAISE directly to MARY, we get the sign PRAISE(MARY), as given in (5.49), where the word *Mary* fills in the object slot.

Let us take stock of the conception of signs that emerges, and their use in a grammar of natural language.

Intermediate summary: *Each word and complex expression is viewed as a* **sign**: *a linguistic entity that is assigned an* **f-type** *and an* **s-type**, *with an* **f-denotation** *and* **s-denotation** *in any given model. The f-type and f-denotation describe aspects of the sign's perceptual dimension involving phonetic entities and functions over them. The s-type and s-denotation describe aspects of the sign's conceptual dimension involving semantic entities, truth-values and functions over them. The* **lexicon** *specifies an abstract type for each lexical sign, which determines its f- and s-type. The lexicon may also specify restrictions on a sign's f- and s-denotations. From these lexical signs, a* **grammar** *derives signs of complex expressions. As our grammatical engine we here use the Lambek-Van Benthem Calculus.*

Let us summarize our notational conventions with signs, by reconsidering the simple sentence *Tina is tall*. For this sentence, we assume signs with the following abstract types:

TINA **NP**
TALL **A**
IS **A** → (**NP** → **S**)

According to the assignment of concrete types to the basic abstract types (Table 5.1), we get the concrete types for these signs. This is done by substituting the concrete types from Table 5.1 for the abstract type:

TINA f e ▷ substitute concrete types for **NP**
TALL f et ▷ substitute concrete types for **A**
IS $f(ff)$ $(et)(et)$ ▷ for concrete f-types, substitute f for **NP**, **A** and **S**
for concrete s-types, substitute e for **NP**, et for **A**, and t for **S**

As with semantic denotations, the f-denotations of some signs are restricted. For the sign IS, the restriction on the f-denotation requires that it puts the copula's phonetic entity *is* between the phonetic entities for the subject and the adjective phrase. The restriction on the s-denotation of IS requires it to be the identity function. Formally, we specify the f-component and the s-component as follows:

$$\text{IS} = \langle \lambda x_f.\lambda y_f.\, y \cdot is \cdot x \,, \, \lambda P_{et}.P \,\rangle$$

The signs TINA and TALL are assumed to have arbitrary denotations in both components. Thus, we make no assumptions about the strings or entities that they can denote.

In Figure 5.1, we summarize the derivation of a sign for the sentence *Tina is tall*. The figure shows the derivation at the abstract level and at each of the components in natural deduction format, as well as in tree format. As we saw in (5.53), we can also use the abstract derivation alone, and spell out the concrete components as derived directly from the abstract result. This is done by spelling out the lexical denotation of each sign in each of the two components, and simplifying the presentation of terms, as desired. As another example for this compact notation, consider the simplifications in (5.54) below for concrete components in Figure 5.1.

Abstract derivation:

$$
\cfrac{\text{TINA}:\textbf{NP} \qquad \cfrac{\text{IS}:\textbf{A}\rightarrow(\textbf{NP}\rightarrow\textbf{S}) \qquad \text{TALL}:\textbf{A}}{\text{IS(TALL)}:\textbf{NP}\rightarrow\textbf{S}}}{\text{IS(TALL)(TINA)}:\textbf{S}}
$$

F component:

$$
\cfrac{tina_f \qquad \cfrac{\lambda x_f.\lambda y_f.\, y\cdot is\cdot x \qquad tall_f}{\lambda y_f.\, y\cdot is\cdot tall}}{tina\cdot is\cdot tall}
$$

S component:

$$
\cfrac{\textbf{tina}_e \qquad \cfrac{\lambda P_{et}.P \qquad \textbf{tall}_{et}}{\textbf{tall}}}{\textbf{tall(tina)}}
$$

Alternative notation:

IS(TALL)(TINA):**S**

```
            IS(TALL)(TINA):S
             /          \
   TINA : NP        IS(TALL):NP→S
                      /        \
        IS:A→(NP→S)          TALL:A
```

$tina\cdot is\cdot tall$

```
        tina·is·tall
         /        \
     tina_f    λy_f. y·is·tall
                /          \
   λx_f.λy_f. y·is·x      tall_f
```

tall(tina)

```
        tall(tina)
         /        \
     tina_e      tall
                /    \
          λP_et.P    tall_et
```

Figure 5.1 Tina is tall – abstract derivation and concrete components.

Table 5.2: Complex abstract types.

Abstract type		F-type	S-type
NP→S	intransitive verb	ff	et
NP→(NP→S)	transitive verb	$f(ff)$	$e(et)$
A→(NP→S)	*be* copula	$f(ff)$	$(et)(et)$
A→A	adjective modifier	ff	$(et)(et)$
S→(S→S)	sentence coordinator	$f(ff)$	$t(tt)$
A→(A→A)	adjective coordinator	$f(ff)$	$(et)((et)(et))$
(NP→S)→S	quantified noun phrase	$(ff)f$	$(et)t$
N→((NP→S)→S)	determiner	$f((ff)f)$	$(et)((et)t)$
(NP→S)→(N→N)	relative pronoun	$(ff)(ff)$	$(et)((et)(et))$

(5.54) Derived sign: IS(TALL)(TINA)

f-component:
$$is_{f(ff)}(\text{tall}_f)(\text{tina}_f)$$
$$= (\lambda x_f.\lambda y_f.\ y\cdot is\cdot x)(tall)(tina)$$
$$= tina\cdot is\cdot tall$$

s-component:
$$\text{IS}_{(et)(et)}(\textbf{tall}_{et})(\textbf{tina}_e)$$
$$= (\lambda P_{et}.\,P)(\textbf{tall})(\textbf{tina})$$
$$= \textbf{tall}(\textbf{tina})$$

More abstract types we use, as well as their f-type and s-type, are given in Table 5.2. Quantificational noun phrases are assumed to have the s-type $(et)t$ of generalized quantifiers, as in Chapter 4. Because such GQs take denotations of intransitive verbs as their argument, we assign quantified NPs the abstract type $(NP→S)→S$. This means that they have the f-type $(ff)f$: of functions that assign a phonetic entity to any function from phonetic entities to phonetic entities. Accordingly, determiners like *some* and *every* are assigned the abstract type $N→((NP→S)→S)$, of functions from nouns to quantified NPs, with the corresponding concrete types: $f((ff)f)$ and $(et)((et)t)$. The s-type is the same as in Chapter 4. The s-denotations are also the same as in Chapter 4. For instance, the s-denotation of the sign EVERY is as in (5.55) below.

(5.55) $\text{EVERY}_{(et)((et)t)} = \lambda A_{et}.\lambda B_{et}.A^* \subseteq B^*$

Now, the f-denotation of the sign EVERY is assumed to be the following function:

$$(5.56) \quad \text{every}_{f((ff)f)} = \lambda y_f.\lambda P_{ff}. P(every \cdot y)$$

In words: this is the function mapping any phonetic entity y (of a noun) to an $(ff)f$ function that lets every ff function of an intransitive verb apply to the correct $every \cdot y$ phonetic entity. To illustrate that, let us consider how the f-denotation of the sentence *every student ran* is analyzed, with the function $\text{run} = \lambda x_f.x \cdot ran$ as the f-denotation of the verb:

$$(5.57) \quad (\text{every}(\text{student}))(\text{run})$$
$$= ((\lambda y_f.\lambda P_{ff}. P(every \cdot y))(student))(\lambda x_f.x \cdot ran)$$
$$= (\lambda P_{ff}.P(every \cdot student))(\lambda x_f.x \cdot ran)$$
$$= (\lambda x_f.x \cdot ran)(every \cdot student)$$
$$= every \cdot student \cdot ran$$

Relative pronouns like *that* are treated as functions from intransitive verbs (NP→S) to noun modifiers (N→N). For instance, consider the following sentence.

(5.58) Every student that ran smiled.

In the noun phrase *every student that ran*, the relative pronoun *that* is assumed to map the intransitive verb *ran* to a clause *that ran*. This clause is treated as a modifier that takes the sign of the noun *man* and maps it to the sign corresponding to the expression *student that ran*. To do that, the relative pronoun provides the functional f-denotation of the verb *run* with an identity element ϵ. This application of the function $\lambda y_f. y \cdot ran$ to the ϵ derives the string $\epsilon \cdot ran$, i.e. the simple phonetic entity *ran*. In this way, the relative pronoun *that* "strips" the phonetic entity that lies at the core of the function $\lambda y_f. y \cdot ran$, and allows it to appear without any representation for a subject. The abstract-level and f-level derivations for sentence (5.58) are given in Figure 5.2. Note the details of our use of ϵ when the f-components of the relative pronoun *that* and the verb *run* combine with each other. The $(ff)(ff)$ function for *that* takes the ff argument for *run* and applies it to ϵ. The result is the concatenation $\epsilon \cdot ran$, i.e. the phonetic entity *ran*. This result is concatenated following the phonetic entity *that*, and hence the ff function for the relative *that ran* is

Table 5.3: Sign-based lexicon.

Sign	Abstract type	F-denotation	S-denotation
TINA	NP	$tina$	$\mathbf{tina}_e$
MARY	NP	$mary$	$\mathbf{mary}_e$
STUDENT	N	$student$	$\mathbf{student}_{et}$
TEACHER	N	$teacher$	$\mathbf{teacher}_{et}$
SMILE	NP $\rightarrow$ S	$\lambda y_f.\, y \cdot smiled$	$\mathbf{smile}_{et}$
RUN	NP $\rightarrow$ S	$\lambda y_f.\, y \cdot ran$	$\mathbf{run}_{et}$
PRAISE	NP $\rightarrow$ (NP $\rightarrow$ S)	$\lambda x_f.\lambda y_f.\, y \cdot praised \cdot x$	$\mathbf{praise}_{e(et)}$
SOME	N $\rightarrow$ ((NP $\rightarrow$ S) $\rightarrow$ S)	$\lambda y_f.\lambda P_{ff}.\, P(some \cdot y)$	SOME$_{(et)((et)t)}$
THAT	(NP $\rightarrow$ S) $\rightarrow$ (N $\rightarrow$ N)	$\lambda P_{ff}.\lambda y_f.$ $y \cdot that \cdot P(\epsilon)$	THAT$_{(et)((et)(et))}$

$\lambda y_f.\, y \cdot that \cdot ran$: the function that sends every phonetic entity y to its concatenation with the phonetic entity $that \cdot ran$. When this function applies to the phonetic entity man we get the string $man \cdot that \cdot ran$ When applying the f-denotation for the determiner $every$ as in (5.56) to this phonetic entity, we derive the right linear order for the sentence. We see here that the thematic subject argument of the verb ran in sentence (5.58) is only *understood* by spelling out the semantic analysis of the sentence: it is the student entities that are being quantified over. However, the abstract analysis of the sentence has no trace for such a subject: the pheno-level component within the sign for the relative pronoun $that$ makes sure that the 'subject requirement' of the verb ran is trivially satisfied by providing the ff function for ran with a dummy argument. This stands in contrast to theories of *syntactic movement* in the generative tradition, which implement dummy arguments as syntactic items, which furthermore contribute to the semantic derivation.

Table 5.3 summarizes some of the signs we have used so far, and some similar ones. Reconsider now sentences (5.11) and (5.14), restated below.

(5.59) a. Some teacher that praised Mary smiled.

  b. Some teacher that Mary praised smiled.

Using the lexicon of Table 5.3, we give the abstract-level analysis of sentences (5.59a) and (5.59b) in Figure 5.3. The derivation of the

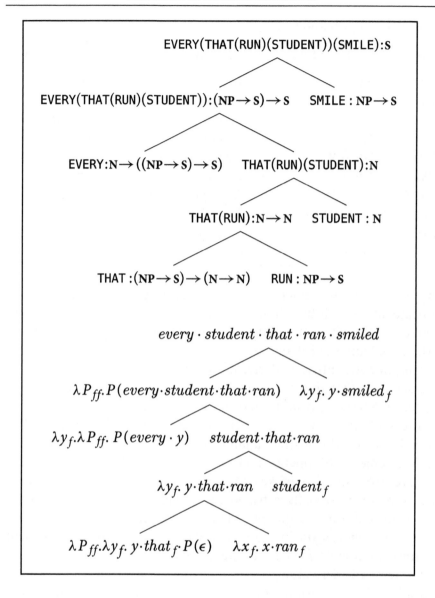

Figure 5.2 Every student that ran smiled – *abstract derivation and f-derivation.*

s-denotations is the same as in our analyses (5.13) and (5.21). However, these s-denotations are within two different derived signs. One sign, for sentence (5.59a), is derived by directly applying the sign PRAISE to the sign MARY. This leads to an f-denotation containing the phonetic entity *praised · mary*. By contrast, sentence (5.59b) is analyzed by letting hypothetical reasoning combine the signs PRAISE and MARY, as in (5.52). This leads to an f-denotation containing the phonetic entity *mary · praised*. We see that the difference between sentences (5.59a) and (5.59b) is analyzed as a local derivational difference: in our sign-based system the string in (5.59a) can only be derived by letting the sign for *Mary* fill in the first argument of the verb's sign. This means that the first *semantic* argument of the verb must also be filled in by the semantic entity for *Mary*. The opposite situation is with the string in (5.59b), which can only be coupled with an s-denotation where the second semantic argument of the verb is filled in by the semantic denotation of *Mary*. However, after the sign for *praised Mary* or *praised Mary* is derived, the rest of the derivation for the two sentences is identical.

You are now advised to solve Exercises 4, 5, 6 and 7 at the end of this chapter.

As we saw in our analysis (5.44) of the sentence *Tina praised every student* (=(5.43)), the Lambek-Van Benthem Calculus helps dealing with quantified NPs in object position. As we see in Exercise 4, this generalizes to our ACG use of the Lambek-Van Benthem Calculus for manipulating signs. The way ACG deals with quantifier NPs in object position also accounts for an additional property of sentences with multiple NPs: the appearance of certain ambiguities that may be associated with different "scopal" relations between quantifiers. Consider for instance the following two sentences.

(5.60) a. Some teacher praised every student.

   b. Every student praised some teacher.

So far we have not analyzed such sentences with two NPs that are treated as generalized quantifiers. In some cases like this, a well-known fact is that speakers may experience a sort of ambiguity known as *scope ambiguity*. For instance, sentence (5.60a) may be considered true if there is one teacher who praised all the students. However, the sentence may also be considered true if no such teacher exists, as long as every student was praised by some or other teacher. The first interpretation is often the preferred one, and it is called the *object narrow scope* reading of sentence (5.60a). The latter interpretation, which in (5.60a) is also possible, is known as the sentence's *object wide scope*

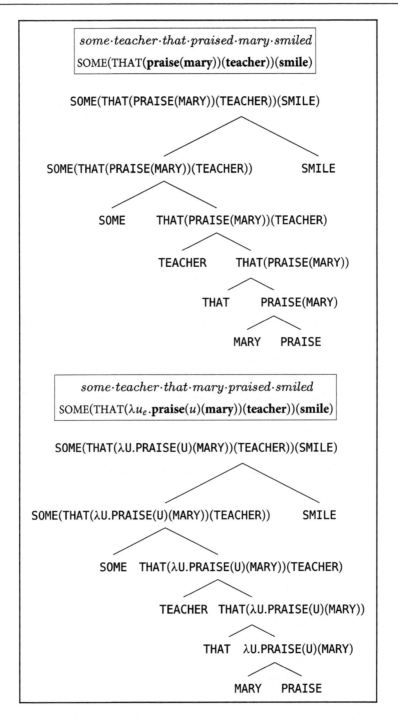

Figure 5.3   Abstract-level analysis of relative clauses.

reading. As we shall see below, our ACG framework describes both kinds of interpretations for sentences as in (5.60) containing multiple quantified NPs.

To see how the ACG framework treats sentences as in (5.60), consider first the two possibilities in which the sign EVERY(STUDENT) can combine with the verb sign PRAISE:

(5.61) a. λ V. EVERY(STUDENT)(λ U. PRAISE(U)(V))

      b. λ U. EVERY(STUDENT)(λ V. PRAISE(U)(V))

In (5.61a) the place-holder U is discharged before the NP sign combines with the verb sign. This place-holder is the first argument of the verb sign, hence it corresponds to the verb's *object* slot. Accordingly, the abstract derivation in (5.61a) leads to the following f-denotation, with the string *every student* occupying the object position.

(5.62) $\lambda v_f.\text{every}(\text{student})(\lambda u_f.\text{praise}(u)(v))$
$= \lambda v_f.(\lambda z_f.\lambda P_{ff}.P(every\cdot z))(student)$
    $(\lambda u_f.(\lambda x_f.\lambda y_f.\, y\cdot praised\cdot x)(u)(v))$
$= \lambda v.(\lambda P.P(every\cdot student))(\lambda u.(\lambda x.\lambda y.y\cdot praised\cdot x)(u)(v))$
$= \lambda v.(\lambda P.P(every\cdot student))(\lambda u.v\cdot praised\cdot u)$
$= \lambda v.(\lambda u.v\cdot praised\cdot u)(every\cdot student)$
$= \lambda v.v\cdot praised\cdot every\cdot student$

By contrast, in (5.61b) the place-holder first discharged is V, corresponding to the verb's *subject* slot. Accordingly, the abstract derivation in (5.61b) leads to the following f-denotation, with *every student* occupying the subject position.

(5.63) $\lambda u_f.\text{every}(\text{student})(\lambda v_f.\text{praise}(u)(v))$
$= \lambda u_f.(\lambda z_f.\lambda P_{ff}.P(every\cdot z))(student)$
    $(\lambda v_f.(\lambda x_f.\lambda y_f.\, y\cdot praised\cdot x)(u)(v))$
$= \lambda u.(\lambda P.P(every\cdot student))(\lambda v.(\lambda x.\lambda y.y\cdot praised\cdot x)(u)(v))$
$= \lambda u.(\lambda P.P(every\cdot student))(\lambda v.v\cdot praised\cdot u)$
$= \lambda u.(\lambda v.v\cdot praised\cdot u)(every\cdot student)$
$= \lambda u.every\cdot student\cdot praised\cdot u$

The derivations in (5.62) and (5.63) are embedded in the two sign derivations on the left-hand side of Figure 5.4 below, which encode derivations of sentences (5.60a) and (5.60b), respectively. What we see here is that in our ACG framework, the order in which signs combine does not uniquely determiner linear order relations within the derived string. In both (5.61a) and (5.61b) the sign for *every student* combines with the sign for the verb before the sign for *some teacher* combines with the result. But these two derivations yield different strings.

The converse is also true: different orders in which signs combine may yield the same string. Specifically, the two topmost derivations in Figure 5.4 both derive the string of sentence (5.60a). Despite the different orders in which the NP signs combine with the verb signs, both derivations let the two NPs fill in the same argument of the verb sign. Accordingly, in both derivations the sign for *some teacher* is analyzed as the subject, and the sign for *every student* is analyzed as the object. By contrast, the different orders in which the subject and object signs are combined with the verb affect the truth-value that is derived for sentence (5.60a). When the object sign is the first to combine with the verb, we get the value in (5.64a) below. By contrast, when the subject sign combines first with the verb, we get (5.64b).

(5.64) a. $\text{SOME}(\textbf{teacher})(\lambda v_e.\text{EVERY}(\textbf{student})(\lambda u_e.\textbf{praise}(u)(v)))$

      b. $\text{EVERY}(\textbf{student})(\lambda u_e.\text{SOME}(\textbf{teacher})(\lambda v_e.\textbf{praise}(u)(v)))$

By spelling out the denotations SOME and EVERY, we get the following equivalence with (5.64a).

(5.65) $\text{SOME}(\textbf{teacher})(\lambda v_e.\text{EVERY}(\textbf{student})(\lambda u_e.\textbf{praise}(u)(v))) = 1$

    $\Leftrightarrow \textbf{teacher}^* \cap (\lambda v_e.\text{EVERY}(\textbf{student})(\lambda u_e.\textbf{praise}(u)(v)))^* \neq \emptyset$

    $\Leftrightarrow \textbf{teacher}^* \cap (\lambda v_e.\textbf{student}^* \subseteq (\lambda u_e.\textbf{praise}(u)(v))^*)^* \neq \emptyset$

    $\Leftrightarrow \textbf{teacher}^*$
    $\cap \{v \in E : \textbf{student}^* \subseteq \{u \in E : \textbf{praise}(u)(v) = 1\}\} \neq \emptyset$

    In words: *there is a teacher v s.t. for every student u, v praised u.*

In a similar way we get the following equivalence with (5.64b).

(5.66) $\text{EVERY}(\textbf{student})(\lambda u_e.\text{SOME}(\textbf{teacher})(\lambda v_e.\textbf{praise}(u)(v))) = 1$

    $\Leftrightarrow \textbf{student}^* \subseteq \{u \in E : \textbf{teacher}^* \cap \{v \in E : \textbf{praise}(u)(v) = 1\}\}$

    In words: *for every student u there is a teacher v s.t. v praised u.*

In sum, we have seen that the string *some teacher praised every student* (=(5.60a)) can be derived with the two signs derived at the top of Figure 5.4, each of which is assigned a different truth-value: (5.65) and (5.66) respectively. According to speaker intuitions about scope ambiguity, this is a desirable result: the first analysis reflects the object narrow scope reading of sentence (5.60a), while the latter reflects its object wide scope reading.

Empirical questions about scope ambiguity are quite complex, and we cannot cover them here in any detail. It suffices to make two remarks. For some cases, e.g. *every student praised some teacher* (=(5.60b)), it has been claimed that the object wide scope analysis would be spurious, since it does not have direct semantic evidence. This is because the object wide scope analysis is logically stronger in this case than the object narrow scope analysis. Therefore, in contrast with sentence (5.60a), the object wide scope analysis does not add to the situations covered by the object narrow scope analysis. This point does not falsify our ACG ambiguity analysis, but it makes it harder to support it in many cases. Furthermore, in other cases, it was pointed out that the multitude of possible scope relations in the ACG analysis would clearly overgenerate. Consider a sentence like the following.

(5.67) Some student who admires no teacher worships a detective who caught every thief.

Only a few of the twenty-four scope relations between the four quantifiers in (5.67) can be empirically demonstrated. However, without further restrictions, our ACG analysis would generate all of them. The restrictions on scope mechanisms as embodied in our ACG treatment have been the subject of much empirical research in linguistics. For some references see the further reading at the end of this chapter.

Let us take stock. As we see in Figure 5.4, in the ACG framework there are two separate issues concerning the composition of signs in simple transitive sentences:

- The argument of the verb sign that is abstracted over before the NP sign combines with it.
- The order in which the NP signs combine with the verb sign.

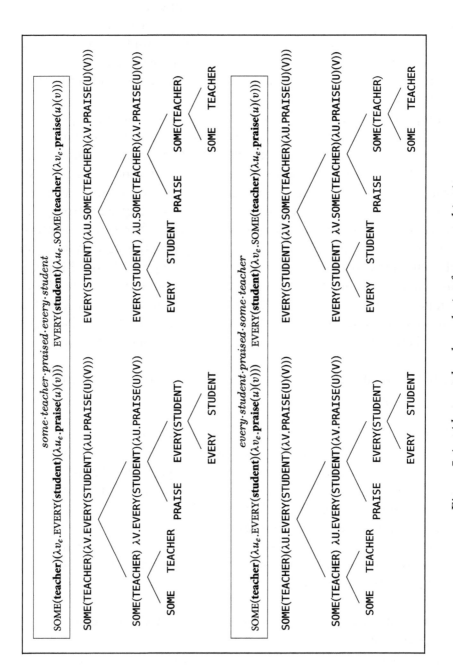

Figure 5.4 Abstract-level analysis of scope ambiguity.

The order of abstraction determines the subject/object analysis of noun phrases; the order of combination determines the scope relations between them. 'Scope ambiguity' of a string ensues when that same string can be derived with different orders of sign combinations.

FURTHER READING

Introductory: On hypothetical reasoning and natural deduction see Barker-Plummer et al. (2011, ch. 8). On positive and comparative adjectives see Lassiter (2015). On the Lambek-Van Benthem Calculus see Carpenter (1997, ch. 5). On de Saussure's life and work see Joseph (2012). On ACG see course notes at ACG (2015).

Advanced: On natural deduction see Prawitz (1965), and, for a historical overview, Pelletier (2000). On positive and comparative adjectives see Klein (1980); Kennedy (2007). The Lambek Calculus was introduced in Lambek (1958), and interpreted in Van Benthem (1986, 1991). For extensive introductions to categorial grammars see Moortgat (2011); Steedman (1997); Moot and Retoré (2012). De Saussure's best-known discussion of signs is in De Saussure (1959). The distinction between tectogrammatics and phenogrammatics was introduced in Curry (1961). Other precursors of the ACG approach are Keenan (1989); Morrill (1994); Oehrle (1994). The ACG framework was proposed by De Groote (2001). Similar approaches were developed in Muskens (2003); Kracht (2003).

EXERCISES (ADVANCED: 2, 6, 7)

1. Consider the following entailments.
   (i) Every man is mortal $\Rightarrow$ If John is a man then John is mortal
   (ii) No man is immortal $\Rightarrow$ If John is a man then John is not immortal
   (iii) Some man is tall $\Rightarrow$ If every man is thin then some man is tall and thin

   a. For entailment (i) find an entailment (i') and develop a line of hypothetical reasoning to justify (i) using (i'). Mimic the way (5.27) is used to justify (5.26) in (5.31).
   b. Repeat the same for (ii) and (iii).

c. Based on your answers for 1a and 1b, complete the following empirical hypothesis about entailments with conditionals in their consequent: the entailment $S_1 \Rightarrow$ *If S_2 then S_3* holds if and only if the entailment _____ holds.

2. Give three more entailments with a conditional in their consequent, similar to (i)–(iii) in Exercise 1. You may base your answers on Boolean operators and generalized quantifiers, discussed in Chapters 3 and 4.

3. For the analysis of the sentence *Tina and every man ran* (=(4.80), page 131), we assume that *Tina* is of type e. For the other words, we assume the same types as in Chapter 4: $\text{AND}^{(et)t}$, $\text{EVERY}_{(et)((et)t)}$, **man**$_{et}$ and **run**$_{et}$. Show that using hypothetical reasoning, we can combine these types and denotations into a derivation with the same results as in (4.80). What is your conclusion about the type lifting operator of (4.77) (page 129)?

4. From the signs TINA, EVERY(STUDENT) and PRAISE, there are two possible strings that we can derive using the Lambek-Van Ben-them Calculus: (i) *tina · praised · every · student* and (ii) *every · student · praised · tina*.

a. Show an abstract-level derivation that leads to string (i), the corresponding derivation of the concrete f-denotation, and the s-denotation associated with it. You can use the derivations in (5.44) and (5.45).

b. Repeat the same for string (ii).

5. Using the lexicon of Table 5.3, show a derivation tree for the following sentence:
(i) *Mary praised some teacher.*
Show that in any model, the derived s-denotations of (i) and sentence (5.59b) (*some teacher that Mary praised smiled*) satisfy: $[\![(5.59b)]\!] \leq [\![(i)]\!]$. Thus, the TCC explains the entailment (5.59b)$\Rightarrow$(i).

6. a. Define the sign BELIEVE. Using this sign and the lexicon of Table 5.3, analyze the following sentences:
(*i*) Tina believes Mary ran.
(*ii*) Some teacher that Tina believes Mary praised ran.
For each sentence give the abstract derivation and the derived f- and s-denotations.

   b. Repeat the same for the sentence *Mary praised some teacher that Tina believes Mary praised.*

7. Verbs like *believe* and *tell* may be followed by the word *that*, in a use that is different than its appearance in relative clauses. By assuming lexical ambiguity of *that*, we analyze the sentences:

   (i) Tina told Mary some story
  (ii) Tina told Mary that some teacher ran
 (iii) Tina told some student that Mary praised some story.

   a. Define the sign TELL that allows us to derive (i) using the lexicon of Table 5.3.
   b. Define new signs for TELL and THAT that also allow us to derive (ii).
   c. Using the three signs you defined, show two abstract derivations for (iii), and the s-denotations they lead to. One s-denotation should explain the entailment from (iii) to "what Tina told some student is that Mary praised some story". The other s-denotation should explain the entailment from (iii) to "what Tina told some student who was praised by Mary is some story".

SOLUTIONS TO EXERCISES

1. a. (i') is the entailment *Every man is mortal and John is a man* $\Rightarrow$ *John is mortal* (Exercise 10 in Chapter 4). The line of inference is:

$$\cfrac{\cfrac{\text{Every man is mortal} \quad [\text{John is a man}]^1}{\text{John is mortal}} \; (i')+\text{MP}}{\text{If John is a man then John is mortal}} \; \text{discharge hypothesis 1}$$

   c. S_1 and $S_2 \Rightarrow S_3$

3. Before composing the entity $\mathbf{tina}_e$ further, we lift it into an $(et)t$ quantifier as follows:

$$\cfrac{\cfrac{\mathbf{tina}_e \quad [P_{et}]^1}{P_{et}(\mathbf{tina})} \; \text{FA}}{\lambda P_{et}.P(\mathbf{tina})} \; \text{discharge hypothesis 1}$$

The rest of the semantic derivation is as in (4.80). The type lifting operator is derived as a corollary of the Lambek-Van Benthem Calculus.

4. See Figure 5.5 for abstract-level derivations. The concrete derivations of the f-denotations are:

(i) $(\lambda v_f.(\text{every}(\text{student})))(\lambda u_f.\text{praise}(u)(v)))(\text{tina})$

$= (\lambda v_f.((\lambda y_f.\lambda P_{ff}.\ P(every\cdot y))(\ student))$
$\quad (\lambda u_f.(\lambda x_f.\lambda y_f.\ y\cdot praised\cdot x)(u)(v)))(tina)$

$= (\lambda v_f.(\lambda P_{ff}.P(every\cdot student))(\lambda u_f.(\lambda x_f.\lambda y_f.\ y\cdot praised\cdot x)(u)$
$\quad (v)))(tina)$

$= (\lambda v_f.(\lambda P_{ff}.P(every\cdot student))(\lambda u_f.v\cdot praised\cdot u))(tina)$

$= (\lambda v_f.v\cdot praised\cdot every\cdot student)(tina)$

$= tina\cdot praised\cdot every\cdot student$

(ii) $(\text{every}(\text{student}))(\text{praise}(\text{tina}))$

$= (\lambda P_{ff}.P(every\cdot student))((\lambda x_f.\lambda y_f.\ y\cdot praised\cdot x)(tina))$

$= (\lambda P_{ff}.P(every\cdot student))(\lambda y.y\cdot praised\cdot tina)$

$= every\cdot student\cdot praised\cdot tina$

5. By substituting the denotations of SOME and THAT in the s-denotation derived on the right-hand side of Figure 5.3, we get:
SOME(THAT($\lambda u_e.\textbf{praise}(u)(\textbf{mary})$)($\textbf{teacher}$))($\textbf{smile}$)$=1$
$\Leftrightarrow (\lambda u_e.\textbf{praise}(u)(\textbf{mary}))^* \cap \textbf{teacher}^* \cap \textbf{smile}^* \neq \emptyset$
$\Rightarrow (\lambda u_e.\textbf{praise}(u)(\textbf{mary}))^* \cap \textbf{teacher}^* \neq \emptyset$
$\Leftrightarrow$ SOME($\textbf{teacher}$)($\lambda u_e.\textbf{praise}(u)(\textbf{mary})$)$=1$.
The last s-denotation is the one derived for the abstract-level sign SOME(TEACHER)(λ U. PRAISE(U)(MARY)), whose f-denotation is the string for *Mary praised some teacher*.

6. a. BELIEVE : S$\rightarrow$(NP$\rightarrow$S) $= \langle \lambda x_f.\lambda y_f.y\cdot believes\cdot x ,\ \textbf{believe}_{t(et)}\rangle$
For the abstract analysis of (i) see Figure 5.6a.
Concrete f-denotation of sentence (i):
believe$_{f(ff)}$(run$_{ff}$(mary$_f$))(tina$_f$)
$= (\lambda x_f.\lambda y_f.y\cdot believes\cdot x)((\lambda z_f.z\cdot ran)(mary))(tina)$
$= tina\cdot believes\cdot mary\cdot ran$

Concrete s-denotation of sentence (i):
$\textbf{believe}_{t(et)}(\textbf{run}_{et}(\textbf{mary}_e))(\textbf{tina}_e)$

For the abstract analysis of (ii) see Figure 5.6b (cf. (5.40)).
Concrete f-denotation of embedded clause in (ii):
$\lambda u_f.$believe$_{f(ff)}$(praise$_{f(ff)}$(u)(mary$_f$))(tina$_f$)
$= \lambda u.(\lambda x_f.\lambda y_f.y\cdot believes\cdot x)((\lambda z_f.\lambda v_f.v\cdot praised\cdot z)(u)(mary))$
$\quad (tina)$
$= \lambda u.(\lambda x_f.\lambda y_f.y\cdot believes\cdot x)(mary\cdot praised\cdot u)(tina)$
$= \lambda u.tina\cdot believes\cdot mary\cdot praised\cdot u$

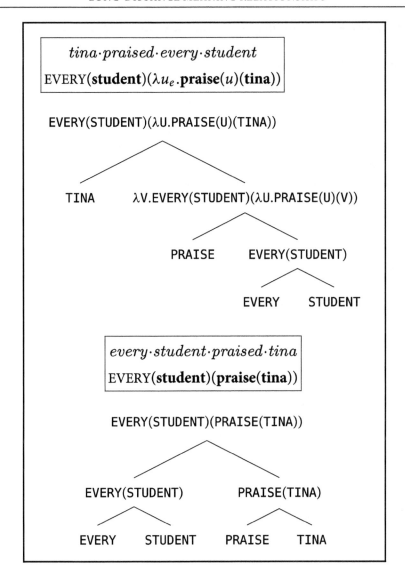

Figure 5.5 Abstract-level analysis with a quantificational noun phrase.

Concrete f-denotation of sentence (ii):

$\text{some}_{f((ff)f)}(\text{that}_{(ff)(ff)}(\lambda u_f.\text{believe}_{f(ff)}(\text{praise}_{f(ff)}(u)(\text{mary}_f))$
$(\text{tina}_f))(\text{teacher}_f))(\text{run}_{ff})$

$= \text{some}_{f((ff)f)}(\text{that}_{(ff)(ff)}(\lambda u_f.\,tina \cdot believes \cdot mary \cdot praised \cdot u)$
$(\text{teacher}_f))(\text{run}_{ff})$

$= (\lambda x_f.\lambda P_{ff}.\ P(some{\cdot}x))((\ \lambda P_{ff}.\lambda y_f.\ y{\cdot}that{\cdot}P(\epsilon))(\lambda u_f.tina \cdot$
$believes \cdot mary \cdot praised \cdot u)(teacher))(\lambda z_f.\ z{\cdot}ran)$

$= (\lambda x_f.\lambda P_{ff}.\ P(some{\cdot}x))(\lambda y_f.y \cdot that \cdot tina \cdot believes \cdot mary \cdot$
$praised(teacher))(\lambda z_f.\ z{\cdot}ran)$

$= some \cdot teacher \cdot that \cdot tina \cdot believes \cdot mary \cdot praised \cdot ran$

Concrete s-denotation of sentence (ii):

$\text{SOME}_{(et)((et)t)}(\text{THAT}_{(et)(et)}(\lambda u_e.\mathbf{believe}_{t(et)}(\mathbf{praise}_{e(et)}(u)(\mathbf{mary}_e))$
$(\mathbf{tina}_e))(\mathbf{teacher}_{et}))(\mathbf{run}_{et})$

$= \mathbf{teacher}^* \cap \{u \in E : \mathbf{believe}(\mathbf{praise}(u)(\mathbf{mary}))(\mathbf{tina}) = 1\}$
$\cap\, \mathbf{run}^* \neq \emptyset \quad (\text{cf. } (5.42))$

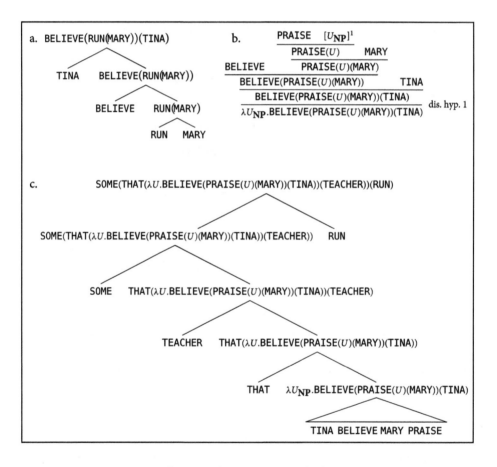

Figure 5.6   *Abstract derivations with the verb* believe.

7. a. TELL : $\mathbf{NP} \to (\mathbf{NP} \to (\mathbf{NP} \to \mathbf{S})) = \langle \lambda x_f . \lambda y_f . \lambda z_f . z \cdot told \cdot x \cdot y ,$
$\mathbf{tell}_{e(e(et))} \rangle$

b. TELL_1 : $\mathbf{NP} \to (\mathbf{S} \to (\mathbf{NP} \to \mathbf{S})) = \langle \lambda x_f . \lambda y_f . \lambda z_f . z \cdot told \cdot x \cdot y ,$
$\mathbf{tell}_{1e(t(et))} \rangle$

THAT_1 : $\mathbf{S} \to \mathbf{S} = \langle \lambda x_f . that \cdot x , \ \lambda x_t . x \rangle$

c. The derived s-denotations are:
SOME$(\lambda z . \mathbf{student}(z) \wedge \mathbf{praise}(z)(\mathbf{mary}))(\lambda x . \mathrm{SOME}(\mathbf{story})$
$(\lambda y . \mathbf{tell}(x)(y)(\mathbf{tina})))$
SOME$(\mathbf{student})(\lambda x . \mathrm{SOME}(\mathbf{story})$
$(\lambda y . \mathbf{tell}_1(x)(\mathbf{praise}(y)(\mathbf{mary}))(\mathbf{tina})))$

CHAPTER 6

INTENSIONALITY AND POSSIBLE WORLDS

This chapter deals with expressions that refer to attitudes, beliefs or possibilities, which we lump together under the title intensional expressions. *The 'psychological' aspects of these expressions systematically challenge the system that we developed in the previous chapters. To address these challenges we add to our models a domain of possible worlds. Denotations involving possible worlds are used as a basic account of intensional expressions. We illustrate systematic ambiguities that appear with these expressions, known as* de dicto/de re *ambiguities, and show that the ACG mechanism of the previous chapter readily treats them as instances of scope ambiguity.*

Language is a rich instrument for discussing psychological aspects of life. All natural languages have means for expressing knowledge, beliefs, wishes, doubts, misunderstandings and errors. We refer to expressions that invoke such concepts as *intensional expressions*. This chapter characterizes some important semantic properties of such expressions and the way they interact with entailments in natural language. When studying entailment with intensional expressions, we will first realize that such expressions systematically block entailment patterns that are otherwise valid with the expressions that we have treated so far. Accordingly, the entailment patterns that we study in this chapter distinguish pre-theoretically between the intensional expressions and other expressions that have so far been treated in this book. Because of their special inferential behavior, intensional expressions reveal a problem for semantic systems like the one we have developed so far, which are based on the basic types e and t. The system we develop in this chapter is based on our system from Chapters 2–5, but it also deals with intensional expressions. To overcome the limitations of our system so far, we will add to it semantic entities known as *possible worlds* or *indices*. The mapping from non-intensional semantics to possible world semantics is pleasantly regular, and involves no new mathematical concepts. This gives us an immediate account of a puzzle that systematically appears with intensional sentences: the problem known as their *de dicto/de re* interpretations. Following our treatment in Chapter 5, we straightforwardly treat such interpretations as manifestations of scope ambiguities.

PUZZLES ABOUT INTENSIONAL EXPRESSIONS

One intensional verb that we encountered in Chapter 5 is the verb *believe*. As we saw, this verb allows embedding sentences within one another, as in the following simple example.

(6.1) John [believes [Mary smiled]].

In structure (6.1), the simple sentence *Mary smiled* is embedded within the belief sentence as a sister of the verb *believe*. Given this structure, it is natural to assume that the verb *believe* operates like a transitive verb, where its 'object' argument in (6.1) is the embedded sentence *Mary smiled*. Under this treatment, the denotation for the verb *believe* in (6.1) takes the truth-value for the embedded sentence *Mary smiled* as its first argument. Its second argument is the entity denoted by the subject *John*. Accordingly, we may let the verb *believe* have the semantic type $t(et)$. This would lead to the following denotation for sentence (6.1).

(6.2) **believe**$_{t(et)}$(**smile**$_{et}$(**mary**$_e$))(**john**$_e$)

From a compositional and type-theoretical point of view, this treatment is perfectly sensible. However, in terms of the denotation it leads to, the analysis in (6.2) does not correctly capture the semantic behavior of sentence (6.1).

To see the problem, suppose that in a given model M the denotation (6.2) of sentence (6.1) is the truth-value 1. Now let let us consider another sentence, where we replace the embedded sentence *Mary smiled* in (6.1) with another sentence, *Tina danced*. This gives us sentence (6.3) below.

(6.3) John [believes [Tina danced]].

Now suppose that in the same model M that we consider, both sentences *Mary smiled* and *Tina danced* have the truth-value 1. In sum, we get:

(6.4) (i) **believe(smile(mary))(john)** = 1, and

     (ii) **smile(mary)** = **dance(tina)** = 1

Now consider what happens when we replace the value **smile(mary)** in the left-hand side of (6.4)(i) (=(6.2)) with the value **dance(tina)**. Because of assumption (6.4)(ii), this replacement does not change the value of (6.4)(i), which remains 1. Thus, in M we get the following denotation of sentence (6.3).

(6.5) **believe(dance(tina))(john)** = 1.

We conclude that any model M that satisfies (6.4)(i) and (6.4)(ii) also satisfies (6.5). This leads us to expect the conjunction in (6.6a) below to entail sentence (6.6b) (=(6.3)).

(6.6) a. Mary smiled, and Tina danced, and John believes Mary smiled.

     b. John believes Tina danced.

This expectation is in conflict with linguistic intuitions. As a matter of fact, there is no entailment from sentence (6.6a) to (6.6b): John may believe that Mary smiled without believing that Tina danced. The factual assertion 'Mary smiled, and Tina danced' in (6.6a) does not change John's beliefs about the state of things. We see that our tentative treatment of belief sentences is problematic: it incorrectly expects an entailment in (6.6).

The problem for our analysis of the belief sentences (6.1) and (6.3) appears when their embedded sentences happen to denote the same truth-value. Let us see another example where this happens. Consider the following sentences.

(6.7) a. John believes Lewis Carroll wrote *Alice*.

     b. John believes Charles Lutwidge Dodgson wrote *Alice*.

Historically, the names *Lewis Carroll* and *Charles Lutwidge Dodgson* referred to the same person (*Lewis Carroll* was the pseudonym of C. L. Dodgson). However, John need not know that, and as a result there is no entailment from (6.7a) to (6.7b). Moreover, there is no such entailment even if we add the following (historically correct) statement.

(6.8) Lewis Carroll is Charles Lutwidge Dodgson.

Analyzing sentence (6.8), let us use the notations **lc** and **cld** for the entity denotations of the respective names. We assume that sentence (6.8) denotes 1 precisely in the models that satisfy the identity statement **lc** = **cld**. This usage of the verb *be* is referred to as *be of identity* (see Exercise 9, Chapter 3). We distinguish such usages of *be* from the use we have so far seen in sentences like *Tina is tall*, which is known as *be of predication*.

Speaking in precise terms about entailment, we can now observe that the conjunction of sentences (6.8) and (6.7a) does not entail (6.7b). Although sentence (6.8) is historically true, John may not know that. Therefore, we may truthfully assert the conjunction of (6.8) and (6.7a), since John may (correctly) believe that Lewis Carroll wrote *Alice*, but John may still not believe that C. L. Dodgson wrote *Alice*. For instance, John may think that Carroll and Dodgson were two different people, or he may not know Carroll's other name. He may even fail to know that *Lewis Carroll* was a pseudonym. In all these cases, common linguistic intuitions show us that no entailment holds from the conjunction of sentences (6.8) and (6.7a) to sentence (6.7b). This is problematic for our tentative treatment of the verb *believe*, which does expect such an entailment. To see the problem, consider any model M where both sentences (6.8) and (6.7a) denote 1. Because (6.8) denotes 1 in M, the denotations **lc** and **cld** are the same entity in M. As a result, the sentences *L. C. wrote 'Alice'* and *C. L. D. wrote 'Alice'* have the same denotation in M. Consequently, the denotations of the belief sentences (6.7a) and (6.7b) must also be equal in M. This means that according to the TCC, our analysis might expect sentences (6.8) and (6.7a) to entail (6.7b), contrary to fact.

Before moving on, let us make two remarks. First, entailments often appear under name replacement when the sentences in question do not involve any intensional verb. For instance, consider the following entailment, which is intuitively valid.

(6.9) Lewis Carroll is Charles Lutwidge Dodgson, and Lewis Carroll
wrote *Alice*
⇒ Charles Lutwidge Dodgson wrote *Alice*.

When we use a non-intensional verb *write* as in (6.9), name replacement intuitively supports the entailment: if Carroll and Dodgson are the same person then Dodgson must have written any book that Carroll did. With our analysis of identity statements, we account for such entailments as a matter of course: as we saw, in any model where the entities **lc** and **cld** are the same, the sentences *L. C. wrote 'Alice'* and *C. L. D. wrote 'Alice'* are assigned the same denotation. This accounts for entailment (6.9) according to the TCC. The entailment in (6.9) is in contrast to what we have seen with the intensional verb *believe* in (6.7). The conclusion is that empirically, name replacement gives us a way to distinguish verbs like *write* from intensional verbs like *believe*. Theoretically, at this stage we are only able to account for the entailment with the former, but not for the lack thereof with the latter.

A second remark that should be made about name replacement is that the linguistic point of our examples above with Carroll and Dodgson is independent of the actual literary facts. We looked at this famous case just because it helps clarify linguistic intuitions about identity sentences. However, our semantic theory is free to contain many models that diverge from the historical facts, i.e. models that *falsify* the statement that Carroll is Dodgson. In such models the two sentences *L. C. wrote 'Alice'* and *C. L. D. wrote 'Alice'* may have different truth-values. This does not affect the validity of our account of the entailment in (6.9): in such 'non-historical' models the antecedent of (6.9) denotes 0, and the TCC is trivially met. Thus, we should view the validity of entailment (6.9) as a linguistic fact, independent of historical facts about the author of *Alice*. A similar entailment would intuitively hold, and be similarly explained, if we replaced the two occurrences of *Charles Lutwidge Dodgson* in (6.9) with *Arnold Schwarzenegger*.

With these two points in mind, let us recapitulate. When we are given an identity statement between two names, substituting one name for another supports the entailment in (6.9), but a similar replacement does not support an entailment in (6.7). Our analysis so far correctly expects the former entailment, but it is also at risk of erroneously expecting an entailment in the latter case. The problem lies in our assumption that the denotation of the verb *believe* applies to a truth-value argument. Intuitively, this assumption leads to problems, because it means that in any model M, John is expected to either believe all sentences that happen to have the same truth-value in M, or disbelieve all of them. However, in reality, when two sentences A and B are assumed to be true, it does not follow that asserting the sentence *John believes A* supports the conclusion *John believes B*. This is an important feature of our ability to talk about other people's mental states, which are always incomplete, and often in disagreement with ours. Because of such disagreements between what is asserted by one agent and what is believed by other agents, our tentative treatment of the verb *believe* empirically fails. This kind of failure is our main challenge in this chapter.

Throughout our discussion above, we have recurrently appealed to a simple *substitution* property of compositional model-theoretic semantics. Suppose that S_1 is a sentence in which an expression exp_1 occurs as a constituent, and let S_2 be the sentence obtained from S_1 by replacing this occurrence of exp_1 with another expression exp_2. Suppose now that in a given model M the expressions exp_1 and exp_2 have the same denotation. As a result the respective sentences S_1 and S_2 also have the same denotation in M. This is a basic property of our framework, and so far we have seen nothing wrong with it. For instance, the correct treatment of entailment (6.9) directly follows from this substitution property. However, the same substitution property leads to unwelcome results with our tentative analysis of the verb *believe*. We refer to this failure by saying that the verb *believe* creates an *intensional context*. For reasons we will discuss later, such intensional environments are also called 'opaque contexts'. As we will see, the problems we have with the intensional context created by the verb *believe* reappear with many other intensional expressions. As we have noted, there is a distinction between intensional belief contexts and simpler cases such as (6.9) above, where the substitution property has desirable results in our current system. For this reason, we informally say that the expression *wrote 'Alice'* in (6.9) is *extensional*, and that it creates an *extensional context*, or a 'transparent' context.

Many other verbs besides the verb *believe* concern mental states. All of these verbs create intensional contexts, and we refer to all of them as *intensional verbs*. Some further examples are given below.

(6.10) **Intensional verbs**: *know, wish, doubt, hope, fear, think, say, discover, want, demand, expect.*

Because it illustrates some major problems of intensionality in natural language, the verb *believe* will be our primary example. However, before moving on to our treatment of this intensional verb, let us see some other examples of intensional expressions, and contrast them with extensional expressions. In all the examples below we use the following premise.

(6.11) Every pianist is a composer, and every composer is a pianist.

Based on our treatment in previous chapters, we know that in every model where the conjunctive sentence (6.11) denotes 1, the nouns *pianist* and *composer* have the same *et* denotation. This allows us to substitute *composer* for *pianist*, or vice versa, as a test for intensionality. Below we examine some contexts as extensional or intensional based on this substitution test.

Example 1. Consider the following two sentences.

(6.12) a. John is looking for a pianist.
         b. John is looking for a composer.

Even when assuming (6.11), sentence (6.12a) does not entail sentence (6.12b): John may be looking for a pianist without being aware that the pianists are the composers. We conclude that the expression *look for* creates an intensional context. Like the verb *believe*, the expression *look for* involves a personal attitude. By contrast, consider the following sentences.

(6.13) a. John is talking to a pianist.
         b. John is talking to a composer.

Here, (6.13a) together with (6.11) do entail sentence (6.13b). Accordingly, we say that the expression *talk to* is extensional.

Example 2. Now consider the following examples.

(6.14) a. Tina is an alleged pianist.
       b. Tina is an alleged composer.

(6.15) a. Tina is a Russian pianist.
       b. Tina is a Russian composer.

In (6.14), from the premise that Tina is an alleged pianist it does not follow that she is an alleged composer, even under the assumption that the composers and the pianists are the same. Thus, we classify the adjective *alleged* as intensional. This is in line with the fact that, like the verbs *believe* and *look for*, this adjective reflects a personal attitude. By contrast, in (6.15) we see that under assumption (6.11), sentence (6.15a) entails (6.15b). This means that the adjective *Russian* in (6.15) is classified as extensional.

Example 3. For another intensionality/extensionality contrast consider the following example.

(6.16) a. In Tina's dream, some pianist is playing.
       b. In Tina's dream, some composer is playing.

(6.17) a. In Tina's room, some pianist is playing.
       b. In Tina's room, some composer is playing.

In (6.16) there is no entailment from (6.16a) to (6.16b): Tina's dream may have pianists that are not composers even under the premise in (6.11). This shows that *in Tina's dream* is an intensional expression, as may be expected from its psychological character. By contrast, with the assumption (6.11), sentence (6.17a) does entail (6.17b). This qualifies *in Tina's room* as an extensional expression.

To sum up, based on our substitution test, we have characterized the following intensional expressions and extensional expressions.

(6.18) **Intensional expressions:** *believe, look for, alleged, in Tina's dream.*
        Extensional expressions: *wrote 'Alice', talk to, Russian, in Tina's room.*

As we saw, intensional expressions and extensional expressions are systematically different in their inferential behavior. This is the main phenomenon we would like to account for in our possible world semantics.

You are now advised to solve Exercise 1 at the end of this chapter.

EXTENSIONS, INTENSIONS AND POSSIBLE WORLDS

A major problem with intensionality appears in our system because we treat sentences as denoting truth-values. As we have seen, truth-values are not rich enough as denotations for embedded sentences appearing as arguments of intensional verbs like *believe*. To overcome this problem, we now change our view on sentence denotations. We introduce a notion of 'possible worlds', and associate sentences with *sets* of such 'worlds'. Intuitively, we will associate every sentence with the set of possible worlds that 'make it true'. Models that contain objects that stand for possible worlds are referred to as *intensional models*. They are contrasted with models like those we have used so far, which are known as *extensional models*. More technically speaking, we view possible worlds, or *indices*, as a special sort of entities. As with *e*-type entities, we do not make special assumptions about what indices are. We simply assume a new basic type *s* for indices, together with the corresponding domain D_s. In intensional models, the domain of indices D_s is allowed to be any non-empty set. Sentences like *Mary smiled* or *Tina danced* are assigned the type *st*. Thus, sentences denote *functions from indices to truth-values*. Such functions characterize sets of indices, and we refer to them as *propositions*. Under this treatment, the first argument of the verb *believe* in sentences like *John believes Mary smiled* is a proposition rather than a truth-value. This will allow us to solve the puzzle we are facing with belief sentences.

To derive *st* propositions as sentence denotations we need to change the types of some lexical entries. A simple way to do that in a sentence like *Mary smiled* is to assume that the verb *smile* denotes a function of type $e(st)$: a function from entities to propositions. Such functions are also known as *one-place properties*. Using $e(st)$ functions, we treat denotations of simple sentences like *Mary smiled* as follows.

(6.19) **smile**$_{e(st)}$(**mary**$_e$)

    = the proposition (*st* function) obtained by applying the one-place property **smile** (an $e(st)$ function) to the entity **mary**.

Similarly, transitive verbs like *praise* will now denote $e(e(st))$ functions, which are referred to as *two-place properties*. These functions come instead of the two-place predicates of type $e(et)$ that we have used so far. The denotations of simple sentences like *Tina praised Mary* are analyzed as follows.

(6.20) $\mathbf{praise}_{e(e(st))}(\mathbf{mary}_e)(\mathbf{tina}_e)$

= the proposition (st function) obtained by applying the two-place property $\mathbf{praise}$ (an $e(e(st))$ function) to the entities $\mathbf{mary}$ and $\mathbf{tina}$.

The move from truth-values to propositions invokes a global type change in our system: from n-place predicates to n-place properties. However, in many ways this move is innocuous, since it allows us to retain all our analyses from previous chapters. To see an example, consider the following entailment.

(6.21) a. Tina danced and Mary smiled
        b. ⇒ Mary smiled.

Assuming that sentences denote propositions, or sets of indices, we let the sentential conjunction *and* in (6.21a) denote the intersection function between sets of indices. In lambda notation, this amounts to the following definition.

(6.22) $\text{AND}^{st} \overset{def}{=} \lambda\varphi_{st}.\lambda\psi_{st}.\lambda i_s.\text{AND}^t(\varphi(i))(\psi(i))$

$$= \lambda\varphi_{st}.\lambda\psi_{st}.\lambda i_s.\psi(i) \wedge \varphi(i)$$

In words: the function AND^{st} maps any two propositions φ and ψ to the proposition $\lambda i.\psi(i) \wedge \varphi(i)$, which is expressed in terms of the extensional propositional conjunction. This function characterizes the intersection of the set of indices that φ and ψ characterize. With the property denotations $\mathbf{dance}_{e(st)}$ and $\mathbf{smile}_{e(st)}$, this leads to the following analysis of sentence (6.21a).

(6.23) $\text{AND}^{st}(\mathbf{smile}_{e(st)}(\mathbf{mary}_e))(\mathbf{dance}_{e(st)}(\mathbf{tina}_e))$

$= \lambda i_s.\mathbf{dance}(\mathbf{tina})(i) \wedge \mathbf{smile}(\mathbf{mary})(i)$

In words, proposition (6.23) sends every index i to 1 whenever both propositions **dance(tina)** and **smile(mary)** send i to 1. Alternatively, we may view the two conjoined propositions in (6.23) as the sets of indices that they characterize: **dance(tina)*** and **smile(mary)***. Under this convention, the proposition defined in (6.23) characterizes the intersection between these sets, as formalized in (6.24) below.

(6.24) **dance(tina)*** $\cap$ **smile(mary)***

As a matter of set theory, the intersection in (6.24) is a subset of the set of indices that the proposition **smile(mary)*** characterizes. In a formula:

(6.25) **dance(tina)*** $\cap$ **smile(mary)*** $\subseteq$ **smile(mary)***

Since (6.25) holds in any intensional model, it accounts for the entailment (6.21). In previous chapters, we used the TCC for explaining entailments like (6.21) as following from the less-or-equal relation $\leq$ between truth-values (see Chapter 2, page 21). Now, when sentences denote propositions, we restate the TCC using the subset relation between sets of indices. This is explicitly stated below.

An *intensional semantic theory* T *satisfies the* **truth-conditionality criterion** *(TCC^I) for sentences* S_1 *and* S_2 *if the following two conditions are equivalent:*

(I)   *Sentence* S_1 *intuitively entails sentence* S_2.

(II) *For all models* M *in* T: $([[S_1]]^M)^* \subseteq ([[S_2]]^M)^*$.

For convenience, we henceforth keep using the term 'TCC' when referring to the intensional version TCC^I of this principle. The notation TCC^E is used when referring to the extensional system of Chapter 3. With this intensional version of the TCC, we keep the essence of our analysis of entailments so far, while letting sentences denote propositions instead of truth-values.

Let us now reconsider belief sentences like *John believes Mary smiled*. Such complex sentences have the same syntactic distribution as simpler sentences, i.e. they occur in the same syntactic environments where simpler sentences occur. For instance, consider the following examples.

(6.26)   a.   Mary smiled, and John believes Mary smiled.

       b.   Mary smiled, or John believes Mary smiled.

(6.27)   Tina believes [John believes [Mary smiled]].

Sentences (6.26a–b) involve a sentential conjunction/disjunction between a simple sentence and a complex sentence. In sentence (6.27), we see a complex belief sentence (*John believes Mary smiled*) embedded within another belief sentence. In this sense, the sentence *John believes Mary smiled* behaves like the simple sentence *Mary smiled* within it. Cases like (6.26a–b) and (6.27) are easy to treat if complex sentences and simple sentences have the same type. Thus, we let complex belief sentences like *John believes Mary smiled* denote propositions, just like simple sentences. Accordingly, we let the verb *believe* denote a function of type $(st)(e(st))$: a function from propositions to one-place properties. The function **believe** sends any proposition φ to a one-place property **believe**(φ). This property sends any entity x to the proposition **believe**$(\varphi)(x)$ ("x believes that φ holds"). For instance, sentence (6.28a) below denotes the proposition in (6.28b).

(6.28)   a.   John believes Mary smiled.

       b.   **believe**$_{(st)(e(st))}$(**smile**$_{e(st)}$(**mary**$_e$))(**john**$_e$)

The "doubly embedded" sentence in (6.27) is analyzed as having the following denotation.

(6.29)   **believe(believe(smile(mary))(john))(tina)**

In (6.29), the 'belief proposition' (6.28b) is itself an argument of a **believe** function. The resulting property applies to the entity **tina** and returns a proposition.

   With this treatment of the verb *believe*, we can get back to analyzing the non-entailment in (6.6), which is restated below.

(6.30)   Mary smiled, and Tina danced, and John believes Mary smiled
      $\not\Rightarrow$ John believes Tina danced.

With our original, 'extensional' system, sentences denoted truth-values, and the TCC incorrectly expected an entailment in (6.30). Now, with our intensional system, we would like to verify that our intensional version of the TCC does not expect an entailment in (6.30). Thus, we would like to find a model where the subset relation does not hold between the propositions denoted by the sentences in (6.30). Formally, we look for a model that makes the following hold.

(6.31) $\textbf{smile}_{e(st)}(\textbf{mary})^* \cap \textbf{dance}_{e(st)}(\textbf{tina})^* \cap$

  $(\textbf{believe}(\textbf{smile}(\textbf{mary}))(\textbf{john}))^*$

  $\not\subseteq (\textbf{believe}(\textbf{dance}(\textbf{tina}))(\textbf{john}))^*$

Intuitively, in our intensional system, the inequality in (6.31) may hold because the propositions for the sentences *Mary smiled* and *Tina danced* may be different, and then John may stand in the relation *believe* to one of them but not to the other. Accordingly, the proposition denotations of the sentences *John believes Mary smiled* and *John believes Tina smiled* may be different, and specifically they may block the subset relation in (6.31). To see a concrete example, consider a model that only contains two indices, w_1 and w_2, and where the following requirements hold.

(6.32) a. In w_1 Mary smiles, and in w_2 she does not.
   b. In both w_1 and w_2, Tina dances.
   c. In both w_1 and w_2, John believes the proposition for "Mary smiled".
   d. In w_2 John believes the proposition for "Tina danced", and in w_1 he does not.

From this description we conclude that the antecedent of (6.30) holds in w_1 but the consequent does not. This accounts for the lack of entailment in (6.30). More formally, we make the following assumptions about the denotations of the verbs *smile*, *dance* and *believe*.

(6.33) a. $\textbf{smile}(m)^* = \{w_1\}$
   b. $\textbf{dance}(t)^* = \{w_1, w_2\}$
   c. $(\textbf{believe}(\mathcal{X}_{\{w_1\}})(j))^* = \{w_1, w_2\}$
   d. $(\textbf{believe}(\mathcal{X}_{\{w_1, w_2\}})(j))^* = \{w_2\}$

The entities m, t and j in (6.33) are the given denotations in M for *Mary*, *Tina* and *John*. In words, (6.33a–b) define the propositions in M for the sentences *Mary smiled* and *Tina danced*: the one-place property **smile** maps m to the proposition $X_{\{w_1\}}$ characterizing the singleton set $\{w_1\}$; the property **dance** maps t to the proposition $X_{\{w_1,w_2\}}$ characterizing the doubleton set $\{w_1, w_2\}$. For each of these two propositions, the denotation **believe** returns a different one-place property: **believe**$(X_{\{w_1\}})$ and **believe**$(X_{\{w_1,w_2\}})$ respectively, which we denote P_1 and P_2. In (6.33c–d) we define P_1 and P_2 for the argument j: when P_1 applies to j, it returns the proposition characterizing the set $\{w_1, w_2\}$; when P_2 applies to j, the result characterizes the set $\{w_2\}$.

When substituting the definitions from (6.33) in (6.31), we get the following inequality, as we anticipated:

$$\{w_1\} \cap \{w_1, w_2\} \cap \{w_1, w_2\} \nsubseteq \{w_2\}$$

In words, when intersecting the sets of indices associated with the conjuncts of the antecedent in (6.30), we get the set $\{w_1\} \cap \{w_1, w_2\} \cap \{w_1, w_2\}$, i.e. the singleton $\{w_1\}$. However, the set of indices for the consequent of (6.30) is the singleton $\{w_2\}$. This means that in the intensional model we have defined, the proposition for the antecedent in (6.30) does not characterize a subset of the set of indices characterized by the consequent's denotation. Thus, according to our intensional version of the TCC, this model accounts for the lack of entailment in (6.30).

We have seen that in natural language two different sentences may be asserted, and yet an agent like John may be reasonably claimed to believe one of them but not the other one. Intensional models make it possible to analyze such belief assertions correctly. This is because denotations of verbs like *believe* apply to propositions denoted by sentences rather than to their truth-values. This distinction between propositions and truth-values is highlighted by the following terminological convention.

> Let S be a sentence denoting a proposition φ in a model M. Let w be an index in M. The proposition φ is called the **intension** of S in M, whereas the truth-value $\varphi(w)$ is called S's **extension** in M relative to w.

For instance, in the model described in (6.32), the intension of the sentence *Mary smiled* is the function sending the index w_1 to 1 and the index w_2 to 0. We say that relative to w_1, the sentence's extension in this model is 1, and relative to w_2 it is 0. The st intension of the sentence *Tina danced* in the same model sends both indices w_1 and w_2 to 1. This proposition is different from the intension for *Mary smiled*. However, relative to the index w_1 the extension of the two sentences is the same: the truth-value 1. In more philosophical terms, originally due to Gottlob Frege, we say the that an intension represents the *sense* (German: *Sinn*) of a sentence, a 'global' aspect of its meaning. By contrast, a truth-value extension is sometimes called the *reference* (German: *Bedeutung*) of a sentence in a given situation. The reference of an expression is viewed as somewhat 'incidental', since we can only derive it from the sense when we are given a specific situation.

The distinction between intensions (senses) and extensions (references) of language expressions is quite general in intensional semantics. For instance, in our example above we let the verb *smile* denote a property of type $e(st)$: a function from entities to propositions. Given the property $\mathbf{smile}_{e(st)}$ and an index w, we define the extension of the verb *smile* in w. This is the et function that is denoted $\mathbf{smile}^w_{e(st)}$, as defined below.

(6.34) $\mathbf{smile}^w_{e(st)} = \lambda x_e.\mathbf{smile}(x)(w)$

In words: $\mathbf{smile}^w_{e(st)}$ is the et function that holds of any entity x for which the index w is in the set of indices characterized by the proposition $\mathbf{smile}(x)$. For instance, suppose that for our model M above, we have the following full definition of the $e(st)$ property $\mathbf{smile}$, defined for each of the three entities in the D_e domain.

(6.35) $(\mathbf{smile}(m))^* = \{w_1\}$ (as in (6.33a))
$\qquad (\mathbf{smile}(t))^* = \{w_2\}$
$\qquad (\mathbf{smile}(j))^* = \{w_1, w_2\}$

With this definition of the one-place property $\mathbf{smile}$, we get the following extensions relative to each of the two indices w_1 and w_2.

(6.36) $(\mathbf{smile}^{w_1})^* = \{m, j\}$
$\qquad (\mathbf{smile}^{w_2})^* = \{t, j\}$

In words: given the property intension in (6.35), the corresponding *et* extension of *smile* relative to the index w_1 characterizes the set of entities {m, j}. This is because w_1 is sent to 1 by both propositions **smile**(m) and **smile**(j), but not by **smile**(t). Similarly, relative to w_2, the *et* extension of *smile* characterizes the set of entities {t, j}. In this way, we get an *et* extension for the property relative to each index. In general, we define this extension as follows.

(6.37) For any one-place property P of type $e(st)$, the *extension of P* relative to an index w is the *et* function $P^w = \lambda x_e.P(x)(w)$.

You are now advised to solve Exercise 2 at the end of this chapter.

The intuitive distinction between extensional and intensional aspects of meaning is also useful when we come back to the puzzle evoked by John's different beliefs about Lewis Carroll and C. L. Dodgson. Reconsider the sentences in (6.7). As we saw, these sentences do not support an entailment from sentence (6.38a) below to sentence (6.38b).

(6.38) a. Lewis Carroll is Charles Lutwidge Dodgson, and John believes Lewis Carroll wrote *Alice*.

b. John believes Charles Lutwidge Dodgson wrote *Alice*.

The puzzle here is how to make the identity statement *Carroll is Dodgson* hold, without forcing John to have identical beliefs about the two names. To solve this puzzle, we can again use the distinction between extension and intension, but here with respect to the meaning of names. Statements like *Carroll is Dodgson* in (6.38a) are analyzed as only requiring identity between the *extensions* of the two names in a given index. Such identity statements allow the names' intensions to remain different. In (6.38a), John's beliefs about Carroll are analyzed as being about the intension of that name. Thus, if the intensions of the names *Carroll* and *Dodgson* are different, John's beliefs about the two names may be different even when the two names have the same extension.

In more technical terms, we now view *e*-type entities as extensional meanings of names. The name's intensional denotation in a model will now be a *function from indices to entities*. We refer to such *se* functions as *individual concepts*, or *i-concepts* for short. For example, in a model M with $D_e = \{a, b\}$ and $D_s = \{w_1, w_2\}$, let us assume the following i-concept denotations for the names *Carroll* and *Dodgson*.

(6.39) $[\![Lewis\ Carroll]\!]^M = \mathbf{lc}_{se} = w_1 \mapsto a\ \ w_2 \mapsto a$
$\quad\quad [\![C.\ L.\ Dodgson]\!]^M = \mathbf{cld}_{se} = w_1 \mapsto a\ \ w_2 \mapsto b$

The i-concepts **lc** and **cld** both map w_1 to the entity a. However, **lc** and **cld** map w_2 to different entities – a and b, respectively. Because of that, **lc** and **cld** are different intensions, although their extension in w_1 is the same.

Now let us go back to the identity statement *Carroll is Dodgson*. Like all sentences in our intensional system, this sentence denotes a proposition, i.e. a function of type st. In the model described in (6.39) we want this 'identity proposition' to map the index w_1 to 1, since the extensions of the two names in w_1 are the same. By contrast, for the index w_2 we want it to return 0, since the two names have different extensions in w_2. More generally, we want the sentence *Carroll is Dodgson* to denote the proposition that holds of an index i when the extensions $\mathbf{lc}(i)$ and $\mathbf{cld}(i)$ are the same. To obtain that, we define the following operator as the denotation of the copula *be* in identity statements.

(6.40) $\text{IS}^I_{id} = \lambda x_{se}.\lambda y_{se}.\lambda i_s.y(i) = x(i)$

In words, the function IS^I_{id} (intensional *be* of identity) applies to two i-concepts x and y, and returns the proposition characterizing the set of indices i where $x(i)$ and $y(i)$ are the same. For instance, for sentence (6.41a) below (=(6.8)) we get the analysis in (6.41b).

(6.41) a. Lewis Carroll is Charles Lutwidge Dodgson.

b. $\text{IS}^I_{id}(\mathbf{cld}_{se})(\mathbf{lc}_{se})$
$\quad = \lambda i_s.\mathbf{lc}(i) = \mathbf{cld}(i)$

Given the model we assumed in (6.39), the function $\text{IS}^I_{id}(\mathbf{cld})(\mathbf{lc})$ is the function $[w_1 \mapsto 1\ \ w_2 \mapsto 0]$, i.e. the proposition characterizing the singleton $\{w_1\}$.

To analyze simple sentences like *Carroll wrote 'Alice'*, we now have to make sure that the denotation of the predicate *wrote 'Alice'* can apply to i-concepts. To this end, properties of type $e(st)$ should be lifted to functions of type $(se)(st)$. Specifically, we lift the property **write_Alice**$_{e(st)}$ to the following $(se)(st)$ function.

(6.42) $\textbf{write\_Alice}^I_{(se)(st)} = \lambda x_{se}.\lambda i_s.\textbf{write\_Alice}_{e(st)}(x(i))(i)$

In words, the function **write_Alice**^{I} maps every i-concept x to the proposition characterizing all the indices i that satisfy the following requirement: the extension of the property **write_Alice** in i holds of x's extension in i. This definition captures the 'extensional' behavior of predicates like *wrote 'Alice'*, which we observed in entailment (6.9) above. It guarantees that in order to know if the sentence *Carroll wrote 'Alice'* is true in a given index i, we do not need to consider the whole intension of the name *Carroll*. Whether the sentence is true in a given index i only depends on the *extensions* that the name *Carroll* and the verb phrase *wrote 'Alice'* have in i. Because of that, if another name, say *Dodgson*, has the same extension in i as the name *Carroll*, then the two sentences *Dodgson wrote 'Alice'* and *Carroll wrote 'Alice'* will have the same truth-value in i. Formally, we account for entailment (6.9) as follows.

(6.43) [[*Lewis Carroll is Charles Lutwidge Dodgson, and Lewis*

     Carroll wrote Alice]]*

$= (\text{IS}^I_{id}(\textbf{cld}_{se})(\textbf{lc}_{se}))^* \cap (\textbf{write\_Alice}^I_{(se)(st)}(\textbf{lc}))^*$

                             ▷ compositional analysis

$= (\lambda i_s.\textbf{lc}(i) = \textbf{cld}(i))^* \cap (\lambda i_s.\textbf{write\_Alice}_{e(st)}(\textbf{lc}(i))(i))^*$

                          ▷ def. IS^I_{id} and **write_Alice**^{I}

$= (\lambda i_s.\textbf{lc}(i) = \textbf{cld}(i) \wedge \textbf{write\_Alice}_{e(st)}(\textbf{lc}(i))(i))^*$

           ▷ characteristic function (Exercise 12d, Chapter 3)

$= (\lambda i_s.\textbf{lc}(i) = \textbf{cld}(i) \wedge \textbf{write\_Alice}_{e(st)}(\textbf{cld}(i))(i))^*$

                       ▷ substitute $\textbf{cld}(i)$ for $\textbf{lc}(i)$

$\subseteq (\lambda i_s.\textbf{write\_Alice}_{e(st)}(\textbf{cld}(i))(i))^*$ ▷ trivially

$= (\textbf{write\_Alice}^I_{(se)(st)}(\textbf{cld}))^*$ ▷ def. **write_Alice**^{I}

$= [[$*Charles Lutwidge Dodgson wrote* Alice$]]^*$

                            ▷ compositional analysis

We conclude that in every model the following relation holds:

[[*Lewis Carroll is Charles Lutwidge Dodgson, and Lewis Carroll wrote 'Alice'*]]*
     $\subseteq$ [[*Charles Lutwidge Dodgson wrote 'Alice'*]]*.

This account of the entailment (6.9) stems from the identity that the operator $\textsc{is}^I_{id}$ imposes on the extensions of the names *Carroll* and *Dodgson* in the indices where the antecedent holds. Our definition (6.42) makes sure that the denotation of the predicate *wrote 'Alice'* is only sensitive to the extensional aspects of its argument, and hence we preserve identity between the extensions of the sentences *Carroll wrote 'Alice'* and *Dodgson wrote 'Alice'*.

You are now advised to solve Exercise 3 at the end of this chapter.

As we saw, the intensions of the names *Carroll* and *Dodgson* may be different even when their extensions are the same. In such situations, the sentences *Carroll wrote 'Alice'* and *Dodgson wrote 'Alice'* may have different intensions. When analyzing belief sentences containing these simple sentences, we let the verb *believe* denote a function that takes the *intension* of the embedded sentence as its argument. It follows that the belief sentences *John believes Carroll wrote 'Alice'* and *John believes Dodgson wrote 'Alice'* may have different extensions even in indices where the the names *Carroll* and *Lewis*, and hence the two embedded sentences, have the same extension. Formally, this means that we expect the following inequality to hold in some intensional model.

(6.44) $(\textsc{is}^I_{id}(\mathbf{cld}_{se})(\mathbf{lc}_{se}))^* \cap$

      $(\mathbf{believe}_{(st)(e(st))}(\mathbf{write\_Alice}^I_{(se)(st)}(\mathbf{lc}))(\mathbf{john}))^*$

      $\nsubseteq (\mathbf{believe}(\mathbf{write\_Alice}^I_{(se)(st)}(\mathbf{cld}))(\mathbf{john}))^*$

This will account for the lack of entailment in (6.38). Let us show a model that satisfies the inequality in (6.44).

Readers who prefer to avoid the technical details of this model may skip to the section "Intensionality and grammar architecture" on page 211.

CONSTRUCTING A MODEL THAT ACCOUNTS FOR THE
NON-ENTAILMENT (6.38A)$\not\Rightarrow$(6.38B)

We would like to see an intensional model where the inequality in (6.44) holds. This inequality involves three propositions, i.e. characteristic functions of sets of indices. In (6.45) below we denote these three sets A, B and C.

$$(6.45) \quad A = (\text{IS}^I_{id}(\textbf{cld}_{se})(\textbf{lc}_{se}))^*$$
$$B = (\textbf{believe}(\textbf{write\_Alice}^I_{(se)(st)}(\textbf{lc}))(\textbf{john}))^*$$
$$C = (\textbf{believe}(\textbf{write\_Alice}^I_{(se)(st)}(\textbf{cld}))(\textbf{john}))^*$$

To support the inequality in (6.44), we need to find a model with an index w_1 that is in A and in B but not in C. The model that we will show is based on the model that we constructed in (6.39) above for the two i-concepts **lc** and **cld**. To have a separate denotation for the name *John* we add an entity j to D_e. Thus, we construct a model M with the following basic domains:

$$D_e = \{a, b, j\} \qquad D_s = \{w_1, w_2\}$$

Reusing the two i-concepts **lc** and **cld** from (6.39), we have in M:

$$(6.46) \quad \textbf{lc}_{se} = w_1 \mapsto a \ \ w_2 \mapsto a$$
$$\textbf{cld}_{se} = w_1 \mapsto a \ \ w_2 \mapsto b$$

Because the index w_1 is the only index in the model where these i-concepts agree on their extension, we know that the identity proposition A in (6.45) equals $\{w_1\}$ in M. We want to make sure that w_1 is in B but not in C. To obtain that, we want the index w_1 to make the entity **john** stand in the relation **believe** to the proposition **write_Alice**^{I}(**lc**), but not to the proposition **write_Alice**^{I}(**cld**). Obviously, this can only happen if we make sure that these two propositions are different. This is not hard to do, since the i-concepts **lc** and **cld** are different. All we have to do is to make sure that the denotation of the expression *wrote 'Alice'* sends these two i-concepts to different propositions. We defined the intensional denotation **write_Alice**$^I_{(se)(st)}$ of this expression on the basis of the property **write_Alice** of type $e(st)$. Thus, in order to define **write_Alice**^{I} in the model M, we need to define the property **write_Alice**. We want the denotation **write_Alice**^{I} to map each of the i-concepts **lc** and **cld** to a different proposition. Therefore, we will use a property **write_Alice** that maps each of the extensions in w_2 of **lc** and **cld** – the entities a and b, respectively – to a different proposition. One way to do that is to impose the following requirements on the property **write_Alice**.

$$(6.47) \quad \textbf{write\_Alice}_{e(st)}(a)(w_1) = 1 \quad \textbf{write\_Alice}_{e(st)}(a)(w_2) = 1$$
$$\textbf{write\_Alice}_{e(st)}(b)(w_1) = 0 \quad \textbf{write\_Alice}_{e(st)}(b)(w_2) = 0$$

In words: the property **write_Alice** holds of the entity a in both indices but does not hold of the entity b in either index. Recall that in the index w_2, we have $\textbf{lc}(w_2) = a$ and $\textbf{cld}(w_2) = b$. Due to this fact, the definition of the function **write_Alice**^{I} as derived from **write_Alice** makes w_2 be in the proposition **write_Alice**^{I}(**lc**) but not in **write_Alice**^{I}(**cld**). In a formula, we have the following facts about these two propositions.

$(6.48) \ (\textbf{write\_Alice}^I_{(se)(st)}(\textbf{lc}))$

$$= \lambda i_s.\textbf{write\_Alice}_{e(st)}(\textbf{lc}(i))(i)$$
$$\qquad\qquad\qquad\qquad \triangleright \text{ by def. } \textbf{write\_Alice}^I \ (6.42)$$

$$= \begin{bmatrix} w_1 \mapsto \textbf{write\_Alice}_{e(st)}(\textbf{lc}(w_1))(w_1) \\ w_2 \mapsto \textbf{write\_Alice}_{e(st)}(\textbf{lc}(w_2))(w_2) \end{bmatrix}$$
$$\qquad\qquad\qquad\qquad \triangleright D_s = \{w_1, w_2\} \text{ in } M$$

$$= \begin{bmatrix} w_1 \mapsto \textbf{write\_Alice}_{e(st)}(a)(w_1) \\ w_2 \mapsto \textbf{write\_Alice}_{e(st)}(a)(w_2) \end{bmatrix}$$
$$\qquad\qquad\qquad\qquad \triangleright \text{ by denotation } \textbf{lc} \ (6.46)$$

$$= \begin{bmatrix} w_1 \mapsto 1 \\ w_2 \mapsto 1 \end{bmatrix} \qquad \triangleright \text{ by denotation } \textbf{write\_Alice} \ (6.47)$$

$(6.49) \ (\textbf{write\_Alice}^I_{(se)(st)}(\textbf{cld}))$

$$= \begin{bmatrix} w_1 \mapsto \textbf{write\_Alice}_{e(st)}(\textbf{cld}(w_1))(w_1) \\ w_2 \mapsto \textbf{write\_Alice}_{e(st)}(\textbf{cld}(w_2))(w_2) \end{bmatrix}$$
$$\qquad\qquad\qquad\qquad \triangleright \text{ as above}$$

$$= \begin{bmatrix} w_1 \mapsto \textbf{write\_Alice}_{e(st)}(a)(w_1) \\ w_2 \mapsto \textbf{write\_Alice}_{e(st)}(b)(w_2) \end{bmatrix}$$
$$\qquad\qquad\qquad\qquad \triangleright \text{ by denotation } \textbf{cld} \ (6.46)$$

$$= \begin{bmatrix} w_1 \mapsto 1 \\ w_2 \mapsto 0 \end{bmatrix} \qquad \triangleright \text{ by denotation } \textbf{write\_Alice} \ (6.47)$$

Taking stock, we see that we have constructed a model where the difference between the i-concepts **lc** and **cld** leads us to different propositions for the sentences *L. C. wrote 'Alice'* and *C. L. D. wrote 'Alice'*. The former proposition is $\chi_{\{w_1, w_2\}}$, the characteristic function of the set $\{w_1, w_2\}$. The latter proposition is $\chi_{\{w_1\}}$, the characteristic function of the singleton set $\{w_1\}$. All that is left now is to require that for the index w_1, the entity for *John* stands in the *believe* relation to $\chi_{\{w_1, w_2\}}$ but not to $\chi_{\{w_1\}}$. This will guarantee that w_1 is in the set B but not in the set C in (6.45) above. Formally, we assume that the denotation **believe**$_{(st)(e(st))}$ satisfies the following.

(6.50) $(\textbf{believe}(\chi_{\{w_1, w_2\}})(j))^* \quad = \{w_1, w_2\}$
$(\textbf{believe}(\chi_{\{w_1\}})(j))^* \quad\;\; = \emptyset$

In words: we assume that in both w_1 and w_2, the relation **believe** holds between John and the proposition $\chi_{\{w_1, w_2\}}$. By contrast, in both w_1 and w_2, **believe** does *not* hold between John and the proposition $\chi_{\{w_1\}}$. Concluding, we have shown a model M where the following holds:

(6.51) $w_1 \in A = (\text{IS}^I_{id}(\textbf{cld}_{se})(\textbf{lc}_{se}))^* = \{w_1\}$

$w_1 \in B = (\textbf{believe}(\textbf{write\_Alice}^I(\textbf{lc}))(\textbf{john}))^*$
$= (\textbf{believe}(\chi_{\{w_1, w_2\}})(j))^* = \{w_1, w_2\}$

$w_1 \notin C = (\textbf{believe}(\textbf{write\_Alice}^I(\textbf{cld}))(\textbf{john}))^*$
$= (\textbf{believe}(\chi_{\{w_1\}})(j))^* = \emptyset$

We conclude that our intensional system correctly expects there not to be an entailment from sentence (6.38a) to sentence (6.38b).

INTENSIONALITY AND GRAMMAR ARCHITECTURE

When looking back on the intensional accounts we have developed so far, we see that they contain two global type changes from previous chapters. One type change involves changing the type of sentences from t (truth-values) to st (propositions). Accordingly, we systematically replaced truth-values by propositions in the complex types for other syntactic categories as well. For instance, since intransitive verbs lead to a sentence when they combine with a referential NP, we changed their type from et (one-place predicates) to $e(st)$ (one-place properties). The 'propositional' type change from t to st is critical in all possible world accounts of intensionality. Another type change that we used handles the intensions of names, and it was based on changing their type from e (entities) to se (i-concepts). This also entailed a global type change in our system. For instance, when using i-concepts, we change the type of intransitive verbs to $(se)(st)$ of properties ranging over i-concepts.

We see that using types st and se instead of t and e for sentences and names invokes a global type change that affects the analysis of many other expressions. In terms of the ACG framework of Chapter 5, we regard such global type changes as modifications of the semantic types associated with *basic abstract types*. Specifically, since we view sentences as signs of abstract type S, we associate this type with the s-type st of propositions. Similarly, when using i-concepts, we associate referential noun phrases of type NP with type se. As soon as s-types for basic abstract types are changed in this way, the s-types for complex abstract types are automatically modified as well. For instance, an intransitive verb of abstract type NP→S will now have the type $e(st)$ when i-concepts are not used, or $(se)(st)$ when they are. We refer to this kind of global type change as *intensionalization*. Table 6.1 summarizes the effects of the 'propositional' type change on the S-types associated with the basic abstract types of Table 5.1 (Chapter 5, page 168).Table 6.2 illustrates how this type change affects the S-types of complex abstract types (cf. Table 5.2, page 173).

Table 6.1 only employs the propositional type change. Here we have not changed the s-type assigned to the abstract type NP, which remains e as in our extensional system. This means that ACG lexicons based on Tables 6.1 and 6.2 cannot make use of i-concepts. Our avoidance of i-concepts is here for the sake of exposition, but there have also been substantial reasons suggested for avoiding i-concepts in intensional semantics (see further reading).

When introducing global type changes as in Tables 6.1 and 6.2, we need to define the changes that ensue in the denotations of lexical items. For instance, in our treatment above we assumed that the property denotations of verbs like *smile* and *praise* are arbitrary, like their extensional parallels. By contrast, the denotation of sentential *and* was changed in (6.22) to be the intersection function between propositions. Unlike the intensionalized denotations of extensional verbs, this denotation of *and* is not arbitrary, but logical

Table 6.1: Basic abstract types and their propositional intensionalization.

Abstract type		F-type	S-type (extensional)	S-type (intensional)	Remark
NP	noun phrase	f	e	e	no use of i-concepts here
S	sentence	f	t	st	
A	adjective	f	et	$e(st)$	
N	noun	f	et	$e(st)$	

Table 6.2: Complex abstract types and their propositional intensionalization.

Abstract type		F-type	S-type (intensional)
NP→S	intransitive verb	ff	$e(st)$
NP→(NP→S)	transitive verb	$f(ff)$	$e(e(st))$
A→(NP→S)	*be* of predication	$f(ff)$	$(e(st))(e(st))$
A→A	adjective modifier	ff	$(e(st))(e(st))$
S→(S→S)	sentence coordinator	$f(ff)$	$(st)((st)(st))$
A→(A→A)	adjective coordinator	$f(ff)$	$(e(st))((e(st))(e(st)))$
(NP→S)→S	quantified noun phrase	$(ff)f$	$(e(st))(st)$
N→((NP→S)→S)	determiner	$f((ff)f)$	$(e(st))((e(st))(st))$
(NP→S)→(N→N)	relative pronoun	$(ff)(ff)$	$(e(st))((e(st))(e(st)))$

(Chapter 3, page 88). In (6.22) we defined the propositional operator ANDst in terms of our extensional operator AND^t of Chapter 3. This definition allowed us to preserve our account of entailments like (6.21) with sentential conjunctions in the extensional system. We would like to have a more general way of moving from extensional denotations to their intensional correlates. Thus, based on a lexicon with extensional denotations over types e and t, we want a systematic method of getting an intensionalized lexicon, where denotations may also range over the type s of indices. In (6.42) we saw that when intensionalizing the denotation of one-place et predicates into $(se)(st)$ functions with i-concept arguments, we must make sure that these $(se)(st)$ functions are systematically derived from (arbitrary) $e(st)$ properties. As in our definition of the ANDst operator, the aim of these semantic assumptions was to preserve our account of entailments in the extensional system (see (6.43)). In general terms, we want our intensionalization procedure to be properly defined for all entries in our extensional lexicon, and to preserve all accounts of entailments in the extensional system. We summarize this desideratum below.

Given a lexicon L_E with extensional denotations ranging over the types e and t, an **intensionalization** *of L_E is a lexicon L_I ranging over the types e, t and s, such that the following two conditions hold.*

(I) *Every sentence S is derivable from L_E iff S is derivable from L_I.*

(II) *For every two sentences S_1 and S_2 derivable from L_E and L_I: every entailment $S_1 \Rightarrow S_2$ is expected according to the TCC^E for L_E iff $S_1 \Rightarrow S_2$ is expected according to the TCC^I for L_I.*

Requirement (I) guarantees that the type change preserves the set of sentences that are analyzed by using the extensional lexicon. This requirement is easy to satisfy when, as in all our examples, we keep the f-denotations of all entries unchanged. Satisfying requirement (II) involves more intricate considerations. This requirement makes sure that, when we go intensional, the essential semantic properties of our extensional lexicon are preserved. More accurately: the entailments that the lexicon L_I allows us to account for are the same entailments accounted for by L_E, where, as usual, the TCC is our guiding principle. Below we will see one example for a proper intensionalization of an extensional lexicon. However, for intensionalization to be general we need to define it for all extensional lexicons in a given framework. Here we do not discuss the formal methods that are needed for defining this process in its full generality. For references see the further reading at the end of this chapter.

When we properly intensionalize an extensional lexicon L_E, the resulting intensional lexicon L_I that we get is only different in the types it uses, not in the entailments it accounts for. However, because of the intensional types it employs, such an intensional lexicon can be enriched by intensional expressions like the verbs *believe* or *look for*. To see an example for intensionalization, consider Table 6.3, which gives the intensionalized version of the extensional lexicon in Table 5.3 (Chapter 5, page 175), together with a new sign for the intensional verb *believe*.

Table 6.3 contains the intensionalized s-types and s-denotations for the extensional lexicon from Chapter 5. The intensionalized denotation for the determiner sign SOME is spelled out below.

Table 6.3: Intensional sign-based lexicon. Except for BELIEVE, all the items are intensionalized from Table 5.3 (Chapter 5, page 175).

Sign	Abstract type	F-denotation	S-denotation (intensional)
TINA	NP	$tina$	$\mathbf{tina}_e$
MARY	NP	$mary$	$\mathbf{mary}_e$
STUDENT	N	$student$	$\mathbf{student}_{e(st)}$
TEACHER	N	$teacher$	$\mathbf{teacher}_{e(st)}$
SMILE	NP $\to$ S	$\lambda y_f.\, y\cdot smiled$	$\mathbf{smile}_{e(st)}$
RUN	NP $\to$ S	$\lambda y_f.\, y\cdot ran$	$\mathbf{run}_{e(st)}$
PRAISE	NP $\to$ (NP $\to$ S)	$\lambda x_f.\lambda y_f.\, y\cdot praised\cdot x$	$\mathbf{praise}_{e(e(st))}$
SOME	N $\to$ ((NP $\to$ S) $\to$ S)	$\lambda y_f.\lambda P_{ff}.\, P(some\cdot y)$	$\mathbf{SOME}^I{}_{(e(st))((e(st))(st))}$
THAT	(NP $\to$ S) $\to$ (N $\to$ N)	$\lambda P_{ff}.\lambda y_f.\, y\cdot that\cdot P(\epsilon)$	$\mathbf{THAT}^I{}_{(e(st))((e(st))(e(st)))}$
BELIEVE	S $\to$ (NP $\to$ S)	$\lambda x_f.\lambda y_f.\, y\cdot believes\cdot x$	$\mathbf{believe}_{(st)(e(st))}$

(6.52) $\mathrm{SOME}^I_{(e(st))((e(st))(st))}$

$$
\begin{aligned}
&\overset{def}{=} \lambda A_{e(st)}.\lambda B_{e(st)}.\lambda i_s.\mathrm{SOME}_{(et)((et)t)}(A^i)(B^i)\\
&= \lambda A_{e(st)}.\lambda B_{e(st)}.\lambda i_s.(A^i)^* \cap (B^i)^* \neq \emptyset \qquad \rhd\,\text{def. SOME}\\
&= \lambda A_{e(st)}.\lambda B_{e(st)}.\lambda i_s.(\lambda x_e.A(x)(i))^* \qquad \rhd\,\text{def. (6.37)}\\
&\qquad\quad \cap (\lambda y_e.B(y)(i))^* \neq \emptyset
\end{aligned}
$$

In words, the function SOME^I maps any two properties A and B to the proposition holding of an index i iff A and B's extensions in i are mapped to 1 by the extensional determiner SOME. In simpler terms, we can say that in every index i, the determiner SOME^I holds of A and B if the intersection of their extensions in i is not empty.

Along similar lines, we define below the intensionalized denotation for the sign of the relative pronoun THAT.

(6.53) $\mathrm{THAT}^I_{(e(st))((e(st))(e(st)))}$

$$
\begin{aligned}
&\overset{def}{=} \lambda A_{e(st)}.\lambda B_{e(st)}.\lambda x_e.\lambda j_s.\mathrm{THAT}_{(et)((et)(et))}(A^j)(B^j)(x)\\
&= \lambda A_{e(st)}.\lambda B_{e(st)}.\lambda x_e.\lambda j_s.B^j(x) \wedge A^j(x) \qquad \rhd\,\text{def. THAT}\\
&= \lambda A_{e(st)}.\lambda B_{e(st)}.\lambda x_e.\lambda j_s.B(x)(j) \wedge A(x)(j) \qquad \rhd\,\text{def. (6.37)}
\end{aligned}
$$

In words, the function THAT^I maps any two properties A and B to the property whose extension in every index j is the extensional function THAT applied to the extensions of A and B in j. By the extensional definition of THAT, this is the property whose extension in every index j characterizes the intersection of the sets characterized by A and B's extensions in j. Equivalently: the function THAT^I maps any two properties A and B to the property that characterizes the intersection of the binary relations (between indices and entities) that A and B characterize.

After having specified an intensionalized lexicon, let us consider the following entailment.

(6.54) Some student that ran smiled $\Rightarrow$ Some student smiled.

Our extensional lexicon in Table 5.3 (Chapter 5, page 175) easily accounts for such entailments. Looking again at this analysis, in (6.55) and (6.56) below we see the extensional treatment of the two sentences in (6.54).

(6.55) SOME(THAT($\mathbf{run}_{et}$)($\mathbf{student}_{et}$))($\mathbf{smile}_{et}$) $= 1$
          iff ($\mathbf{student}^* \cap \mathbf{run}^*$)$\cap \mathbf{smile}^* \neq \emptyset$

(6.56) SOME($\mathbf{student}_{et}$)($\mathbf{smile}_{et}$) $= 1$
          iff $\mathbf{student}^* \cap \mathbf{smile}^* \neq \emptyset$

When using the intensional lexicon in Table 6.3, the derivations and f-denotations of the sentences in (6.54) are the same as when using the extensional lexicon. The semantic denotations are different, but because the intensional lexicon was derived from the extensional lexicon by a general intensionalization method, we get essentially the same account of the entailment. To see that, consider how the sentences in (6.54) are analyzed in (6.57) and (6.58) below, when using the denotations of the intensional lexicon in Table 6.3.

(6.57) SOME^I(THAT^I($\mathbf{run}_{e(st)}$)($\mathbf{student}_{e(st)}$))($\mathbf{smile}_{e(st)}$)

$= $ SOME^I(($\lambda A.\lambda B.\lambda x_e.\lambda j_s$.THAT($A^j$)($B^j$)($x$))
          ($\mathbf{run}$)($\mathbf{student}$))($\mathbf{smile}$) $\triangleright$ denotation THAT^I

$$= \text{SOME}^I(\lambda x_e.\lambda j_s.\text{THAT}(\mathbf{run}^j)(\mathbf{student}^j)(x))(\mathbf{smile})$$
$$\triangleright \text{ simplification}$$

$$= (\lambda A.\lambda B.\lambda i_s.\text{SOME}(A^i)(B^i))$$
$$(\lambda x_e.\lambda j_s.\text{THAT}(\mathbf{run}^j)(\mathbf{student}^j)(x))(\mathbf{smile})$$
$$\triangleright \text{ denotation SOME}^I$$

$$= \lambda i_s.\text{SOME}(\lambda x_e.\text{THAT}(\mathbf{run}^i)(\mathbf{student}^i)(x))(\mathbf{smile}^i)$$
$$\triangleright \text{ simplification}$$

$$= \lambda i_s.\text{SOME}(\text{THAT}(\mathbf{run}^i)(\mathbf{student}^i))(\mathbf{smile}^i) \quad \triangleright \text{ eta-reduction}$$

(6.58) $\text{SOME}^I(\mathbf{student}_{e(st)})(\mathbf{smile}_{e(st)})$

$$= (\lambda A_{e(st)}.\lambda B_{e(st)}.\lambda i_s.\text{SOME}(A^i)(B^i))(\mathbf{student})(\mathbf{smile})$$
$$\triangleright \text{ denotation SOME}^I$$

$$= \lambda i_s.\text{SOME}(\mathbf{student}^i)(\mathbf{smile}^i) \qquad \triangleright \text{ simplification}$$

For the justification of the last simplification in (6.57), see Exercise 10, Chapter 3. The proposition in (6.57) holds of any index i based on the *extensional* condition that we described in (6.55) using the extensional operators SOME and THAT. For this reason, proposition (6.57) holds of an index i if and only if the intersection of the set extensions in i of the properties for *student, run* and *smiled* is not empty. Similarly, proposition (6.58) holds of indices i where the intersection of the sets associated with the properties for *student* and *smiled* is not empty. Thus, the intensionalized denotations for *some* and *that* account for the entailment in (6.54) by using the same principles that we used in our extensional accounts so far.

The intensional lexicon in Table 6.3 only contains one additional lexical entry that does not appear in the extensional lexicon: the sign for the verb *believe*. Assuming that this verb has type $(st)(e(st))$, we added it to a lexicon that only contains extensional expressions, whose intensional types and denotations were systematically derived from their extensional types and denotations. This process allowed us to capture intensionality effects that we saw earlier in this chapter. More generally, we can now add to our lexicon various intensional expressions, maintaining the principles of our analysis (see Exercises 4, 5, and 9). In this way, having a systematic intensionalization procedure has helped us to work in a conservative, modular way. Our use of possible worlds only becomes pregnant when treating intensional expressions. This modularity makes sure that extensional phenomena that were treated correctly in Chapters 2–5 are similarly treated in our intensional system. It also has some welcome linguistic implications, as we will presently see.

You are now advised to solve Exercises 4, 5 and 6 at the end of this chapter.

DE DICTO/DE RE INTERPRETATIONS AND SCOPE AMBIGUITY

Suppose that John's bike was stolen, and that the following sentence is asserted.

(6.59) Tina believes some Englishman is the thief.

Upon hearing (6.59), we may easily infer that Tina thinks she knows the nationality of the thief. For instance, if Tina believes that *Mr. X* is the thief, then we may conclude from sentence (6.59) that Tina thinks Mr. X is an Englishman. Because the thief's nationality is reported in (6.59) according to what Tina herself said, or otherwise conveyed, we classify this use of the sentence as its *de dicto* interpretation (Latin: 'about what is said'). In this usage, sentence (6.59) makes no claim about the thief's actual nationality: it only describes Tina's belief about it. In other words: when understanding sentence (6.59) under its *de dicto* interpretation, we see that it does not entail that the thief is an Englishman. This is again a peculiar property of the intensional verb *believe*, since the embedded sentence *some Englishman is the thief* in (6.59) surely does entail that the thief is an Englishman. However, in the *de dicto* interpretation of (6.59), the verb *believe* "hides", so to speak, a clear consequence of its sentential complement. For this reason, intensional expressions that lead to *de dicto* interpretations are said to create an *opaque context*.

De dicto interpretations are distinguished from another use of belief sentences like (6.59). To see this interpretation, let us again suppose that Tina believes that Mr. X is the thief. However, this time, let us assume that she has no belief about X's nationality. Interestingly, in such a case we may still utter (6.59) truthfully. Suppose that Mr. X is an

Englishman, but Tina happens not to know that. We can use sentence (6.59) to express *our own belief* about the thief's nationality, without making any commitment on Tina's beliefs about it. As an illustration of this possibility, consider the following context.

(6.60) John's bike was stolen last night. Tina claims that she saw the thief, but she says she has no idea who the person was. The police figure out that the thief must have been one of three people who had been seen at the place shortly before John's bike was stolen. Two of these people, X and Y, are Englishmen. The third person, Z, is a Frenchman. In a police lineup, Tina claims she recognizes X as the thief. A police inspector describes it as follow:

Tina believes some Englishman is the thief. (=(6.59))

The police inspector in (6.60) knows quite well that Tina has no beliefs about X's nationality. Thus, the inspector's utterance of sentence (6.59) does not convey any statement about Tina's beliefs regarding X's nationality. Rather, the inspector uses sentence (6.59) to make an *assertion of his own* about X's nationality. We classify this interpretation of sentence (6.59) as *de re* (Latin: 'about the thing'). The *de re* interpretation of sentence (6.59) supports the entailment that the thief is an Englishman. More generally, *de re* interpretations allow logical consequences to "percolate" upward in the sentence. Because of that, we sometimes say that *de re* interpretations make the intensional context become *transparent*.

Summarizing, below we describe the intuitive *de dicto* and *de re* interpretations of sentence (6.59).

(6.61) a. *De dicto*: Tina believes the sentence "some Englishman is the thief".

b. *De re*: There is some Englishman X, such that Tina believes the sentence "X is the thief".

Based on these intuitions, we can more exactly discern the two facets of sentence (6.59) by teasing apart two different entailment relations in which it partakes. These two entailments are given in (6.62a) and (6.62b) below.

(6.62) a. Tina believes X is the thief, and Tina believes X is an Englishman ⇒ (6.59)

b. Tina believes X is the thief, and X is an Englishman ⇒ (6.59)

When we see sentence (6.59) supporting the entailment in (6.62a), we say that we recognize (6.59)'s *de dicto* interpretation. When we observe entailment (6.62b), we expose (6.59)'s *de re* interpretation.

As another example of the *de dicto/de re* distinction, consider the following sentence with the verb *look for*.

(6.63) Tina is looking for the author of *Alice*.

Under the *de dicto* interpretation of (6.63), Tina is trying to find the person that satisfies the description "the author of *Alice*". By contrast, under its *de re* interpretation, sentence (6.63) may be true if Tina has no special interest in *Alice*. For instance, suppose that Tina wants to find the person who satisfies the description "the author of *The Hunting of the Snark*". This makes (6.63) true even if Tina doesn't know that the same person wrote both books. It is again useful to recognize two different entailments with these *de dicto* and *de re* interpretations of sentence (6.63), as given in (6.64a–b) below, respectively.

(6.64) a. Tina is looking for X, and Tina believes X wrote *Alice* ⇒ (6.63)

b. Tina is looking for X, and X wrote *Alice* ⇒ (6.63)

For another similar example, consider the intensional sentence (6.65) below. This sentence supports the *de dicto/de re* entailments in (6.66a–b), respectively.

(6.65) In Tina's dream, she met the author of *Alice*.

(6.66) a. Tina dreamt she met X, and, in her dream, X was the author of *Alice* ⇒ (6.65)

For instance: (6.65) is true if Tina dreamt she met Bill Gates, and, in her dream, Gates was the author of *Alice*.

    b. Tina dreamt she met X, and X is the author of *Alice* $\Rightarrow$
       (6.65)

       For instance, (6.65) is true if Tina dreamt she met C. L. Dodgson, whom she knows from school, but Tina has no idea that her childhood friend is the celebrated author of *Alice*.

Contrasts between *de dicto* and *de re* interpretations constitute an intriguing puzzle for our account of intensionality. A common solution to this puzzle is based on the idea that these interpretations are an instance of scope ambiguity, similar to the effects we saw in Chapter 5. In example (5.60) (page 177), we saw that our ACG treatment derives two scope relations between object NPs and subject NPs, as intuitively required. We will now use the same mechanism as our account for *de dicto/de re* effects. As we will see, such effects can be described as resulting from different scope relations between NPs like *some Englishman* in (6.59) and the verb *believe*. To illustrate our analysis of *de dicto* and *de re* interpretations, consider the following sentence, which is similar to (6.59) above, but is more convenient for this presentation.

(6.67) Tina believes some witch smiled.

Similarly to our intuitive analysis of sentence (6.59), we paraphrase the *de dicto* and *de re* interpretations of (6.67) as follows.

(6.68) a. *De dicto*: Tina believes the sentence "some witch smiled".
       b. *De re*: There is some witch *u*, such that Tina believes the sentence "*u* smiled".

It should be noted that the *de dicto* interpretation (6.68a) does not entail anything about the existence of witches that smiled: Tina may surely be mistaken in her belief. Furthermore, under its *de dicto* interpretation, sentence (6.67) may also be true if there are no witches at all: the sentence may simply report Tina's superstitious belief, without making any statement on its content. In this *de dicto* interpretation, the assertion about the existence of witches remains "buried" in the opaque intensional environment. By contrast, the *de re* interpretation of (6.67) does make a statement about the existence of witches: it entails that whatever the object of Tina's belief may be, that object is a witch. For instance, under the *de re* interpretation of sentence (6.67), Tina may only believe that Mary smiled, without believing that Mary is a witch. In such a situation sentence (6.67) may still be truthfully used, when the speaker wants to assert that Mary, the object of Tina's belief, is a witch.

To analyze the two interpretations of sentence (6.67), we add an entry for the noun *witch* to our lexicon in Table 6.3:

Sign : WITCH
Abstract type : **N**
F-denotation : *witch*
S-denotation : $\mathbf{witch}_{e(st)}$

Figure 6.1 shows two sign-level derivations we obtain for sentence (6.67) using our assumed lexicon. On the left of Figure 6.1, we see the derivation of sentence (6.67)'s *de dicto* interpretation. This derivation is straightforward, since with our assumed abstract types, it only consists of applications. As Figure 6.1 summarizes, it leads to the following proposition.

(6.69) **believe**(SOME^I(**witch**)(**smile**))(**tina**)

The proposition SOME^I(**witch**)(**smile**) in (6.69) is the denotation of the embedded sentence *some witch smiled*. In (6.69), this proposition is the argument of the function **believe**. When we denote this proposition φ, sentence (6.67) denotes the proposition that holds of the indices where Tina believes the proposition φ. This captures the *de dicto* interpretation of (6.67) as in paraphrase (6.68a).

For the analysis of the *de re* interpretation of (6.67), we observe that in our ACG system, the signs TINA, BELIEVE and SMILE can be directly composed by providing a hypothetical argument to the sign SMILE. Thus, without introducing the sign for the subject *some witch* of the verb *smile*, we get the following derivation.

(6.70)

$$
\begin{array}{c}
\dfrac{\mathrm{BELIEVE} : \mathbf{S} \to (\mathbf{NP} \to \mathbf{S}) \qquad \dfrac{\mathrm{SMILE} : \mathbf{NP} \to \mathbf{S} \quad [\, \mathrm{U}_{\mathrm{NP}} \,]^1}{\mathrm{SMILE}(\mathrm{U}) : \mathbf{S}}}{\mathrm{BELIEVE}(\,\mathrm{SMILE}(\mathrm{U})\,) : \mathbf{NP} \to \mathbf{S}}
\end{array}
$$

$$
\dfrac{\mathrm{TINA} : \mathbf{NP} \qquad \mathrm{BELIEVE}(\,\mathrm{SMILE}(\mathrm{U})\,) : \mathbf{NP} \to \mathbf{S}}{\dfrac{\mathrm{BELIEVE}(\,\mathrm{SMILE}(\mathrm{U})\,)(\,\mathrm{TINA}\,) : \mathbf{S}}{\lambda\, \mathrm{U}_{\mathrm{NP}}.\ \mathrm{BELIEVE}(\,\mathrm{SMILE}(\mathrm{U})\,)(\,\mathrm{TINA}\,) : \mathbf{NP} \to \mathbf{S}}}\ \text{discharge hypothesis 1}
$$

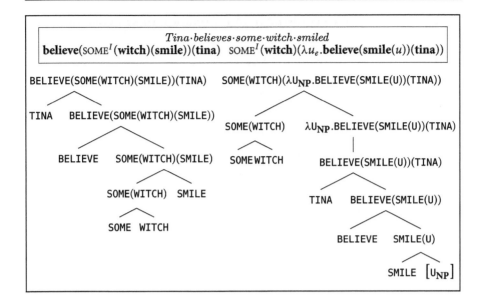

Figure 6.1   Abstract-level analysis of de dicto/de re *ambiguity.*

This derivation resembles derivation (5.40) (page 157), which we observed in our preliminary treatment of the verb *believe* in Chapter 5. In (6.70), the verb sign SMILE takes the hypothetical argument U. The resulting sentence is used as an argument for the sign BELIEVE, which then applies to its subject sign TINA. At this point the hypothetical argument U is 'discharged'. The semantic denotation of the derived sign is the following.

(6.71) $\lambda u_e.\textbf{believe}_{(st)(e(st))}(\textbf{smile}_{e(st)}(u))(\textbf{tina}_e)$

In words, this is the function sending every entity u to the proposition resulting from applying the function **believe** to the proposition **smile**(u) and the entity **tina**. Informally, this function sends every entity u to the proposition: "Tina believes the sentence 'u smiled'". Combining the function in (6.71) with our denotation of *some witch* leads to the following proposition.

(6.72) $\text{SOME}^I(\textbf{witch}_{e(st)})(\lambda u_e.\textbf{believe}_{(st)(e(st))}(\textbf{smile}_{e(st)}(u))(\textbf{tina}_e))$

This proposition reflects the *de re* interpretation of sentence (6.67) as paraphrased in (6.68b). The sign-level derivation of this proposition is given on the right-hand side of Figure 6.1.

In both the *de dicto* derivation and the *de re* derivation, the sign SOME(WITCH) is linked to the argument of the sign SMILE. Because of that, the two derivations in Figure 6.1 lead to the same string: *Tina·believes·some·witch·smiled* (see Exercise 7). Consequently, our grammar associates this string with two different denotations: the *de dicto* proposition (6.69) above, and the *de re* proposition in (6.72). In terms of entailments, we can also verify (see Exercise 8) that proposition (6.72) accounts for the entailment from sentence (6.73) below to sentence (6.67)'s *de re* interpretation.

(6.73) Tina believes Mary smiled, and Mary is a witch.

Further, we also want to verify that our analysis of sentence (6.67)'s *de dicto* interpretation in (6.69) accounts for the entailment from sentence (6.74) below to sentence (6.67).

(6.74) Tina believes Mary smiled, and Tina believes Mary is a witch.

In our system, this would amount to establishing the following relation.

(6.75) $(\textbf{believe}(\textbf{smile}(\textbf{mary}))(\textbf{tina})^* \cap$

$(\textbf{believe}(\textbf{witch}(\textbf{mary}))(\textbf{tina}))^*$

$\subseteq (\textbf{believe}(\text{SOME}^I(\textbf{witch})(\textbf{smile}))(\textbf{tina}))^*$

In words, (6.75) asserts that the intersection of the sets of indices characterized by the propositions for "Tina believes Mary smiled" and "Tina believes Mary is a witch" is a subset of the set of indices characterized by the *de dicto* proposition for "Tina believes some witch smiled". In order to establish (6.75), we would have to make non-trivial assumptions about the denotation of the word *believe*. So far we have made no assumption about this denotation, which was left arbitrary. However, *de dicto* entailments such as (6.74)$\Rightarrow$(6.67) tell us something about Tina's logical abilities. Specifically, this entailment expresses the intuition that if Tina believes in the existence of an entity that smiled

(Mary), and Tina believes that the same entity is a witch, then Tina must believe in the existence of a witch that smiled. This reasoning seems trivial, but it reflects an important fact about the verb *believe* and the arrangement of beliefs that it presupposes. We can informally describe this line of reasoning as follows.

(6.76) a. Tina believes the sentence "Mary smiled", and Tina believes the sentence "Mary is a witch" (=(6.74))

b. $\Rightarrow$ Tina believes the sentence "Mary smiled and Mary is a witch"

c. $\Rightarrow$ Tina believes the sentence "some witch smiled" (=*de dicto* interpretation of (6.67)).

Studies in intensional semantics analyze entailments such as (6.76a)$\Rightarrow$(6.76b) as a result of the simpler entailments from the sentences "Mary smiled" and "Mary is a witch" to their conjunction. Similarly, the entailment (6.76b)$\Rightarrow$(6.76c) is analyzed as caused by the entailment from the sentence "Mary smiled and Mary is a witch" to the sentence "some witch smiled". In this way, entailments with complex belief sentences are related to extensional entailments with the embedded sentences.

A note of caution is in place about this connection between beliefs and simple extensional entailments. While in the examples above the connection is plausible, and explains the entailment from sentence (6.74) to (6.67), we should be careful with attempts to generalize it. Generalizing the line of reasoning in (6.76) may lead us to think that Tina is an "infallible believer": that if she believes a sentence S_1, she never fails to believe any other sentence S_2 that is entailed from S_1. In other words, Tina is a perfect deducer of inferences: the set of sentences she believes in are *closed under entailment*. Of course, ascribing such infallibility to Tina, or any other human being, would be grossly incorrect. Avoiding such gross over-simplifications in our analysis of belief expressions and other intensional expressions is a major challenge. As you see in the further reading suggested at the end of this chapter, the precise semantic treatment of intensional verbs like *believe* is the center of much debate in logic and philosophy of language. We will not be able to dive into this big problem.

Let us summarize what we have seen and done, which is quite a lot already. Belief sentences, as well as other intensional sentences, show two kinds of interpretations that we characterized as *de dicto* and *de re*. In belief sentences with indefinite descriptions, such as *Tina believes some witch smiled*, we treated the *de dicto* and *de re* interpretations as cases of scope ambiguity, which are modeled by our ACG-based account in precisely the same way as they were in Chapter 5. The hypothesis about the scopal origins of *de dicto/de re* interpretations was originally suggested by the philosopher Willard Van Orman Quine (1908–2000), and was first fully formalized in Richard Montague's work. We summarize this general hypothesis below.

> **The Quine-Montague Hypothesis**: De dicto *and* de re *interpretations of intensional sentences can be described by the same general mechanisms that derive scope ambiguity.*

The Quine-Montague Hypothesis embodies a modular approach to grammar. Scope mechanisms like the hypothetical reasoning principle of Chapter 5 are held responsible for ambiguities with intensional expressions. Such scope mechanisms are assumed independently of possible worlds semantics. They are motivated by phenomena like long-distance dependencies and quantifier scope, which are also observed in 'purely extensional' environments. The Quine-Montague Hypothesis proposes that once scope mechanisms are "plugged into" an intensional system, *de dicto* and *de re* interpretations follow as their by-product. In line with this modularity assumption, our introduction of possible worlds in this chapter was based on the extensional system of Chapters 2–5. This conservative treatment has allowed us to systematically employ our analysis of extensional expressions, while extending it to some complex intensional phenomena that involve psychological dimensions of language use.

You are now advised to solve Exercises 7, 8 and 9 at the end of this chapter.

FURTHER READING

Introductory: For an easy introduction to Frege's classic article, see McGinn (2015). For the basics of intensionality in classical Montague semantics, see Dowty et al. (1981); Gamut (1982). For a more recent introduction to intensional semantics in natural language, see Von Fintel and Heim (2011), which also surveys limitations of the Quine-Montague Hypothesis, including so-called "scope paradoxes" and additional interpretations to *de dicto/de re*.

Advanced: Frege (1892) is one of the earliest modern works on intensionality, and a major influence on further work. On *be* sentences and other copular constructions, see Mikkelsen (2011). For a philosophical introduction to possible world semantics and its origins, see Menzel (2014). For an extensive introduction, see Fitting and Mendelsohn (1998). On the use of individual concepts in philosophy and semantics see Abbott (2011). For a general intensionalization method, see De Groote and Kanazawa (2013). On logics of belief and other related puzzles about epistemic logic, see Hendricks and Symons (2014). The Quine-Montague hypothesis is based on Quine (1956) and Montague (1973). For further linguistic work about intensionality, see Von Heusinger et al. (2011, part XII) as well as Fodor (1970); Boye (2012); Portner (2009); Von Fintel (2006).

EXERCISES (ADVANCED: 4, 9)

1. For each of the intensional adjectives *former, fake, false* and *imaginary* show an entailment that it does not respect, similarly to the adjective *alleged* in (6.14). For each of your examples, show an extensional adjective that does respect the entailment (like *Russian* in (6.15)).

2. a. In an intensional model with $D_s = \{w_1, w_2\}$ and $D_e = \{a, b\}$, describe the $e(st)$ property **smile**, where for w_1, a smiles but b does not, and for w_2, both a and b smile.

   b. Give the sets characterized by the extensions **smile**^{w_1} and **smile**^{w_2}.

   c. Suppose that for w_1, a believes b smiles, and that for w_2, a does not believe b smiles. Based on the denotation of **smile** above, write the respective claims as requirements on the $(st)(e(st))$ denotation **believe**. Use the notation f_A for the characteristic function of A.

3. In an intensional model with $D_s = \{w_1, w_2, w_3, w_4\}$ and $D_e = \{a, b\}$, we define the two individual concepts **lc** and **cld** as follows: $\mathbf{lc}(w_1) = \mathbf{lc}(w_3) = a$, $\mathbf{lc}(w_2) = \mathbf{lc}(w_4) = b$, $\mathbf{cld}(w_2) = \mathbf{cld}(w_3) = a$, $\mathbf{cld}(w_1) = \mathbf{cld}(w_4) = b$.

a. What is the set of indices that the proposition $\text{IS}^I_{id}(\textbf{lc})(\textbf{cld})$ characterizes?

b. Suppose that the property $\textbf{write\_Alice}_{e(st)}$ satisfies: $(\textbf{write\_Alice}(a))^* = \{w_1, w_2\}$ and $(\textbf{write\_Alice}(b))^* = \{w_1, w_4\}$. Using the definition of $\textbf{write\_Alice}^I$ in (6.42), specify the sets of indices that each of the propositions $\textbf{write\_Alice}^I(\textbf{lc})$ and $\textbf{write\_Alice}^I(\textbf{cld})$ characterizes.

4. In Table 3.2 (Chapter 3, page 89) we defined the intersective modifier $\textbf{chinese}^{\text{mod}}$ of type $(et)(et)$ as based on an et function. Using our intensional typing, we now define the intersective modifier $\textbf{chinese}^{\text{Imod}}$ of type $(e(st))(e(st))$ as based on the $e(st)$ property $\textbf{chinese}$:

$\textbf{chinese}^{\text{Imod}} = \lambda P_{e(st)}.\lambda x_e.\lambda i_s.\textbf{chinese}(x)(i) \wedge P(x)(i)$.

a. In an intensional model with $D_s = \{w_1, w_2, w_3, w_4\}$ and $D_e = \{a, b\}$, we define the $e(st)$ properties $\textbf{teacher}$, $\textbf{smile}$ and $\textbf{chinese}$ as follows:

$(\textbf{teacher}(w_1))^* = \{a\}$	$(\textbf{smile}(w_1))^* = \{a, b\}$	$(\textbf{chinese}(w_1))^* = \{b\}$
$(\textbf{teacher}(w_2))^* = \{b\}$	$(\textbf{smile}(w_2))^* = \{b\}$	$(\textbf{chinese}(w_2))^* = \{b\}$
$(\textbf{teacher}(w_3))^* = \{a, b\}$	$(\textbf{smile}(w_3))^* = \{a\}$	$(\textbf{chinese}(w_3))^* = \{a\}$
$(\textbf{teacher}(w_4))^* = \{a\}$	$(\textbf{smile}(w_4))^* = \{b\}$	$(\textbf{chinsese}(w_4))^* = \{a\}$

Based on these denotations, and the denotation SOME^I in (6.52), find the sets of indices characterized by the denotations of the following sentences in the given model:

(i) [Some [Chinese teacher]] smiled.

(ii) [Some teacher] smiled.

In agreement with the entailment (i)$\Rightarrow$(ii), verify that the former is a subset of the latter.

b. In contrast to the entailment (i)$\Rightarrow$(ii), consider the lack of entailment from (iii) below to (ii):

(iii) [Some [alleged teacher]] smiled.

In view of this lack of entailment, we want to make sure that in the given model, the adjective alleged may have a denotation s.t. the set of indices characterized by the denotation of (iii) is not a subset of the set characterized by the denotation of (ii). Give a restriction on the denotation $\textbf{alleged}$, of type $(e(st))(e(st))$, that guarantees that.

c. Prove that the entailment (i)$\Rightarrow$(ii) is respected in all intensional models we define with the typing above and the denotations $\textbf{chinese}^{\text{Imod}}$ and SOME^I. Thus: show that in any model, the set of indices characterized by the denotation of (i) is a subset of the set characterized by the denotation of (ii).

5. Consider the following sentences:

(i) *Birds lay eggs.*

(ii) *Necessarily, birds lay eggs.*

Intuitively, (ii) entails (i), but (i) does not entail (ii). In view of such patterns, we assume that the denotation NECESSARILY, of type $(st)(st)$, satisfies the following for every model, for every proposition φ_{st}:

(iii) $(\text{NECESSARILY}(\varphi))^* \subseteq \varphi^*$.

a. Define NECESSARILY, and make sure your definition satisfies (iii).

b. With this definition, show a model M and a proposition φ in M s.t. $\varphi^* \nsubseteq (\text{NECESSARILY}(\varphi))^*$.

6. Repeat Exercise 5 from Chapter 5 for the intensional lexicon in Table 6.3: using this intensional lexicon, prove that in any model, the derived s-denotations of the sentences *some teacher that Mary praised smiled* (=(5.59b), page 175) and *Mary praised some teacher* (i) satisfy: $[\![(5.59b)]\!] \le [\![(i)]\!]$. Thus, the TCC explains the entailment (5.59b)$\Rightarrow$(i) also with the intensionalized version (Table 6.3) of the extensional lexicon in Table 5.3 (page 175).

7. Based on the lexicon of Table 6.3 and the sign WITCH, show that the two derivations in Figure 6.1 lead to the same string.

8. Accounting for the *de re* entailment (6.73)$\Rightarrow$(6.67), show that the following subset relation holds in any model:

$(\textbf{believe}_{(st)(e(st))}(\textbf{smile}_{e(st)}(\textbf{mary}))(\textbf{tina}))^* \cap (\textbf{witch}_{e(st)}(\textbf{mary}))^*$
$\subseteq (\text{SOME}^I(\textbf{witch})(\lambda u_e.\textbf{believe}(\textbf{smile}(u))(\textbf{tina})))^*$

9. a. Consider the following sentence:

(i) *Tina is talking to some witch.*

Based on Table 6.3, show the object narrow/wide scope derivations, with a sign TALK_TO of type NP$\rightarrow$(NP$\rightarrow$S). Verify that the two s-denotations derived are equivalent.

b. Consider now the following sentence:

(ii) *Tina is looking for some witch.*

Paraphrase the *de dicto* and *de re* interpretations of (ii) similarly to paraphrases (6.68a–b) of (6.67).

c. Consider the sign LOOK_FOR for the verb in (ii), of an abstract type ((NP$\rightarrow$S)$\rightarrow$S)$\rightarrow$(NP$\rightarrow$S), and the following f-denotation and s-denotation:

$\lambda X_{(ff)f}.\lambda y_f.\ X(\lambda x_f.y\cdot is\text{-}looking\text{-}for\cdot x)$ $\textbf{look\_for}_{((e(st))(st))(e(st))}$
Show two abstract derivations of (ii) that derive different s-denotations by employing object narrow/wide scope strategies. For the object wide scope derivation, rely on the following partial derivation, with double use of hypothetical reasoning:

$$\cfrac{\text{LOOK\_FOR} \quad \cfrac{\cfrac{[\ \mathsf{U_{NP}}]^1 \quad [\ \mathsf{P_{NP\to S}}]^2}{\mathsf{P_{NP\to S}}(\ \mathsf{U_{NP}})}}{\lambda\ \mathsf{P_{NP\to S}}.\ \mathsf{P}(\ \mathsf{U_{NP}})}\text{ discharge hypothesis 2}}{\text{LOOK\_FOR}(\lambda\ \mathsf{P_{NP\to S}}.\ \mathsf{P}(\ \mathsf{U_{NP}}))}$$

Verify that your two abstract derivations lead to the same f-denotation, i.e. the string in (ii). Further, derive and simplify the s-denotations that your two abstract derivations lead to.

SOLUTIONS TO SELECTED EXERCISES

1. every manager is a committee member; every committee member is a manager; a *former* manager smiled $\not\Rightarrow$ a *former* committee member smiled every manager is a committee member; every committee member is a manager; a *blond* manager smiled $\Rightarrow$ a *blond* committee member smiled

2. a. $\textbf{smile} = \begin{bmatrix} a \mapsto [w_1 \mapsto 1\ w_2 \mapsto 1] \\ b \mapsto [w_1 \mapsto 0\ w_2 \mapsto 1] \end{bmatrix}$

   b. $(\textbf{smile}^{w_1})^* = \{a\}$; $(\textbf{smile}^{w_2})^* = \{a, b\}$.
   c. $\textbf{believe}(f_{\{w_2\}})(a)(w_1) = 1$; $\textbf{believe}(f_{\{w_2\}})(a)(w_2) = 0$.

3. a. $\{w_3, w_4\}$
   b. $(\textbf{write\_Alice}^I(\textbf{lc}))^* = \{w_1, w_4\}$,
      $(\textbf{write\_Alice}^I(\textbf{cld}))^* = \{w_1, w_2, w_4\}$.

4. a. $[\![(i)]\!]^* = \{w_2, w_3\} \subset [\![(ii)]\!]^* = \{w_1, w_2, w_3\}$
   b. $\textbf{alleged}(\textbf{teacher})(b)(w_4) = 1$.
   c. Similarly to (6.57)–(6.58), by def. of SOME^I and $\textbf{chinese}^{\text{lmod}}$
      we have:
      $(\text{SOME}^I(\textbf{chinese}^{\text{lmod}}(\textbf{teacher}))(\textbf{smile}))^*$
      $= (\lambda i_s.\ ((\textbf{teacher}^i)^* \cap (\textbf{chinese}^i)^*) \cap (\textbf{smile}^i)^* \neq \emptyset)^*$
      $\subseteq (\lambda i_s.\ (\textbf{teacher}^i)^* \cap (\textbf{smile}^i)^* \neq \emptyset)^* = (\text{SOME}^I(\textbf{teacher})(\textbf{smile}))^*$.

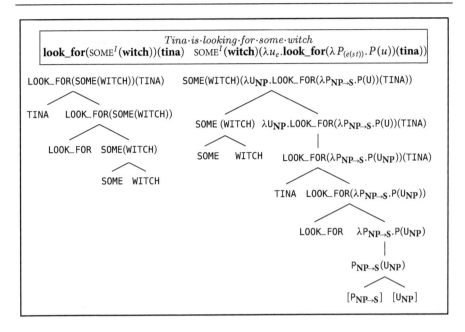

Figure 6.2   Exercise 9 – abstract-level analysis of de dicto/de re *ambiguity.*

5. a. NECESSARILY $= \lambda \psi_{st} . \begin{cases} \psi & \text{if } \psi^* = D_s \\ \lambda i_s.0 \text{ if } \psi^* \neq D_s \end{cases}$

In words: NECESSARILY sends a proposition ψ to itself, in cases when ψ sends every index to 1; otherwise, NECESSARILY sends ψ to the proposition characterizing the empty set of indices.

b. In any model where $\varphi^* \neq \emptyset$ and $\varphi^* \neq D_s$ (e.g. $D_s = \{w_1, w_2\}$ and $\varphi^* = \{w_1\}$), we have $(\text{NECESSARILY}(\varphi))^* = \emptyset$. Hence: $(\text{NECESSARILY}(\varphi))^* \subseteq \varphi^*$, but $\varphi^* \not\subseteq (\text{NECESSARILY}(\varphi))^*$.

9. b. Tina is looking for an object that would satisfy the description "witch"; there is some witch u, such that Tina is looking for u.

c. For abstract derivations see Figure 6.2.

CONCLUSION AND FURTHER TOPICS

With the principles and techniques that were covered in the previous chapters, we can now recapitulate what we have done, and look at further topics and directions.

RECAPITULATION

Throughout this book, two principles have played a key role:

(i) entailment as an empirical phenomenon revealing important aspects of meaning
(ii) the compositionality principle as a bridge between meaning and form

Chapter 2 presented the concept of *models* and the Truth-Conditionality Criterion as a basis for the compositional analysis of entailment. Compositionality helped us to treat structural ambiguity as a syntactic phenomenon that leads to semantic ambiguity, i.e. systematic uncertainty in certain judgments about entailment. Chapter 3 developed one of the essential ingredients of formal semantics: the use of functions for linguistic denotations. We saw the role that functions of different types play in the compositional treatment of entailment, and how functions are represented in formal semantic analysis. In Chapter 4, we used functions for handling natural language quantification, concentrating on quantified noun phrases. We saw that many complex entailments in language involving monotonicity, coordination and classical syllogisms are immediately accounted for when generalized quantifiers are used as noun phrase denotations. Chapter 5 revealed a connection between three apparently unrelated phenomena: long-distance dependencies, scope ambiguity and verbs with quantified objects. These three phenomena were treated by adding a new compositional principle, *hypothetical reasoning*, to a grammar architecture that manipulates pairs of forms and meanings packed in linguistic *signs*. Chapter 6 extended our framework in another direction: the analysis of *intensional* expressions – words and phrases that refer to psychological states and imaginary situations. We saw that, using our initial system from Chapter 3, we can analyze complex intensional phenomena by adding a basic domain of possible worlds. Relying on the extended framework emanating from Chapters 5 and 6, we captured the intuitive relation between scope ambiguity and *de dicto/de re* ambiguities with intensional expressions.

WHERE TO GO FROM HERE?

Readers of different backgrounds and interests may choose to follow a number of different directions to further explore formal semantics and related areas. The recommendations below suggest a few possible avenues.

1. Readers who are novices to theoretical linguistics may first like to learn more about some of the general topics in the field. The three linguistic areas that are most closely related to formal semantics are syntactic theory, lexical semantics and pragmatics. In each of these vast areas there are many competing theories and approaches. Some of them which are closely related to formal semantics are covered in the textbooks Fromkin et al. (2014, ch. 3) and Carnie (2013) (on syntax); and Cruse (1986) and Murphy (2010) (on lexical semantics). Within the topics related to formal semantics and pragmatics, studies of implicature and presupposition are a good place to start (see below).
2. If you are interested in formal semantics proper, you can use some of the topics and references in the next section.
3. On psycholinguistic approaches to formal semantics, see Crain (2012); Pylkkänen (2008); Chemla and Singh (2014). For further ongoing work in experimental semantics and pragmatics, see the web pages of the Experimental Pragmatics conference (XPRAG 2015).
4. For a selection of work in artificial intelligence that strongly relies on formal semantics, see Dagan et al. (2013); Bos (2011); Liang and

Potts (2015). For further ongoing work in computational semantics, see the web page of the Special Interest Group on Computational Semantics (SIGSEM 2015).

MORE TOPICS AND READINGS IN FORMAL SEMANTICS

The topics discussed throughout this book only scratch the surface of state-of-the-art formal semantics. Many of the ideas and principles in this book have gradually developed since the end of the nineteenth century, on the basis of work in philosophy of language and on the foundations of mathematics. A good way to deepen your understanding of formal semantics is by exploring some of the core philosophical writings in these fields. McGinn (2015) gives penetrable summaries and explanations of some of the classical works in this area. Another good idea is to consult more than one textbook. Zimmermann and Sternefeld (2013) and Jacobson (2014) give excellent overviews, from different perspectives, of some of the topics discussed in this book, and many others. Heim and Kratzer (1997) will further broaden your horizons with regards to current approaches in formal semantics.

Once you feel that your formal semantic basics are strong enough, you can dive further into specific topics. The list below summarizes some of the outstanding problems in formal semantics, with recommendations on further reading when available. Some handbooks with excellent survey articles are mentioned at the end of this list.

QUANTIFICATION. In Chapter 4, as in much work on quantification in formal semantics, we concentrated on quantified *noun phrases*. For an advanced monograph on generalized quantifier theory in relation to natural language, see Peters and Westerståhl (2006). Another advanced book, with more linguistic topics related to quantified NPs, is Szabolcsi (2010). Much further work in formal semantics is currently being done on *mass term* quantification using words like *much* or *little*, and on adverbs of quantification using words like *usually* and *seldom*.

ANAPHORA. In Chapter 3, we quickly treated the reflexive pronoun *herself*. We have not discussed other pronouns like *she* and *her*, which also show special semantic interactions with noun phrases. Pronouns – and more generally, anaphoric expressions – have been extensively treated in different semantic frameworks. You can familiarize yourself with work in this area by consulting the textbooks Büring (2005); Heim and Kratzer (1997); Jacobson (2014). The more advanced book Kamp and Reyle (1993) gives an overview of one influential semantic theory – Discourse Representation Theory (DRT) – which concentrates on pronouns and anaphoric expressions in general. Another anaphoric phenomenon that has been extensively studied in formal semantics is *verb phrase ellipsis*, as in *Tina smiled, and Mary <u>did too</u>*. Heim and Kratzer's and Jacobson's books contain useful accounts of VP ellipsis in relation to nominal anaphora.

DEFINITE AND INDEFINITE DESCRIPTIONS. While proper names and quantified NPs were treated throughout this book, we have said little on the interpretation of definite NPs like *the boy* and indefinite NPs like *a boy*. The properties of such descriptions are central to philosophy of language, and have led to much work in formal semantics and pragmatics since the early 1980s. In particular, the semantic relations between descriptions and pronouns have led to much research in DRT and related frameworks in formal semantics. Another important property of definite and indefinite descriptions is their *generic* interpretations, as in *dogs bark* or *the dog is a social animal*. Krifka et al. (1995) is a useful introduction on generic descriptions.

PLURALITY. Plural NPs have also not been extensively treated in this book. They are especially important for formal semantics because of their "collective" interpretation. For instance, sentences like *the boys met, Sue and Dan met* and *all the boys gathered* have interpretations that cannot be analyzed by quantifying over simple entities. Theories of plurals normally address such challenges by distinguishing arbitrary entities, like the denotation of *Sue*, from *collections* of such entities. The latter are used as denotations of plural noun phrases like *Sue and Dan*. For two advanced monographs on plurals, see Lasersohn (1995); Winter (2001).

TENSE AND ASPECT. The different tenses that languages allow, e.g. *Tina smiles* vs. *Tina smiled*, have important effects on sentence meaning. Many of the relations between morphological tense and the temporal meaning of sentences are much more complex than they may at first seem. Further, languages often let tensed sentences (or in some languages, tense-neutral sentences) appear in different *aspects*. For instance, we can consider the distinction that English makes between the past tense sentences *Tina smiled* and *Tina was smiling*. Tense and aspect phenomena bring another dimension to formal semantic analysis: the way languages describe the occurrence of events in time. Logical and mathematical theories have developed sophisticated methods to deal with temporal expressions and the aspectual effects that languages show. Formal semantics uses some of these logical methods. For overviews, see Goranko and Galton (2015); Hamm and Bott (2014).

SPATIAL EXPRESSIONS. Just as languages allow speakers to express complex temporal relations, they also have rich mechanisms for talking about space. In English, space is prominent, with prepositions like *on, outside* and *to*, as well as with verbs that describe motion or location, such as *put, pull, intersect* and *overlap*. To appreciate the complexities of spatial reference in English, you can look at the descriptive work in Herskovits (1986) (on prepositions) and Levin (1993, part 2) (on verbs). Formal semantic accounts of spatial expressions draw on various elements from mathematical theories, especially the notions of *regions* and *vectors* in topology and linear algebra.

ADJECTIVES. In Chapter 3, we touched upon the compositional behavior of adjectives and their ability both to modify nouns and to appear as independent predicates. Many works in formal semantics also address other important properties of adjectives: their comparative and superlative forms (*taller, tallest*), their combination with measures (*6 feet tall*), their complex interactions with the context of utterance, and the many different ways to classify adjectives. For an overview, see McNally and Kennedy (2008).

ADVERBS AND ADVERBIAL MODIFICATION. Adverbs like *quickly* show some of the compositional complexities of adjectives, but in a way that is even more puzzling. If we treat adverbs as being derived from *et* predicates, it is not clear how they combine with verbs. For instance, *Sue danced beautifully* does not mean that Sue herself was beautiful. In a major attempt to overcome this outstanding challenge, many works use the semantic notion of *events* as a link between the denotation of adverbs and the denotation of verbs.

Events are useful for many adverbial modifiers, including spatial adverbials (*Sue ran in the park*) and temporal adverbials (*Sue ran at night*). For more on event semantics, see Maienborn (2011).

INTENSIONALITY AND MODALS. Intensionality phenomena interact with many of the other phenomena mentioned above: anaphoric expressions, indefinite and definite descriptions, quantification, scope ambiguity, adjectives and adverbs, and tense and aspect (tense itself may be seen as an intensional phenomenon). One well-researched area within intensionality phenomena is the semantics of *modal expressions* like *may, can, must* or *would*. These and other topics are systematically addressed, with ample references, in the advanced (yet unpublished) lecture notes Von Fintel and Heim (2011).

IMPLICATURES AND PRESUPPOSITIONS. A large domain of research, with many new developments, studies *implicatures*: apparently defeasible, but logically systematic, inferences that can be drawn on the basis of natural language utterances. For instance, the sentence *some boy ran* implicates that *not every boy ran*, although this is certainly not an indefeasible entailment of the former sentence. For this reason, classically, this sort of implication was studied outside the realm of formal semantics proper. However, a large body of recent literature addresses many implicatures as part of formal semantics. For two rival approaches, see Chierchia et al. (2012); Geurts (2010). Another important semantic-pragmatic phenomenon is *presupposition*, like the inferences from *the dictator is smiling* to *there is a dictator* and, furthermore, to *there is a unique dictator*. Such entailments show very different properties from the ones we have been addressing in this book, especially with respect to their behavior when sentences are embedded within one another. For an advanced introductory article on presupposition, which clarifies some of the most important issues, see Von Fintel (2004). For other advanced introductions, see Beaver and Geurts (2014); Potts (2015).

QUESTIONS AND IMPERATIVES. Throughout this book we treated sentences that are used for reporting facts. However, natural language sentences may also have other functions in a conversation: to ask questions, give orders or make requests. These different usages often require adjustments in the semantics we have been using, especially in relation to the TCC. Questions, or *interrogative* sentences, are an especially lively area within formal semantics, with different approaches competing for the right way to model their semantics and pragmatics.

For more advanced introductions to these topics, you may find it useful to consult some of the survey articles in the following handbooks:

- Van Benthem and ter Meulen (2011)
- Maienborn et al. (2011, 2012); Von Heusinger et al. (2011)
- Lappin and Fox (2015)
- Riemer (2016)

APPENDIX TO CHAPTER 3

Throughout Chapter 3 we have relied on three basic procedures. First, we assigned types and denotations to words. Second, we used these lexical types and denotations to assign types and denotations to complex expressions, based on their syntactic structure and the compositionality principle. Third, we let certain lexical denotations be systematically restricted. In this appendix we formally summarize the semantic framework of Chapter 3 by fleshing out these three procedures. This leads to a slightly revised version of the Truth-Conditionality Criterion, which takes some more formal details into account.

TYPES AND DENOTATIONS OF WORDS

Suppose that we are given a finite *vocabulary* Σ of the words in our language. The type of a word in Σ is assumed to remain constant even when its denotation changes. For instance, even though the name *Tina* may denote different objects in different models, those objects must all be of the same type: e. We let denotations vary but remain of a constant type by defining a *typing function* over our vocabulary. This function, which we call T, maps every word w in Σ to a type $T(w)$ in the set of types $\mathcal{T}$. Formally:

Definition 6. *Let Σ be a finite vocabulary. A **typing function** T over Σ is any function from Σ to the set of types $\mathcal{T}$.*

We adopt the following terminological convention:

> *A* **typed lexicon**, *or in short a 'lexicon', is a pair $\langle \Sigma, T \rangle$ of a vocabulary Σ and a typing function T over Σ.*

Based on a word's type in a lexicon, we assign it a denotation. The function responsible for assigning denotations to words is called an *interpretation function*. This function, denoted I, maps every word w in Σ to an element of the domain of w's type $T(w)$. To define interpretation functions, we first collect all the domains together into one set that we call a *frame*. The choice of the basic domain of entities $D_e = E$ determines our frame completely. This is because the other basic domain, D_t, is fixed, and all other domains are derived from these two basic domains by Definition 2. To highlight the dependency of domains on the set of entities E, we write D_τ^E rather than D_τ. The frame $\mathcal{F}^E$ is the union of all domains relative to a set of entities E. Formally:

Definition 7. *Let E be a non-empty set. The* **frame** $\mathcal{F}^E$ *over E is defined by:*

$$\mathcal{F}^E \overset{def}{=} \bigcup_{\tau \in T} D_\tau^E.$$

With these notions of a lexicon and a frame, interpretation functions are defined as follows:

Definition 8. *Let L be a typed lexicon $\langle \Sigma, T \rangle$. An* **interpretation function** *over L and a non-empty set of entities E is any function I from Σ to the frame $\mathcal{F}^E$ that satisfies the following, for every word w in Σ: $I(w) \in D_{T(w)}^E$.*

In words: an interpretation function maps any word w to an element in the domain of the type assigned to w.

We now adopt the following terminological convention:

> A **model** *over a lexicon L is a pair $\langle E, I \rangle$ of a non-empty set of entities E and an interpretation function I over L and E.*

Given a model $\langle E, I \rangle$, the objects in the frame are determined by E, and word denotations are determined by I. Table A.1 illustrates a small lexicon with the words *Tina*, *Mary*, *smiled* and *praised* and a small model over this lexicon. Note that in this example the name *John* is not in our vocabulary, and the entity j is not denoted by any word.

Table A.1: A typed lexicon L_1 and a model M_1 over that lexicon.

Lexicon $L_1 = \langle \Sigma_1, T_1 \rangle$	Model $M_1 = \langle E_1, I_1 \rangle$
Vocabulary:	**Entities:**
$\Sigma_1 = \{\text{Tina, Mary, smiled, praised}\}$	$E_1 = \{\text{t, m, j}\}$
Typing function T_1 from Σ_1 to $\mathcal{T}$:	**Interpretation function I_1 from Σ_1 to $\mathcal{F}^{E_1}$:**
Tina $\mapsto e$	Tina $\mapsto$ t
Mary $\mapsto e$	Mary $\mapsto$ m
smiled $\mapsto et$	smiled $\mapsto s' = [\text{t} \mapsto 0 \;\; \text{j} \mapsto 1 \;\; \text{m} \mapsto 1]$
praised $\mapsto e(et)$	praised $\mapsto p' = \begin{bmatrix} \text{t} & \mapsto & [\text{t} \mapsto 0 \;\; \text{j} \mapsto 0 \;\; \text{m} \mapsto 1] \\ \text{j} & \mapsto & [\text{t} \mapsto 0 \;\; \text{j} \mapsto 0 \;\; \text{m} \mapsto 1] \\ \text{m} & \mapsto & [\text{t} \mapsto 1 \;\; \text{j} \mapsto 0 \;\; \text{m} \mapsto 1] \end{bmatrix}$

This is harmless: our definition of models allows entities, as well as other objects in the frame, not to have any name in our vocabulary.

TYPES AND DENOTATIONS OF COMPLEX EXPRESSIONS

A model is used for deriving denotations of complex expressions. The compositionality principle requires that the only information needed for deriving a denotation for a complex expression is the denotations of its immediate parts in the syntactic structure. For instance, to derive the denotation of *Tina praised Mary*, we only need to know the denotations of the subject *Tina* and the verb phrase *praised Mary*. In all our treatments above we have assumed that complex expressions have such binary structures. We define a binary structure as an ordinary binary tree, whose leaf nodes contain occurrences of words in the vocabulary. Accordingly we adopt the following inductive definition.

Definition 9. *A **binary structure** over a vocabulary Σ is one of the following:*

(I)   *An occurrence of a word w in Σ.*

(II)   *A sequence $[S_1\ S_2]$, where S_1 and S_2 are binary structures over Σ.*

For the sentence *Tina praised Mary* we assumed the binary structure [*Tina* [*praised Mary*]], where each of the two parts is also by definition a binary structure. The term "binary tree" is quite awkward when referring to single words like *Tina*, but this is an innocuous formality that follows from the recursion in the statement of Definition 9.

Given a typed lexicon and a model over this lexicon, we assign denotations to binary structures inductively, based on their structure and the rule of function application. Our use of function application for composing types and denotations is defined below, for any two types $\alpha\beta$ and α, and denotations f, x of these types, respectively:

$$\alpha\beta + \alpha = \alpha + \alpha\beta = \beta$$
$$f + x = x + f = f(x)$$

These are the rules of the Ajdukiewicz Calculus for type composition. When used in conjunction with our model definition, we apply these rules for assigning types and denotations to binary structures. This is defined below:

Definition 10. *Let $M = \langle E, I \rangle$ be a model over a typed lexicon $L = \langle \Sigma, T \rangle$. Let S be a binary structure over Σ. The type $\tau(S)$ of S in L and its denotation $[\![S]\!]^M$ in M are defined by:*

(i)   *If S is a word w in Σ:*
      $\tau(S) = T(w)$ *and* $[\![S]\!]^M = I(w)$.

(ii) *If S = $[S_1 \, S_2]$, where S_1 and S_2 are binary structures:*
      $\tau(S) = \tau(S_1) + \tau(S_2)$ *and* $[\![S]\!]^M = [\![S_1]\!]^M + [\![S_2]\!]^M$.

Definition 10 specifies types and denotations of words by the lexical typing function and the interpretation function respectively. Types and denotations of complex binary structures are inductively defined by function application. For an illustration of this inductive procedure see the analysis of the sentential structure *Tina [praised Mary]* in Table A.2, which uses the lexicon and model of Table A.1.

RESTRICTING DENOTATIONS AND THE REVISED TRUTH-CONDITIONALITY CRITERION

Lexicon L_1 in Table A.1 only contains words to which we assigned *arbitrary* denotations. This means that all models over L_1 are permitted when evaluating the TCC. Now we should also consider words whose denotations are restricted, e.g. as summarized in Table 3.2 (Chapter 3).

Table A.2: Analysis of structure *Tina [praised Mary]* in lexicon L_1 and model M_1 of Table A.1.

Types in L_1	Denotations in M_1
$\tau(praised\ Mary)$	$[\![praised\ Mary]\!]^{M_1}$
$= \tau(praised) + \tau(Mary)$	$= [\![praised]\!]^{M_1} + [\![Mary]\!]^{M_1}$ ▷ def. 10, clause (II)
$= T_1(praised) + T_1(Mary)$	$= I_1(praised) + I_1(Mary)$ ▷ def. 10, clause (I)
$= e(et) + e$	$= p' + m$ ▷ lexicon and model (Table A.1)
$= et$	$= p'(m)$ ▷ application
	$= [t \mapsto 1\ j \mapsto 0\ m \mapsto 1]$ ▷ def. of p' (Table A.1)
$\tau(Tina\ [praised\ Mary])$	$[\![Tina\ [praised\ Mary]]\!]^{M_1}$
$= \tau(Tina) + \tau(praised\ Mary)$	$= [\![Tina]\!]^{M_1} + [\![praised\ Mary]\!]^{M_1}$
	▷ def. 10, clause (II)
$= T_1(Tina) + et$	$= I_1(Tina) + p'(m)$
	▷ def. 10, clause (I); analysis of *praised Mary* above
$= e + et$	$= t + p'(m)$ ▷ lexicon and model (Table A.1)
$= t$	$= (p'(m))(t)$ ▷ application
	$= 1$ ▷ def. of p' in model (Table A.1)

The models we use make sure that words such as *not* or *skillful* are assigned the desired denotations in their type's domain. This means that we are only interested in some of the models that specify $(et)(et)$ denotations for these words. Specifically, we only want those models where the denotation of *not* is predicate negation, the denotation of *skillful* is a subsective function, etc. We refer to the models that satisfy these restrictions as *intended models*. For example, Table A.3 defines the intended models we assume for a lexicon containing the words *a*, *is*, *not* and the adjective *Chinese* in its modificational use. We said that the first three words have a "constant" denotation. What we mean by that is that, in any intended model $\langle E, I \rangle$, the interpretation function I sends these words to a unique element in the domain $D_{(et)(et)}^E$. The modificational adjective *Chinese* also has a restricted interpretation: **chinese**^{mod}. However, in any domain $D_{(et)(et)}^E$ there may be many such functions, since the *et* function **chinese** may denote any member of the domain D_{et}^E.

Table A.3:   A typed lexicon L_2 and the intended models M over that lexicon.

Lexicon $L_2 = \langle \Sigma_2, T_2 \rangle$		Intended models $M = \langle E, I \rangle$
Vocabulary:		**Entities:**
$\Sigma_2 = \{$Tina, pianist, chinese, is, a, not$\}$		$E \neq \emptyset$
Typing function T_2 from Σ_2 to $\mathcal{T}$:		**Interpretation functions I from Σ_2 to $\mathcal{F}^E$:**
Tina	$\mapsto e$	Tina $\mapsto$ **tina** (arbitrary)
pianist	$\mapsto et$	pianist $\mapsto$ **pianist** (arbitrary)
Chinese	$\mapsto (et)(et)$	Chinese
		$\mapsto \lambda f_{et}.\lambda x_e.\textbf{chinese}(x) \wedge f(x),$ for some function **chinese** $\in D_{et}^E$
is	$\mapsto (et)(et)$	is $\mapsto \lambda g_{et}.g$
a	$\mapsto (et)(et)$	a $\mapsto \lambda g_{et}.g$
not	$\mapsto (et)(et)$	not $\mapsto \lambda g_{et}.\lambda x_e.1 - g(x)$

The restrictions we have assumed allow the TCC to formally account for entailments such as the following:

(A.1) Tina [is [not [a pianist]]]
   $\Rightarrow$ Tina [is [not [a [Chinese pianist]]]]

This is achieved by letting our revised definition of the TCC refer to intended models, excluding models that do not respect the lexical restrictions we assume. For instance, referring to intended models guarantees that the word *not* denotes the complement function, *is* and *a* denote the identity function, and *Chinese* is an intersective modifier. The restrictions that we assume for the sake of analyzing entailment (A.1) are summarized again in Table A.3.

Using the restrictions in Table A.3 and our method of assigning denotations to complex expressions (Definition 10), we can show that, for each intended model M, the following relation holds between the truth-values that M assigns to the structures in (A.1):

(A.2) $[\![Tina\ [is\ [not\ [a\ pianist]]]]\!]^M$
   $\leq [\![Tina\ [is\ [not\ [a\ [Chinese\ pianist]]]]]\!]^M$

More generally, below we explicitly restate the Truth-Conditionality Criterion, based on our notion of intended models:

> Let $L = \langle \Sigma, T \rangle$ *be a typed lexicon in a theory* T. *The theory* T *is said to satisfy the* **TCC** *for the binary structures* S_1 *and* S_2 *of sentences over* Σ, *if the following two conditions are equivalent:*
>
> (I)   *Structure* S_1 *intuitively entails structure* S_2.
> (II)   *For all intended models* M *in* T: $[\![S_1]\!]^M \leq [\![S_2]\!]^M$.

There are two modifications in this formal statement of the TCC, compared to the informal version in Chapter 2 (page 20): (i) because of our assumptions on structural ambiguity, we relativize the intuitive notion of entailment to *binary structures* of sentences, rather than to sentences; (ii) in clause (II), rather than quantifying over all models, we here make sure that only *intended models* matter for the TCC. This is because only these models satisfy the restrictions that we assume for lexical denotations.

BIBLIOGRAPHY

Abbott, B. (1999), 'The formal approach to meaning: Formal semantics and its recent developments', *Journal of Foreign Languages* **119**, 2–20. https://www.msu.edu/~abbottb/formal.htm. Accessed: March 24, 2015.

Abbott, B. (2011), 'Support for individual concepts', *Linguistic and Philosophical Investigations* **10**, 23–44.

ACG (2015), 'The Abstract Categorial Grammar Homepage', http://www.loria.fr/equipes/calligramme/acg/. Accessed: March 4, 2015.

Adler, J. E. and Rips, L. J., eds (2008), *Reasoning: Studies of Human Inference and Its Foundation*, Cambridge University Press, New York.

Ajdukiewicz, K. (1935), 'Die syntaktische konnexität', *Studia Philosophia* **1**, 1–27.

Austin, J. L. (1962), *How to Do Things with Words: The William James Lectures delivered at Harvard University in 1955*, edited by J. O. Urmson, Clarendon, Oxford.

Bach, E., Jelinek, E., Kratzer, A. and Partee, B. B. H., eds (1995), *Quantification in Natural Languages*, Kluwer, Dordrecht.

Barendregt, H., Dekkers, W. and Statman, R. (2013), *Lambda Calculus with Types*, Cambridge University Press, Cambridge.

Barker, C. and Jacobson, P. (2007), Introduction: Direct compositionality, *in* C. Barker and P. Jacobson, eds, *Direct Compositionality*, Oxford University Press, Oxford, pp. 1–22.

Barker-Plummer, D., Barwise, J. and Etchemendy, J. (2011), *Language, Proof, and Logic*, 2nd edn, CSLI Publications, Stanford.

Barwise, J. and Cooper, R. (1981), 'Generalized quantifiers and natural language', *Linguistics and Philosophy* **4**, 159–219.

Beaver, D. I. and Geurts, B. (2014), Presupposition, *in* E. N. Zalta, ed., *The Stanford Encyclopedia of Philosophy*, winter 2014 edn.

Bos, J. (2011), 'A survey of computational semantics: Representation, inference and knowledge in wide-coverage text understanding', *Language and Linguistics Compass* **5**(6), 336–66.

Boye, K. (2012), *Epistemic Meaning: A Crosslinguistic and Functional-Cognitive Study*, De Gruyter, Berlin.

Brewka, G., Dix, J. and Konolige, K. (1997), *Nonmonotonic Reasoning: An Overview*, CSLI Publications, Stanford.

Büring, D. (2005), *Binding Theory*, Cambridge University Press, Cambridge.

Carlson, G. (2011), Genericity, *in* Von Heusinger et al. (2011), pp. 1153–85.

Carnie, A. (2013), *Syntax: A Generative Introduction*, 3rd edn, Wiley-Blackwell, Malden.

Carpenter, B. (1997), *Type-Logical Semantics*, MIT Press, Cambridge, MA.

Chemla, E. and Singh, R. (2014), 'Remarks on the experimental turn in the study of scalar implicature, part I', *Language and Linguistics Compass* **8**(9), 373–86.

Chierchia, G. and McConnel-Ginet, S. (1990), *Meaning and Grammar: An Introduction to Semantics*, MIT Press, Cambridge, MA.

Chierchia, G., Fox, D. and Spector, B. (2012), Scalar implicature as a grammatical phenomenon, *in* Maienborn et al. (2012), pp. 2297–332.

Crain, S. (2012), *The emergence of meaning*, Cambridge University Press, Cambridge.

Cruse, D. A. (1986), *Lexical Semantics*, Cambridge University Press, Cambridge.

Curry, H. B. (1961), Some logical aspects of grammatical structure, *in* R. O. Jakobson, ed., *Structure of Language and its Mathematical Aspects*, Vol. 12 of *Symposia on Applied Mathematics*, American Mathematical Society, Providence , pp. 56–68.

Dagan, I., Roth, D., Sammons, M. and Zanzotto, F. M. (2013), *Recognizing Textual Entailment: Models and Applications*, Morgan & Claypool.

De Groote, P. (2001), Towards Abstract Categorial Grammars, *in Proceedings of the 39th Annual Meeting of the Association for Computational Linguistics (ACL)*, pp. 252–9.

De Groote, P. and Kanazawa, M. (2013), 'A note on intensionalization', *Journal of Logic, Language and Information* **22**, 173–94.

De Saussure, F. (1959), *Course in General Linguistics*, Philosophical Library, New York. Translation of *Cours de Linguistique Générale*, Payot, Paris, 1916.

Dehaene, S. (2014), *Consciousness and the Brain: Deciphering How the Brain Codes Our Thoughts*, Viking Penguin, New York.

Dowty, D., Wall, R. and Peters, S. (1981), *Introduction to Montague Semantics*, D. Reidel, Dordrecht.

Elbourne, P. (2011), *Meaning: A Slim Guide to Semantics*, Oxford University Press, Oxford.

Fitting, M. and Mendelsohn, R. L. (1998), *First-Order Modal Logic*, Kluwer, Dordrecht.

Fodor, J. D. (1970), 'The linguistic description of opaque contexts', PhD thesis, Massachusetts Institute of Technology.

Frege, G. (1892), 'Über sinn und bedeutung', *Zeitschrift für Philosophie und philosophische Kritic* **100**, 25–50. Translated as 'On sense and reference' in Geach and Black (1960), pp. 56–78.

Fromkin, V., Rodman, R. and Hyams, N. (2014), *An Introduction to Language*, 10th edn, Wadsworth, Cengage Learning.

Gamut, L. T. F. (1982), *Logica, Taal en Betekenis*, Het Spectrum, De Meern. In two volumes. Translated as *Logic, Language and Meaning*, University of Chicago Press, Chicago, 1991.

Geach. P and Black M., eds (1960), *Translations from the Philsosophicals Writings of Gottlob Frege*, 2nd edn, Blackwell, Oxford.

Geurts, B. (2010), *Quantity Implicatures*, Cambridge University Press, Cambridge.

Goranko, V. and Galton, A. (2015), Temporal logic, *in* E. N. Zalta, ed., *The Stanford Encyclopedia of Philosophy*, summer 2015 edn.

Grice, H. P. (1975), Logic and conversation, *in* P. Cole and J. L. Morgan, eds, *Syntax and Semantics, Vol. 3, Speech Acts*, Academic Press, New York, pp. 41–58.

Groenendijk, J. and Stokhof, M. (1984), 'Studies on the semantics of questions and the pragmatics of answers' PhD thesis, University of Amsterdam.

Groenendijk, J. and Stokhof, M. (2011), Questions, *in* Van Benthem and ter Meulen (2011), pp. 1059–132.

Gunter, C. (1992), *Semantics of Programming Languages: Structures and Techniques*, MIT Press, Cambridge, MA.

Halmos, P. R. (1960), *Naive Set Theory*, Springer Science & Business Media.

Hamm, F. and Bott, O. (2014), Tense and aspect, *in* E. N. Zalta, ed., *The Stanford Encyclopedia of Philosophy*, spring 2014 edn.

Haspelmath, M. (2004), Coordinating constructions: an overview, *in* M. Haspelmath, ed., *Coordinating Constructions*, John Benjamins, Amsterdam/Philadelphia, pp. 3–39.

Heim, I. (2011), Definiteness and indefiniteness, *in* Von Heusinger et al. (2011), pp. 996–1024.

Heim, I. and Kratzer, A. (1997), *Semantics in Generative Grammar*, Blackwell, Oxford.

Hendricks, V. and Symons, J. (2014), Epistemic logic, *in* E. N. Zalta, ed., *The Stanford Encyclopedia of Philosophy*, spring 2014 edn.

Hendriks, H. (1993), 'Studied flexibility: Categories and types in syntax and semantics', PhD thesis, University of Amsterdam.

Herskovits, A. (1986), *Language and Spatial Cognition: An Interdisciplinary Study of the Prepositions in English*, Cambridge University Press, Cambridge.

Hindley, J. R. and Seldin, J. P. (1986), *Introduction to Combinators and the Lambda-Calculus*, Cambridge University Press, Cambridge.

Horn, L. R. and Kato, Y. (2003), Introduction: Negation and polarity at the millennium, *in* L. R. Horn and Y. Kato, eds, *Negation and Polarity: Syntactic and Semantic Perspectives*, Oxford University Press, Oxford, pp. 1–20.

Hutton, G. (2007), *Programming in Haskell*, Cambridge University Press, Cambridge.

Jacobson, P. (1999), 'Towards a variable-free semantics', *Linguistics and Philosophy* **22**, 117–85.

Jacobson, P. (2014), *Compositional Semantics: An Introduction to the Syntax/Semantics Interface*, Oxford University Press, Oxford.

Janssen, T. M. V. (1983), 'Foundations and applications of Montague Grammar', PhD thesis, Mathematisch Centrum, Amsterdam.

Janssen, T. M. V., with B. H. Partee (2011), Compositionality, *in* Van Benthem and ter Meulen (2011), pp. 495–554.

Joseph, J. E. (2012), *Saussure*, Oxford University Press, Oxford.

Kamareddine, F., Laan, T. and Nederpelt, R. (2004), *A Modern Perspective on Type Theory*, Kluwer, Dordrecht.

Kamp, H. and Reyle, U. (1993), *From Discourse to Logic: Introduction to Modeltheoretic Semantics of Natural Language, Formal Logic and Discourse Representation Theory*, Kluwer, Dordrecht.

Keenan, E. L. (1989), Semantic case theory, *in* R. Bartsch, J. van Benthem and P. van Emde Boas, eds, *Semantics and Contextual Expression*, Foris, Dordrecht, pp. 33–57.

Keenan, E. L. (1996), The semantics of determiners, *in* Lappin (1996), pp. 41–64.

Keenan, E. L. (2003), 'The definiteness effect: semantics or pragmatics?', *Natural Language Semantics* **11**(2), 187–216.

Keenan, E. L. (2006), Quantifiers: Semantics, *in* E. K. Brown, ed., *Encyclopedia of Language & Linguistics*, 2nd edn, Vol. 10, Elsevier, Amsterdam, pp. 302–8.

Keenan, E. L. (2007), 'On the denotations of anaphors', *Research on Language and Computation* **5**, 5–17.

Keenan, E. L. (2011), Quantifiers, *in* Von Heusinger et al. (2011), pp. 1058–87.

Keenan, E. L. and Faltz, L. (1978), *Logical Types for Natural Language*, UCLA Occasional Papers in Linguistics 3, Department of Linguistics, UCLA.

Keenan, E. L. and Faltz, L. (1985), *Boolean Semantics for Natural Language*, D. Reidel, Dordrecht.

Keenan, E. L. and Paperno, D., eds (2012), *Handbook of Quantifiers in Natural Language*, Springer, Dordrecht.

Keenan, E. L. and Westerståhl, D. (2011), Generalized quantifiers in linguistics and logic, *in* Van Benthem and ter Meulen (2011), pp. 859–910.

Kennedy, C. (2007), 'Vagueness and grammar: The semantics of relative and absolute gradable adjectives', *Linguistics and Philosophy* **30**, 1–45.

Kennedy, C. (2011), Ambiguity and vagueness: An overview, *in* Maienborn et al. (2011), pp. 507–35.

Klein, E. (1980), 'A semantics for positive and comparative adjectives', *Linguistics and Philosophy* **4**, 1–45.

Koons, R. (2014), Defeasible reasoning, *in* E. N. Zalta, ed., *The Stanford Encyclopedia of Philosophy*, spring 2014 edn.

Kracht, M. (2003), *The Mathematics of Language*, De Gruyter, Berlin.

Krifka, M., Pelletier, F. J., Carlson, G. N., ter Meulen, A., Chierchia, G. and Link, G. (1995), Genericity: An introduction, *in* G. N. Carlson and F. J. Pelletier, eds, *The Generic Book*, University of Chicago Press, Chicago, pp. 1–124.

Lambek, J. (1958), 'The mathematics of sentence structure', *American Mathematical Monthly* **65**, 154–69.

Lappin, S., ed. (1996), *The Handbook of Contemporary Semantic Theory*, Blackwell, Oxford.

Lappin, S. and Fox, C., eds (2015), *The Handbook of Contemporary Semantic Theory*, 2nd edn, Wiley-Blackwell, Malden.

Lasersohn, P. (1995), *Plurality, Conjunction and Events*, Kluwer, Dordrecht.

Lasersohn, P. (2011), Mass nouns and plurals, *in* Von Heusinger et al. (2011), pp. 1131–53.

Lassiter, D. (2015), Adjectival modification and gradation, *in* Lappin and Fox (2015), pp. 143–67.

Laurence, S. and Margolis, E. (1999), Introduction, *in* E. Margolis and S. Laurence, eds, *Concepts: Core Readings*, MIT Press, Cambridge, MA, pp. 3–82.

Levin, B. (1993), *English Verb Classes and Alternations: A Preliminary Investigation*, University of Chicago Press, Chicago.

Levinson, S. C. (1983), *Pragmatics*, Cambridge University Press, Cambridge.

Liang, P. and Potts, C. (2015), 'Bringing machine learning and compositional semantics together', *Annual Review of Linguistics* **1**(1), 355–76.

Maienborn, C. (2011), Event semantics, *in* Maienborn et al. (2011), pp. 802–29.

Maienborn, C., Heusinger, K. V. and Portner, P., eds (2011), *Semantics: An International Handbook of Natural Language Meaning*, Vol. 1, De Gruyter, Berlin.

Maienborn, C., Heusinger, K. V. and Portner, P., eds (2012), *Semantics: An International Handbook of Natural Language Meaning*, Vol. 3, De Gruyter, Berlin.

Matthewson, L., ed. (2008), *Quantification: A Cross-Linguistic Perspective*, Emerald Group, Bingley.

McAllester, D. A. and Givan, R. (1992), 'Natural language syntax and first-order inference', *Artificial Intelligence* **56**, 1–20.

McGinn, C. (2015), *Philosophy of Language: The Classics Explained*, MIT Press, Cambridge, MA.

McNally, L. (2011), Existential sentences, *in* Von Heusinger et al. (2011), pp. 1829–48.

McNally, L. and Kennedy, C. (2008), Introduction, *in* L. McNally and C. Kennedy, eds, *Adjectives and Adverbs: Syntax, Semantics, and Discourse*, Oxford University Press, Oxford, pp. 1–15.

Menzel, C. (2014), Possible worlds, *in* E. N. Zalta, ed., *The Stanford Encyclopedia of Philosophy*, fall 2014 edn.

Mikkelsen, L. (2011), Copular clauses, *in* Von Heusinger et al. (2011), pp. 1805–29.

Montague, R. (1970a), English as a formal language, *in* B. Visentini, ed., *Linguaggi nella Società e nella Technica*, Edizioni di Communità, Milan, pp. 189–223. Reprinted in Thomason (1974).

Montague, R. (1970b), 'Universal grammar', *Theoria* **36**, 373–98. Reprinted in Thomason (1974).

Montague, R. (1973), The proper treatment of quantification in ordinary English, *in* J. Hintikka, J. Moravcsik and P. Suppes, eds, *Approaches to Natural Languages: Proceedings of the 1970 Stanford Workshop on Grammar and Semantics*, D. Reidel, Dordrecht, pp. 221–42. Reprinted in Thomason (1974).

Moortgat, M. (2011), Categorial type logics, *in* Van Benthem and ter Meulen (2011), pp. 95–190.

Moot, R. and Retoré, C. (2012), *The Logic of Categorial Grammars: A Deductive Account of Natural Language Syntax and Semantics*, Springer, Berlin.

Morrill, G. (1994), *Type Logical Grammar: Categorial Logic of Signs*, Kluwer, Dordrecht.

Moss, L. S. (2010), Natural logic and semantics, *in* M. Aloni, H. Bastiaanse, T. de Jager and K. Schulz, eds, *Proceedings of the Seventeenth Amsterdam Colloquium*, Vol. 6042 of *Lecture Notes in Computer Science*, Springer, pp. 84–93.

Murphy, M. L. (2010), *Lexical Meaning*, Cambridge University Press, Cambridge.

Muskens, R. (2003), Language, lambdas, and logic, *in* G.-J. Kruijff and R. Oehrle, eds, *Resource Sensitivity in Binding and Anaphora*, Studies in Linguistics and Philosophy, Kluwer, Dordrecht, pp. 23–54.

Oehrle, R. (1994), 'Term-labeled categorial type systems', *Linguistics and Philosophy* **17**, 633–78.

Pagin, P. and Westerståhl, D. (2010), 'Compositionality I: Definitions and variants', *Philosophy Compass* **5**, 265–82.

Partee, B. H. (1984), Compositionality, *in* F. Landman and F. Veltman, eds, *Varieties of Formal Semantics*, Foris, Dordrecht, pp. 281–311. Reprinted in Partee (2004).

Partee, B. H. (1996), The development of formal semantics in linguistic theory, *in* Lappin (1996), pp. 11–38.

Partee, B. H. (2004), *Compisitionality in Formal Sementics: Selected Papers by Barbara H. Partee*, Blackwell, Malden.

Partee, B. H. (2015), *History of Formal Semantics*. Materials for a book in preparation, Oxford University Press, http://people.umass.edu/partee/Research.htm. Accessed: March 24, 2015.

Partee, B. H., ter Meulen, A. and Wall, R. (1990), *Mathematical Methods in Linguistics*, Kluwer, Dordrecht.

Pelletier, F. J. (2000), A history of natural deduction and elementary logic textbooks, *in* J. Woods and B. Brown, eds, *Logical Consequence: Rival approaches*, Vol. 1, Hermes Science Oxford, pp. 105–38.

Penka, D. and Zeijlstra, H. (2010), 'Negation and polarity: An introduction', *Natural Language and Linguistic Theory* **28**, 771–86.

Peters, S. and Westerståhl, D. (2006), *Quantifiers in Language and Logic*, Oxford University Press, Oxford.

Portner, P. (2009), *Modality*, Oxford University Press, Oxford.

Potts, C. (2015), Presupposition and implicature, *in* Lappin and Fox (2015), pp. 168–202.

Prawitz, D. (1965), *Natural Deduction: A Proof-Theoretical Study*, Almqvist & Wiksell, Stockholm.

Pylkkänen, L. (2008), 'Mismatching meanings in brain and behavior', *Language and Linguistics Compass* **2**, 712–38.

Quine, W. V. O. (1956), 'Quantifiers and propositional attitudes', *Journal of Philosophy* **53**, 177–87.

Riemer, N., ed. (2016), *The Routledge Handbook of Semantics*, Routledge, London and New York.

Saeed, J. I. (1997), *Semantics*, Blackwell, Oxford.

Sánchez, V. (1991), 'Studies on natural logic and categorial grammar', PhD thesis, University of Amsterdam.

Schönfinkel, M. (1924), 'Über die bausteine der mathematischen logik', *Mathematische Annalen* **92**(3), 305–16.

Schroeder-Heister, P. (2014), Proof-theoretic semantics, *in* E. N. Zalta, ed., *The Stanford Encyclopedia of Philosophy*, summer 2014 edn.

Searle, J. R. (1969), *Speech Acts*, Cambridge University Press, Cambridge.

SIGSEM (2015), 'Website of SIGSEM, the Special Interest Group on Computational Semantics, Association for Computational Linguistics (ACL)', http://www.sigsem.org. Accessed: June 26, 2015.

Smith, E. E. (1988), Concepts and thought, *in* R. J. Sternberg and E. E. Smith, eds, *The Psychology of Human Thought*, Cambridge University Press, Cambridge, pp. 19–49.

ST (2015), 'Set theory – Wikibooks', http://en.wikibooks.org/wiki/Set_Theory. Accessed: March 25, 2015.

Steedman, M. (1997), *Surface Structure and Interpretation*, MIT Press, Cambridge, MA.

Stenning, K. and van Lambalgen, M. (2007), *Human Reasoning and Cognitive Science*, MIT Press, Cambridge, MA.

Suppes, P. (1957), *Introduction to Logic*, Van Nostrand Reinhold, New York.

Szabolcsi, A. (1987), Bound variables in syntax: Are there any?, *in Proceedings of the 6th Amsterdam Colloquium*, pp. 331–5.

Szabolcsi, A. (2010), *Quantification*, Cambridge University Press, Cambridge.

Taylor, J. R. (1989), *Linguistic Categorization: Prototypes in Linguistic Theory*, Oxford University Press, Oxford.

Thomason, R., ed. (1974), *Formal Philosophy: Selected Papers of Richard Montague*, Yale, New Haven.

Thompson, S. (1991), *Type Theory and Functional Programming*, Addison-Wesley, Wokingham.

Van Benthem, J. (1986), *Essays in Logical Semantics*, D. Reidel, Dordrecht.

Van Benthem, J. (1991), *Language in Action: Categories, Lambdas and Dynamic Logic*, North-Holland, Amsterdam.

Van Benthem, J. and ter Meulen, A., eds (2011), *Handbook of Logic and Language*, 2nd edn, Elsevier, Amsterdam.

Van Eijck, J. and Unger, C. (2010), *Computational Semantics with Functional Programming*, Cambridge University Press, Cambridge.

Von Fintel, K. (2004), Would you believe it? The king of France is back! (Presuppositions and truth-value intuitions), *in* M. Reimer and A. Bezuidenhout, eds, *Descriptions and Beyond*, Oxford University Press, Oxford, pp. 315–41.

Von Fintel, K. (2006), Modality and language, *in* D. M. Borchert, ed., *Encyclopedia of Philosophy*, 2nd edn, MacMillan Reference USA, Detroit, pp. 315–41.

Von Fintel, K. and Heim, I. (2011), Intensional semantics. Unpublished lecture notes, Massachusetts Institute of Technology, http://web.mit.edu/fintel/fintel-heim-intensional.pdf, Accessed: March 10, 2015.

Von Heusinger, K., Maienborn, C. and Portner, P., eds (2011), *Semantics: An International Handbook of Natural Language Meaning*, Vol. 2, De Gruyter, Berlin.

Werning, M., Hinzen, W. and Machery, E., (2012), *The Oxford Handbook of Compositionality*, Oxford University Press, Oxford.

Westerståhl, D. (2015), Generalized quantifiers in natural language, *in* Lappin and Fox (2015), pp. 9–39.

Winter, Y. (2001), *Flexibility Principles in Boolean Semantics: Coordination, Plurality and Scope in Natural Language*, MIT Press, Cambridge, MA.

Winter, Y. and Scha, R. (2015), Plurals, *in* Lappin and Fox (2015), pp. 77–113.

XPRAG (2015), 'Homepage of the Experimental Pragmatics conference', https://lucian. uchicago.edu/blogs/xprag2015/. Accessed: June 26, 2015.

Zamparelli, R. (2011), Coordination, *in* Von Heusinger et al. (2011), pp. 1713–41.

Zimmermann, T. E. and Sternefeld, W. (2013), *Introduction to Semantics: An Essential Guide to the Composition of Meaning*, De Gruyter, Berlin.

INDEX

Abstract Categorial Grammar (ACG), 166
abstract type *see* type
abstraction *see* function abstraction
adjective, 236
  adjective phrase, 31–2
  attributive *see* adjective, modificational use
  comparative, 150, 185, 236
  extensional, 197
  intensional, 197
  intersective, 80–8
  modificational use, 80
  predicative use, 80
  subsective, 80–8
adverb, 87, 95, 109, 236–7
  of quantification, 234
Ajdukiewicz, K., 53; *see also* Ajdukiewicz Calculus
Ajdukiewicz Calculus, 52–4, 242
ambiguity, 30–5
  scope ambiguity, 177–83; *see also de dicto; de re*
  structural ambiguity, 30–4
  see also vagueness
anaphora, 234–5; *see also* pronoun
antecedent (of an entailment) *see* premise
arbitrary denotation *see* denotation
aspect, 235–6

basic abstract type *see* type, abstract
basic domain *see* domain
basic type *see* type
be of identity, 193, 206
be of predication, 193
Bedeutung, 204
beta-reduction, 68; *see also* lambda calculus
binary function *see* function
binary relation, 9, 56; *see also* determiner; predicate

binary structure, 241
Boolean algebra *see* Boolean structure
Boolean structure, 80, 91, 126, 129

calculus *see* Ajdukiewicz Calculus; lambda calculus; Lambek Calculus; Lambek-Van Benthem Calculus; type calculus
cancellable reasoning *see* defeasible reasoning
cardinality, 9
cartesian product, 9
characteristic function, 46–9, 101; *see also* set characterized by a function
coherence, 16
combinator, 88
common noun *see* noun
comparative *see* adjective, comparative
complement *see* complement function; complement set; sentential complement
complement function, 32
complement set, 9
complex expression, 17–18; *see also* complex nominal; lexical item
complex nominal, 115
complex type (= non-basic type) *see* type
compositionality, 27–30
computational semantics, 233–4
concatenation, 162–3
concept, 14, 35, 160–2; *see also* individual concept
conceptual *see* concept
conceptual model *see* model
conclusion (of an entailment), 13
concrete type *see* type
conditional sentence, 148–9
  monotonicity of conditionals *see* monotonicity